Retaking Rationality

RICHARD L.
REVESZ

MICHAEL A.
LIVERMORE

Retaking Rationality

How Cost-Benefit Analysis Can

Better Protect the Environment

and Our Health

OXFORD
UNIVERSITY PRESS
2008

OXFORD
UNIVERSITY PRESS

Oxford University Press, Inc., publishes works that further Oxford University's objective of excellence in research, scholarship, and education.

Oxford New York
Auckland   Cape Town   Dar es Salaam   Hong Kong   Karachi   Kuala Lumpur   Madrid   Melbourne
Mexico City   Nairobi   New Delhi   Shanghai   Taipei   Toronto

With offices in
Argentina   Austria   Brazil   Chile   Czech Republic   France   Greece   Guatemala   Hungary   Italy   Japan
Poland   Portugal   Singapore   South Korea   Switzerland   Thailand   Turkey   Ukraine   Vietnam

Library of Congress Cataloging-in-Publication Data
Revesz, Richard L., 1958-
    Retaking rationality: how cost-benefit analysis can better protect the environment and our health / Richard L. Revesz and Michael A. Livermore.
        p. cm.
    Includes bibliographical references and index.
    ISBN 978-0-19-536857-4 (cloth: alk. paper) 1. Trade regulation—United States—Cost effectiveness.
2. Environmental law—United States—Cost effectiveness. 3. Public health laws—United States—Cost effectiveness.
4. Administrative agencies—United States—Decision making. I. Livermore, Michael. II. Title.
    HD3616.U47R486 2008
    320.60973—dc22
                                                                                      2007040930

1 2 3 4 5 6 7 8 9

Printed in the United States of America
on acid-free paper

Note to Readers
This publication is designed to provide accurate and authoritative information in regard to the subject matter covered. It is based upon sources believed to be accurate and reliable and is intended to be current as of the time it was written. It is sold with the understanding that the publisher is not engaged in rendering legal, accounting, or other professional services. If legal advice or other expert assistance is required, the services of a competent professional person should be sought. Also, to confirm that the information has not been affected or changed by recent developments, traditional legal research techniques should be used, including checking primary sources where appropriate.

(Based on the Declaration of Principles jointly adopted by a Committee of the American Bar Association and a Committee of Publishers and Associations.)

You may order this or any other Oxford University Press publication by visiting the Oxford University Press website at www.oup.com

For Vicki, Joshua and Sarah, with enormous love and admiration.

— RR

For our fragile planet, and the people who dedicate themselves to protecting it. And for Patti and Jennifer, with love and gratitude.

— ML

CONTENTS

PROLOGUE: REASON AND COMPASSION

MAKING DECISIONS is a basic part of the human experience. Sometimes these decisions don't matter much—if we pick a bad movie, we waste only a little time and money. Other decisions are more important: choosing a spouse or purchasing a home; picking a daycare provider for a child; providing the right level of discipline for a teenager; or deciding on the best care for an elderly parent. We devote a great deal of our thinking lives to making choices, trying to maximize our own happiness and the well-being of the people we care about. And, perhaps most importantly, we attempt to avoid making the really bad decisions that can have major negative consequences.

Governments are also constantly making decisions. Some governmental decisions are more important than others, but even the smallest can have major consequences. When a government makes a major decision, the effects can be far-reaching—witness the choice of the United States to go to war in Iraq, or the successive decisions made over many years not to improve the levees in New Orleans. Governmental authorities have tremendous power over our lives and the decision to exercise that power—or not to exercise it—can be highly beneficial, but can also be disastrous.

Both governmental and individual decisions are made by people, with all of our human imperfections. Our picture of the world is always incomplete. But despite our inherent flaws and limitations, we are still capable of making decisions in good faith, taking advantage of our natural capacity for reason to best help others and ourselves.

Because of the importance of governmental decisions, and our limited capacity as human beings, government has a responsibility to use the most powerful tools at its disposal to make the best decisions it can.

When policymakers make decisions without gathering all available information, looking at alternative courses of action, and anticipating the likely consequences of their actions, they are as foolish as someone who fails to consult a map when driving in unfamiliar territory. When governmental officials ignore the latest scientific developments, suppress new information, or make decisions that are rationalized after the fact, bad policy is made, resulting in loss of life, squandered economic resources, and the needless destruction of natural resources.

However, making good decisions at the governmental level requires more than looking at a map. Many of these decisions are mind-bendingly complex. Regulations intended to protect the environment or public health often address thorny toxicological questions and engineering or technological challenges that involve diverse sectors of the economy and staggering amounts of data. Regulators must master the physiological, economic, engineering, ecological, and social consequences of regulations in order to make good decisions. When regulators tally the "pros" and "cons" of a decision, they frequently create weighty, multi-volume documents.

Governmental decisions are also fundamentally different from personal decisions in that they often affect people in the aggregate. In our individual lives, we come into contact with at least some of the consequences of our decisions. If we fail to consult a map, we pay the price: losing valuable time driving around in circles and listening to the complaints of our passengers. We are constantly confronted with the consequences of the choices that we have made. Not so for governments, however, which exercise authority by making decisions at a distance.

Perhaps one of the most challenging aspects of governmental decisions is that they require a special kind of compassion—one that can seem, at first glance, cold and calculating, the antithesis of empathy. The aggregate and complex nature of governmental decisions does not address people as human beings, with concerns and interests, families and emotional relationships, secrets and sorrows. Rather, people are numbers stacked in a column or points on a graph, described not through their individual stories of triumph and despair, but by equations, functions, and dose-response curves. The language of governmental decisionmaking can seem to—and to a certain extent does—ignore what makes individuals unique and morally important.

But, although the language of bureaucratic decisionmaking can be dehumanizing, it is also a prerequisite for the kind of compassion that is needed in contemporary society. Elaine Scarry has developed a comparison between *individual compassion* and *statistical compassion*.[1] Individual compassion is familiar—when we see a person suffering, or hear the story of some terrible tragedy, we are moved to take action. Statistical compassion seems foreign—we hear only a string of numbers but must comprehend "the concrete realities embedded there."[2] Individual compassion derives from our social nature, and may be hardwired directly into the human brain.[3] Statistical compassion calls on us to use our higher reasoning power to extend our natural compassion to the task of solving more abstract—but no less real—problems.

Because compassion is not just about making us feel better—which we could do as easily by forgetting about a problem as by addressing it—we have a responsibility to make the best decisions that we can. This book argues that cost-benefit analysis, properly conducted, can improve environmental and public health policy. Cost-benefit analysis—the translation of human lives and acres of forest into the language of dollars and cents—can seem harsh and impersonal. But such an approach is also necessary to improve the quality of decisions that regulators make. Saving the most lives, and best protecting the quality of our environment and our health—in short, exercising our compassion most effectively—requires us to step back and use our best analytic tools. Sometimes, in order to save a life, we need to treat a person like a number. This is the challenge of statistical compassion.

This book is about making good decisions. It focuses on the area of environmental, health and safety regulation. These regulations have been the source of numerous and hard-fought controversies over the past several decades, particularly at the federal level. Reaching the right decisions in the areas of environmental protection, increasing safety, and improving public health is clearly of high importance. Although it is admirable (and fashionable) for people to buy green or avoid products made in sweatshops, efforts taken at the individual level are not enough to address the pressing problems we face—there is a vital role for government in tackling these issues, and sound collective decisions concerning regulation are needed.

There is a temptation to rely on gut-level decisionmaking in order to avoid economic analysis, which, to many, is a foreign language on top of seeming cold and unsympathetic. For government to make good decisions, however, it cannot abandon reasoned analysis. Because of the complex nature of governmental decisions, we have no choice but to deploy complex analytic tools in order to make the best choices possible. Failing to use these tools, which amounts to abandoning our duties to one another, is not a legitimate response. Rather, we must exercise statistical compassion by recognizing what numbers of lives saved represent: living and breathing human beings, unique, with rich inner lives and an interlocking web of emotional relationships.

The acres of a forest can be tallied up in a chart, but that should not blind us to the beauty of a single stand of trees. We need to use complex tools to make good decisions while simultaneously remembering that we are not engaging in abstract exercises, but that we are having real effects on people and the environment.

In our personal lives, it would be unwise not to shop around for the best price when making a major purchase, or to fail to think through our options when making a major life decision. It is equally foolish for government to fail to fully examine alternative policies when making regulatory decisions with life-or-death consequences. This reality has been recognized by four successive presidential administrations. Since 1981, the cost-benefit analysis of major regulations has been required by presidential order. Over the past twenty-five years, however, environmental and other progressive groups have declined to participate in the key governmental proceedings concerning the cost-benefit analysis of federal regulations, instead preferring to criticize the technique from the outside. The resulting asymmetry in political participation has had profound negative consequences, both for the state of federal regulation and for the technique of cost-benefit analysis itself. Ironically, this state of affairs has left progressives open to the charge of rejecting reason, when in fact strong environmental and public health programs are often justified by cost-benefit analysis. It is time for progressive groups, as well as ordinary citizens, to retake the high ground by embracing and reforming cost-benefit analysis.

The difference between being unthinking—failing to use the best tools to analyze policy—and unfeeling—making decisions without compassion—is unimportant: Both lead to bad policy. Calamities can result from the failure to use either emotion or reason. Our emotions provide us with the grounding for our principles, our innate interconnectedness, and our sense of obligation to others. We use our powers of reason to build on that emotional foundation, and act effectively to bring about a better world.

We are all far from infallible. We make mistakes all the time. That is part of learning and acting. The only time that we are truly guilty for our mistakes, however, is when we should have known better. For instance, when governments make bad decisions, people may die. If this outcome is the result of lack of information, or just bad luck, we must accept it as an unfortunate but unavoidable consequence of human limitations. But, in our complex world, government has an obligation to engage reality, to confront and examine problems as directly as possible, and arrive at the best answers it can. When government fails to use its best analytic tools, when bad decisions are made that could have been avoided, it is time to demand a change.

This book makes the case for why cost-benefit analysis is necessary. It also points to many flaws in how this analysis is currently carried out, and suggests what caused these flaws and how they can be remedied. This book does not aspire to be the last word on the economic analysis of regulation. Quite the contrary, the intention is to contribute to a wider dialogue, with a significantly larger pool of participants. For several decades, the conversation has been dominated by foes of regulation, and has largely excluded the public. In order for the future dialogue to be adequately deliberative and sufficiently democratic, more of the voices of Americans affected by regulation—which is to say all of us—must be heard.

PART I | Decisions Are
Made by Those Who
Show Up[4]

The Case for Cost-Benefit Analysis

Domestic issues are back on the table. After the terrorist attacks of September 11, 2001, the nation's attention was focused almost entirely overseas—to issues of terrorism, war, and foreign policy. The administration of President George W. Bush has aggressively argued that the nation is engaged in a "war on terror." The Iraq war and ensuing occupation and civil conflict further relegated domestic issues to the back burner. Security was on people's minds in the 2004 presidential election, and opposition to the Iraq war helped propel Democratic majorities to the House of Representatives and the Senate in 2006. However, domestic issues can remain dormant for only so long, and there has been a resurgence of concern over traditional bread-and-butter domestic issues like health care, job creation, education, and environmental protection.

One debate that has remained latent over the last half-dozen years concerns the proper role of regulation in the American economy. Regulation has a very significant impact on our lives—regulations govern the safety of our workplaces, control the purity of our air and water, and determine the goods available to us as consumers. One would be hard pressed to find a completely unregulated area of contemporary life. And although these regulations generate large benefits, they also impose great costs. In one estimate, the cost of complying with U.S. environmental regulations adopted in the last ten years alone is $20 billion per year.[5]

The debate over weighing the costs and benefits of regulation—dubbed *cost-benefit analysis*—has played an important role in shaping regulatory policy for the past quarter-century. In this debate, there are two main camps. The conservative camp generally wants to reduce or relax economic regulation, and has used cost-benefit analysis to do so. The liberal camp is skeptical of both deregulation and cost-benefit analysis, which it sees as a technique that has historically been invoked to justify deregulation or less stringent regulation.

This book challenges the liberal camp to rethink its position on cost-benefit analysis. Although cost-benefit analysis, as currently practiced, is indeed biased against regulation, those biases are not inherent to the methodology. If those biases were identified and eliminated, cost-benefit analysis would become a powerful tool for neutral policy analysis. In short, this book argues that progressive groups should seek to mend, not end, cost-benefit analysis.

The goal of cost-benefit analysis is straightforward: It seeks to maximize the net benefits of regulation. Net benefits are calculated by subtracting the *costs* of regulation—such as compliance costs, job loss, and the reduced consumer well-being resulting from price increases—from the *benefits*—such as lives saved or protected from disease and disability, wilderness preservation, and the creation of jobs or recreational opportunities. In practice, of course, the question of counting costs and benefits gets very complicated very quickly. But the core idea is simple and intuitive.

The roots of the antiregulatory bias within cost-benefit analysis are historical rather than conceptual. They stem from the shunning of cost-benefit analysis by proregulatory interests—such as consumer, environmental, and labor groups—which had the unintended effect of leaving antiregulatory interests free to shape the use of the technique toward their purposes. Starting in the early 1980s, conservatives used cost-benefit analysis to squelch economic regulation. Groups more sympathetic to regulation found themselves on the defensive. Many liberal groups fought back by rejecting the validity of cost-benefit analysis altogether, claiming that technical and moral problems rendered it worthless.[6] These groups essentially boycotted not just cost-benefit analysis, but any debate over how it should be conducted.

That boycott continued even when these groups had the ear of a sympathetic administration. During Bill Clinton's second term, the Environmental Protection Agency (EPA) initiated a process to create guidelines for how the agency would perform cost-benefit analysis. Most of the relevant players knew that this process would determine crucial methodological issues, such as how to assign a dollar value to life-saving regulations. The antiregulatory camp, including industry, was well represented. But environmentalists avoided the meetings as if they were being held on a Superfund site filled with fifty-gallon drums of benzene.[7] As a result, the guidelines were created with empty chairs in the room.

By ceding the field, liberals ensured that their belief about cost-benefit analysis became a reality. For the past two decades, antiregulatory interests have had nearly free rein to develop cost-benefit analysis. No surprise, then, that the tool has taken the shape of its master's hand. Today, cost-benefit analysis is indeed shot through with many antiregulatory biases. Those biases, however, reflect the character of the masters, and not of the tool. Purged of those biases, cost-benefit analysis can be reclaimed as a neutral instrument.

There are two general classes of antiregulatory bias in contemporary cost-benefit analysis: substantive biases and institutional biases. *Substantive biases* are analytic distortions such as bad assumptions, miscounted costs, and ignored benefits. "Part II: Eight Fallacies of Cost-Benefit Analysis," discusses eight substantive fallacies within cost-benefit analysis that bias the technique against regulation. *Institutional biases* are distortions that arise because particular decisionmaking procedures are poorly structured. "Part III: Instituting Regulatory Rationality," discusses flaws in the structure of regulatory review and how these flaws can be corrected.

Because of these biases, we regulate less, and less stringently, than we should. Under rules that have been in place since the early days of the Reagan administration, most major new environmental, health and safety regulations must pass a cost-benefit test before they can be adopted. Because current cost-benefit analysis is biased against regulation, efficient and worthwhile regulations do not pass the test. For regulatory agencies like the EPA and the Occupational Safety and Health Administration (OSHA), watering down their rules has been the price of getting rules. The result? Less safety, worse health, and a dirtier environment.

Proregulatory interests can no longer cling to the possibility that a boycott can shut down the game; they must now get in the game. Cost-benefit analysis has enormous currency in the federal policymaking apparatus. It is statutorily required for important environmental, health and safety programs.[8] It has been embraced by four successive presidential administrations, both Democratic and Republican. It is institutionally structured into the administrative decisionmaking process through Office of Management and Budget (OMB) review of regulations. Many influential federal judges are strong supporters of cost-benefit analysis,[9] and important court decisions have turned on how administrative agencies apply the technique.[10] Cost-benefit analysis is here to stay.

Now is a good time for liberals to enter the conversation. Proregulatory interests had little opportunity to participate in cost-benefit analysis for a dozen years during the administrations of Presidents Ronald Reagan and George H. W. Bush. At that time, it was more politically expedient for progressives to issue blanket criticisms than develop more nuanced positions. But entrenchment in that position cost proregulatory groups an opportunity to reform cost-benefit analysis during the Clinton years, when they had the ear of White House officials. When the Supreme Court decided the 2000 election in favor of George W. Bush, progressive groups lost access. With a new administration entering office in January 2009, groups may again have an opportunity to participate—they should take advantage of it this time.

CHOOSING COST-BENEFIT ANALYSIS

This book makes the case for cost-benefit analysis not only because such analysis is inevitable, but also because it is desirable. We live in a world of finite resources. Some social problems will resist being fully resolved, even if we spend every dollar we have to address them. Consider "no-threshold pollutants"—environmental contaminants that have adverse health effects even at very low concentrations. To eliminate the risk associated with a no-threshold pollutant, we would have to eliminate or capture every single molecule of the contaminant in the environment—clearly an impossible task. Yet although we cannot achieve zero risk, we can always reduce risk just a bit further. In the absence of an obvious endpoint, we need a mechanism that tells us when to stop spending money. Cost-benefit analysis is that mechanism; it allows us to spend money to the point at which the last dollar spent buys one dollar of risk reduction. If we spend beyond that point, we will pay more than we receive. But if we spend any less, we forego risk reductions that are socially desirable.

For certain kinds of governmental programs, the use of cost-benefit analysis is a requirement of basic rationality. When considering any regulation aimed at increasing economic efficiency, a responsible regulator must estimate the economic costs and benefits. Otherwise, it is impossible to know at what point to stop spending money to achieve one goal and start spending to achieve another. Even for regulation motivated by goals other than efficiency—protecting rights, redistributing wealth, or fulfilling moral obligations—the economic impacts are clearly a relevant consideration.[11]

Cost-benefit analysis also makes decisionmakers more accountable by making their decisions more transparent. Cost-benefit analysis is here to stay, but in some sense it has always been with us. Most political decisions involve some form of cost-benefit analysis, however crude, with some costs not counted at all (such as those imposed on the politically weak) and some benefits given undue weight (such as those accruing to the politically powerful). By providing a more accurate assessment of the real costs and benefits of a decision, formalized cost-benefit analysis reveals the distortions of politics—the backroom deals and special-interest politics—for what they are. And when the bum deals are measured against an objective scale, it is easier for voters to act by "throwing the bums out."

The money spent by governments is accounted for in budgets. Taxpayers are acutely aware of the money they must send to the federal government every year. However, budgets and tax burdens do not capture the economic costs imposed by governmental regulation. It is harder to discern these economic costs because they are borne by individuals and private firms rather than directly by the government. In the absence of some form of cost-benefit analysis, regulations are equivalent to uncounted—and unaccountable—governmental spending. In the typical formulation of both budgets and regulations, it is important for decisionmakers to know how much money they are spending, and what results they are buying. Just as the environmental effects of government actions must be accounted for in an environmental impact statement, the economic effects should be acknowledged as well.

Another important justification for cost-benefit analysis is that it imposes structure on the vast discretion that is given to administrative agencies. In an ideal democracy, the people, or the elected representatives of the people, make the laws and determine their enforcement. That approach is impossible, however, in a complex society such as ours. In order to regulate the American economy, an army of bureaucrats, scientists, lawyers, and economists is needed to gather and process information, and make decisions. Because of the technical nature of many regulatory decisions, bureaucrats and experts deep in the bowels of the federal government wield substantial power over our lives. Cost-benefit analysis can be used to ensure that their decisions are based on reasoned analysis and not, for instance, on the unaccountable whim of an official or a bargain-hunting special interest.

CRITICISMS OF COST-BENEFIT ANALYSIS

Several criticisms of cost-benefit analysis have been advanced.[12] Perhaps the most prevalent argument against cost-benefit analysis is that it leads to immoral commodification. Opponents of cost-benefit analysis have attempted to trump the opposition with the rhetorical attack that such analysis "places a dollar value" on human life or other special kinds of goods like wilderness areas.[13] But this criticism confuses pricing with commodification. Pricing, a mechanism used to allocate society's resources, is the most effective way to aggregate information and allocate scarce resources to produce the most benefit. Prices may reflect an unfair distribution of wealth, but the problem is not prices, but inequity—a problem that can and should be addressed through governmental intervention. Commodification has to do with the social significance of pricing—the fear that assigning a price to the good things in life obscures their inherent worth.[14] Yet pricing does not necessarily result in commodification. After all, many of the goods we hold dear are openly traded on markets, including pets, homes, fine art, medical care, wedding rings, and nature preserves.

Cost-benefit analysis has also been criticized for delivering the impression, but not the reality, of scientific certainty. It is true that cost-benefit analysis has the aura of mathematical accuracy. It is also true that cost-benefit analysis must inevitably incorporate uncertainty. Neither the health effects of a contaminant nor the economic effects of the regulation that seeks to contain it will ever be crystal clear. For some, this inescapable uncertainty renders cost-benefit analysis nearly worthless.[15] But, conducted properly, cost-benefit analysis can help quantify areas of uncertainty to improve decisionmaking. If anything, formal cost-benefit analysis is especially useful in confronting imperfect information; it allows us to clarify the contours of our uncertainty and the distribution of potential outcomes, thereby improving our ability to make smart choices in the face of the unknown.

A third criticism of cost-benefit analysis is that it unfairly distributes regulatory benefits. One of the premises of cost-benefit analysis is that the value of a regulation can be measured by what people would be willing to pay to receive its benefit. Because of widespread inequalities in wealth, however, a willingness to pay does not necessarily track well-being—someone who is very poor may be willing to pay very little for a benefit that nonetheless may improve his or her life a great deal. Thus, relying on the willingness to pay as a metric may result in the diversion of resources to regulations that are not welfare maximizing or that favor the interests of the wealthy over the poor.

The problem underlying this critique is the large gap between the rich and the poor. The appropriate remedy for this problem is the adoption of redistributional policies, not the abandonment of cost-benefit analysis. It is generally thought that the best way to improve overall well-being is to maximize wealth by managing the economy effectively, and then redistributing wealth through the tax-and-transfer system.[16] Cost-benefit analysis, then, helps with the first step—wealth maximization.

In addition, cost-benefit analysis has been altered somewhat in practice to take account of wealth disparities. For example, the value of the benefit typically assigned to life-saving regulations is the same no matter what the target population. As currently conducted, cost-benefit analysis does not value regulations according to the population affected—an average value derived from the whole population is used, thus treating each person equally. In general, this use of average values has a redistributive effect from richer to poorer.

A final and related criticism is that cost-benefit analysis may produce regulatory pariahs.[17] Regulations that benefit some at the expense of others may pass a cost-benefit test. Over a large number of regulations, the disparities will often balance out, as the beneficiaries of one regulation are burdened by another. But there may be systemic biases against specific populations that will make them losers in the overall regulatory scheme. A fundamental concern about fairness arises if certain Americans receive less than they contribute to the regulatory system, while being asked to pay, over and over, for the regulatory benefits delivered to others.

This criticism is powerful, but it does not invalidate the use of cost-benefit analysis. Rather, it suggests that further study is needed to ensure fair distributional impacts of the regulatory system. If necessary, we must redistribute society's wealth in a more egalitarian manner through, for example, the tax-and-transfer and public works programs. Nothing in the redistributive imperative, however, requires us to jettison cost-benefit analysis.

In the end, many of the criticisms of cost-benefit analysis take aim at those who tout cost-benefit analysis as a master decisionmaking procedure capable of trumping all other values. This book makes no such claim. Treating cost-benefit analysis as a master procedure is actually an abuse of the technique. Cost-benefit analysis is only one input into public policy, but it is important. We need a formal and systematic way of measuring the impacts of proposed regulations and comparing them across a common economic scale. To either pick cost-benefit analysis as a master procedure or absolutely reject it is a false choice—cost-benefit analysis can be useful without being the alpha and omega of policy analysis. In the process of making vastly important decisions that affect billions of dollars and every single American, under conditions of great uncertainty, we should take advantage of every available tool to make the best possible choices, without over-relying on any particular technique.

Proregulatory interest groups will often be pleased with the results of properly conducted cost-benefit analysis. The benefits of saving lives, preserving nature for future generations, and avoiding environmental catastrophe, properly calculated, will often outweigh the short-term costs of regulation. As a nation, we are willing to make sacrifices to preserve natural resources for future generations and to protect our health and safety. By retaking rationality as the basis for the regulatory agenda, and embracing appropriate cost-benefit analysis in the regulatory decisionmaking process, proregulatory voices can again rally America to make needed sacrifices and create a better and more sustainable future.

For some, cost-benefit analysis has become a dirty word, a stand-in for a deregulatory agenda that simultaneously blocks important new environmental, health and safety initiatives and seeks to undo past progress. But this need not be so. Cost-benefit analysis—reformed and placed in an improved executive structure—can be a technique embraced by proregulatory interests. Cost-benefit analysis has the potential to increase agency transparency, facilitate the centralization and coordination of agency action, and bring increased rationality to federal regulation. These are outcomes and values that proregulatory interests should support. By fighting to improve cost-benefit analysis, rather than fighting against cost-benefit analysis, proregulatory interests will become more effective and influential in the halls of power and with an American public that is keenly aware of both the great potential and danger of government regulation. Retaking rationality means discarding an entrenched but counterproductive position. It is an opportunity both to gain greater political power and to use this power wisely.

BEYOND TRAGIC CHOICES

A recent article titled, "Dark Side of the New Economy," described the harmful effects of the Long Beach port in California on the local environment, and the general problem of pollution associated with the large American ports that export and import billions of dollars of goods each day. The article, published by the Natural Resources Defense Council in its *OnEarth* magazine, is extremely compelling, providing both human detail and several shocking statistics to drive home the point that port pollution is a serious problem. It opens by contrasting a seemingly bucolic southern California, where "children of many colors play tetherball and basketball in the warm sun" and "palm fronds rustle in the gentle breeze" with the pollution that is carried on that breeze—pollution so strong that "children get sick: [t]he air can irritate eyes, noses, throats, and lungs." The story ends with a local resident, who moved away after 38 years, saying, "And who's left behind? The people who can't leave. Well, God have mercy on them. If that's not environmental injustice, I don't know what is."[18]

Pollution from ports results largely from the unregulated nature of port traffic. An expert quoted in the article, Peter Greenwald, believes that the resulting emissions could be cut by 90 percent or more using existing technology. Container ships, which transport consumer goods into and out of the country, burn an extremely low-grade and polluting form of diesel fuel. These ships typically keep their engines running even when stationary, in order to power up their dockside operations. Many lack even basic pollution controls, the equivalent of catalytic converters on cars, which can reduce emissions very significantly at relatively low cost.

The article casts the problem of port pollution in moral terms, and seeks to elicit strong compassion for the people suffering the consequences of port traffic. The profits of large faceless corporations—many foreign—are set alongside the health of ordinary working Americans. The interest of economic growth is shown as being at odds with the interest of public health and environmental protection. Both the ports and the United States government are portrayed to be in violation of basic moral duties; the former, private firms, are causing serious foreseeable harm to people's health; the latter, our federal government, is abdicating its basic role of protecting the disadvantaged.

In addition to the moral perspective—which is clearly relevant—cost-benefit analysis provides another viewpoint on the problem of port pollution. If it is relatively inexpensive for ports to clean up—by requiring ships to meet air-quality standards through fuel shifting and other relatively cheap mechanisms—and the problems of port pollution, including sickness and death, are severe—then the lack of regulation is not only a moral problem, but also an economic problem. According to such an analysis, prosperity and environmental protection are not in opposition—environmental protection also means increased prosperity. The lack of regulation in this area is understood to have a very large and deleterious effect on America's wealth. The pollution coming from ports does not facilitate economic development; it retards it.

When people are presented with choices between prosperity and environmental protection, they often choose environmental protection. Still, many people understand the choices to be difficult: jobs versus clean air, material wealth versus endangered species, economic development versus the moral duty to future generations. In a number of cases, these choices may seem to require truly tragic compromises—for example, if fulfilling the moral duty to justly distribute environmental goods requires us to slow down economic growth. Cost-benefit analysis, however, shows us that many times, the choices are *not* tragic. Environmental protection is not only the moral thing to do, it also maximizes wealth.

One of the most famous cases in all of environmental law is *TVA v. Hill*,[19] in which the Supreme Court stopped the construction of the Tellico Dam on the Little Tennessee River in order to protect a species of fish called the snail darter. In that decision, the Court determined that the Endangered Species Act prevented the consideration of costs if federal action would imperil an endangered animal. The message of the decision, that environmental values could trump economic values, was hailed by environmentalists and loathed by industry. But the long-term message of *TVA v. Hill* may be that environmental and economic values often go hand in hand. Indeed, it turns out that the Tellico Dam was such a huge waste of money that even by the time the construction was mostly finished, it had became clear that the benefits that could be produced by the dam did not justify completing the project—even without taking the survival of the snail darter into consideration.[20]

In those cases in which protecting the environment is justified by cost-benefit analysis, there is no tragic choice between environmental and economic values, only the tragedy of failed democracy. The Clean Air Act includes provisions to "grandfather" old, dirty power plants, and subjects only new plants to its strict pollution control provisions. When the act was passed, thirty-seven years ago, the thinking was that, eventually, the old plants would become obsolete and go off line. However, that turned out to be incorrect; these ancient, decrepit, pollution-spewing plants are still in operation. Any cost-benefit analysis would show that there are clear economic benefits to shutting down these plants and building newer, more efficient models. If it would be good for the environment, and economically justified, then why has it not been done? In these cases, the resulting lack of regulation is not attributable to differences of values, or the difficulty of making tough choices. The explanation is simpler and sadder: A democratic institution—the legislature, an agency, or the executive—is not functioning properly because of the influence of special interests, short-sighted ideology, incompetence, or some other problem. Cost-benefit-justified regulations that are not undertaken point to the basic failure of policymakers and pathologies within our system of government.

Cost-benefit analysis, then, can be an enormously powerful tool for proregulatory groups. It can show that the interests they represent—the environment, consumers, or workers—are not opposed to the economy. Instead, regulation is necessary to preserve economic value and maximize wealth because protecting the environment and protecting health and safety are an essential part of a well-functioning economy. Without regulation, we would all be much poorer. And if cost-benefit analysis shows that regulations are justified, proregulatory groups have a strong argument that the obstacles are not competing values, but simply the failures of politicians or regulators to serve the interests of the American public. Cost-benefit analysis, then, can be a radical tool, useful to challenge the existing order. Even Ronald Reagan did not stop the phaseout of leaded gasoline when presented with a powerful cost-benefit analysis showing its net benefits.

Progressive groups have had many important successes in challenging the status quo by framing their arguments in terms of individual rights. The civil rights movement provided the template for other important social justice movements like the women's and gay rights movements, and the environmental justice movement. There are important tactical advantages to arguing in terms of rights—perhaps most importantly, for these groups, has been access to the courts as a lever of power to move their agendas. Rights-based arguments are also professionally attractive to the cadre of lawyers that staff many proregulatory groups.[21] And the rhetoric of rights resounds strongly within the American public. Because cost-benefit analysis argues in terms of aggregate welfare, rather than individual rights, it is unfamiliar to many progressive organizations. That does not mean, however, that it is ineffective.

The same story can be told in many ways. In order to reach as broad an audience as possible, proregulatory groups must be able to tell their stories so that every sector of American society can hear them. Environmental, consumer, and labor organizations know how to tell compelling narratives of the consequences of governmental failure—the children with asthma, the young father crushed in an industrial accident. These stories are important and should be told. They galvanize public support, and speak to our essential humanity by calling on our compassion for the troubles of our fellow human beings. But such narratives can lose their power in judicial or regulatory proceedings—in the eyes of judges or regulatory agencies, these are soft and unscientific, mere anecdotes that lack concrete, quantifiable meaning. And there are many Americans who require not only individual stories, but hard numbers to convince them that regulation is justified. It is in these contexts that proregulatory groups can reach for cost-benefit analysis. The heart of any movement may be individual stories of hardship and struggle, of injustice and redemption. But at some point, reason—coolly calculating, rational, disinterested—must be applied. Proregulatory groups need not lose their souls in order to embrace cost-benefit analysis. They only need to be reminded that reason is often on their side as well.

The Walls Go Up

Conservative think tanks, academics, and policy makers have taken an entirely different approach to cost-benefit analysis. Unlike proregulatory groups, conservatives have embraced this tool wholeheartedly—pushing to expand its use, and combing for ways to reform it to their liking. At every stage in the development of cost-benefit analysis, commentators and decisionmakers committed to deregulation have faithfully pursued the goals of placing cost-benefit analysis at the center of the administrative state and shaping it towards their agenda. When the political climate was in their favor, they quickly moved to implement their vision of cost-benefit analysis. When they faced opposition in the White House, they used whatever levers they had at their disposal in Congress, and bided their time until better conditions arose.

PREPARATION, PREPARATION, PREPARATION

William A. Niskanen, an economist trained at the University of Chicago, was one of several conservative academics who slowly built support for the antiregulatory agenda in the 1970s. Niskanen's most important academic contribution came in 1971, with the publication of his book *Bureaucracy and Representative Government*. In that book, he offers the theory of the "empire-building" bureaucrat. Under this theory, high-level regulatory officials act as economic utility-maximizers by seeking increases in the size of their agencies' budgets and mandates. Their thirst for power results in a bureaucracy that, in size, is vastly out of proportion to the economy, resulting in reductions in economic growth and prosperity.

The empire-building theory of agencies had a broad impact, both inside the academy and in the larger political debate. Perhaps more importantly, it was used with considerable success by opponents of regulation to justify the need to control regulators. Niskanen's theories helped undercut the classical idea of the regulator as a public-minded civil servant. By recasting bureaucrats as opportunists, Niskanen justified controlling them more strictly.

Another important early player responsible for the increased role of cost-benefit analysis of federal regulation was Murray L. Weidenbaum. A conservative economist, Weidenbaum first became involved in regulatory politics while a professor at Washington University in St. Louis, where he founded the Center for the Study of American Business in 1975.[22] In 1977, he issued an independent analysis of federal regulation, claiming that the prior year's regulations imposed $66.1 billion in costs on the United States economy.[23] It was one of the first studies done on this topic.[24] In the late 1970s, Weidenbaum authored several articles that sought to estimate the costs imposed by federal regulation, and argued strenuously that deregulation was needed to spur economic growth.[25]

Weidenbaum's analysis of the impact of regulation on the economy, and the overall well-being of the American public, was informed by his views about how regulation came about. He argued that the standard economic theory of regulation, asserting that regulated industry captured the political process, had to be updated to reflect new times:

> [T]he core of the economist's version of the "capture" theory still holds—public policy tends to be dominated by the organized and compact pressure groups who attain their benefits at the expense of the more diffused and larger body of consumers. But the nature of those interest groups have changed in recent years. Instead of the railroad baron . . . the villain of the piece has become a self-styled representative of the Public Interest, who has succeeded so frequently in identifying his or her personal prejudices with the national well-being. The business firm, in contrast, performing the traditional middleman function, typically serves the unappreciated and involuntary role of proxy for the overall consumer interests.

With this story, Weidenbaum gives his account of why overly burdensome environmental, health and safety regulations come about, and why concerted action on behalf of the embattled business community was needed to scale back the "growing intrusion of the public bureaucracy into the private sector."[26]

One of Weidenbaum's most important contributions at this stage was to suggest cost-benefit analysis as a tool to rein in the regulatory state. He argued that pleas for deregulation were not sufficient. He acknowledged that some regulation was necessary to address market failures. But he also suggested that substantial deregulation could be achieved through "the methodologies developed in the field of public finance" including "benefit-cost tests and cost-effectiveness studies." He acknowledged that "to an eclectic economist, government regulation should be carried to the point where the incremental costs equal the incremental benefits," and cited the early conservative economic theorist Friedrich Hayek for the proposition that "a free market system does not exclude [all regulation] on principle."[27] Nevertheless, Weidenbaum clearly believed that cost-benefit analysis could be used to reduce the overall impact of regulation on the economy, with the primary goal of stopping new regulation and encouraging deregulation.

Several other conservative scholars argued for deregulation from perches such as the American Enterprise Institute (AEI), publishing in academic journals and publications like *Regulation* magazine. Two such scholars, who would later play important roles in the Reagan administration, were James C. Miller III and Christopher DeMuth. Miller was a resident scholar and director of the Center for the Study of Government Regulation at AEI, a think tank with a long history of opposing governmental regulation. He had also served as an economist (Miller has a PhD in economics from the University of Virginia) in the Nixon and Ford administrations, working at the Council on Wage and Price Stability, which undertook early efforts at conducting centralized regulatory review. During those years, Miller published books and articles on cost-benefit analysis[28] and regulatory reform.[29]

DeMuth was also active in regulatory politics. He served in the Nixon administration as a staff assistant and ultimately as the chairman of the White House Task Force on Environmental Policy. He also spent time at Harvard University, where he was a lecturer at the Kennedy School of Government and the director of the Harvard Faculty Project on Regulation.

Writing in *American Spectator* in 1978, DeMuth argued that an Agency for Consumer Advocacy—proposed by President Jimmy Carter—might not be a bad idea, so long as it was used to counteract the "splurge of new health, safety, and environmental laws," that DeMuth saw as "hostile toward traditional business values and paternalistic toward the consumer."[30] DeMuth believed, however, that "in the hands of anti-business ideologues or those who believe they can judge the consumer interest better than consumers themselves," a new Consumer Advocate might do great harm. To DeMuth, the only appropriate role for a federal consumer advocacy agency was to reduce consumer regulation in the hopes that an unleashed free market would provide consumers the best possible choices and prices—a role he called "defending consumers against regulation."[31] Prior to his governmental appointment, DeMuth also published several antiregulatory articles arguing, for example, that regulation tended to reduce the economic competitiveness of the United States in global markets,[32] and that tighter control needed to be exerted over spendthrift federal agencies.[33]

The Reagan administration was not the first to try to reduce regulation and impose more centralized control of governmental agencies, but earlier efforts had not been very effective. President Nixon began the process by requiring agencies to circulate proposed environmental, consumer, and health and safety rules among other agencies for comment.[34] Battling the continuing threat of inflation, President Ford required agencies to assess the impact of new regulations on inflation, a requirement that was administered by the Council on Wage and Price Stability.[35] President Carter also required agencies to prepare statements of the impacts of their regulations, and created a Regulatory Analysis Review Group to comment on certain major rules.[36]

The antiregulatory arguments made by conservative scholars and industry had started to convince important policymakers that something far more significant had to be done to gain control of the new administrative agencies that were issuing environmental, health and safety rules. Though these efforts were tentative and somewhat ineffective, they were the early signs that the power of the antiregulatory movement was beginning to be translated into public policy. Under the Reagan administration, the steps taken by opponents of regulation shifted from tentative to surefooted.

REAGAN AND THE RISE OF COST-BENEFIT ANALYSIS

After developing his academic ideas about the origin of burdensome regulation, and his views about the costs imposed by the regulatory state, Murray Weidenbaum became involved in Ronald Reagan's presidential campaign. He played a prominent role in the campaign's emphasis on deregulation, serving as the chairman of its task force on regulation, which ultimately recommended a one-year moratorium on all environmental, health and safety regulation.[37] The Reagan campaign consistently emphasized deregulation as an important plank in its platform; for example, in a debate with President Carter, then Governor Reagan said:

I am suggesting that there are literally thousands of unnecessary regulations that invade every facet of business, and indeed, very much of our personal lives, that are unnecessary; that Government can do without; that have added $130 billion to the cost of production in this country; and that are contributing their part to inflation. And I would like to see us a little more free, as we once were.[38]

The work of Weidenbaum and his intellectual peers laid the foundation for Reagan's deregulation agenda. The Reagan campaign was able to cast regulation and the federal bureaucracy as the enemy of economic growth, and the friend of inflation. By tapping into the deep anxiety of the working and middle class about their financial prospects, Reagan successfully positioned his agenda of deregulation and tax cutting as the key to creating jobs and increasing overall prosperity. This narrative was an important part of the Reagan campaign's success at unseating President Carter and gaining the White House.

Reagan rewarded the cadre of antiregulatory intellectuals with appointments to several key positions in his new administration. For his efforts, Weidenbaum was named the first chairman of Reagan's Council of Economic Advisers. Niskanen, the scholar who developed the theory of the empire-building bureaucrat, was given one of the two other posts on the council and charged with focusing on regulatory matters, among other areas.[39] Miller was appointed to head up the new Office of Information and Regulatory Affairs (OIRA) within the Office of Management and Budget (OMB).

Within a month of his inauguration in 1981, President Reagan issued Executive Order 12,291, asserting an unprecedented level of control over the administrative apparatus.[40] This executive order created the essential architecture for the central review of agency action that is in place today. Agencies were required to prepare detailed cost-benefit analyses of proposed regulations with a significant impact on the economy, and if a regulation's expected costs exceeded its expected benefits, then the regulation could not go forward. Officials within OIRA would oversee this process, and were empowered to determine whether proposed regulations passed muster under cost-benefit analysis. This entire process of OIRA review was largely shrouded in secrecy, with the relationships between OIRA officials and agency representatives, and OIRA and the affected industry, kept from the public view. When the executive order was announced, political commentators credited Weidenbaum, along with Vice President George H. W. Bush and James Miller, for having developed the strategy behind the order.[41]

As the head of OIRA, James Miller became the first "regulatory czar," as the newly empowered OIRA administrator would come to be called.[42] He was also the first executive director of Reagan's Presidential Task Force on Regulatory Relief. In that capacity, he helped implement the program of deregulation that was one of the central pieces of the Reagan economic agenda. The task force, chaired by Vice President Bush, ran for almost three years, and claimed responsibility for "saving U.S. businesses and consumers $150 billion."[43] In particular, it played a prominent role in the reduction of environmental, health and safety regulations. One oft-quoted statistic: *The Federal Register* ran 82,012 pages the year before the task force, and 58,494 afterwards.[44]

Reagan's OIRA team also included James Tozzi. Tozzi joined OMB during the Nixon administration and was given the task of reviewing the environmental protection rules that were coming out of the newly formed Environmental Protection Agency (EPA). There, and in his previous post at the U.S. Army, he sought an expanded role for centralized review, using cost-benefit analysis, to advance his "market-based conservative" ideology.[45] He stayed on through the Ford administration; President Carter also kept him, promoting Tozzi to assistant director of OMB, where he became the Carter administration's "point man"[46] on the Paperwork Reduction Act, which first created OIRA within OMB.

With Reagan's election, Tozzi's dream of a centralized reviewer, deploying cost-benefit analysis, with broad authority over the federal regulation-making apparatus, became a reality. Under Reagan, Tozzi was appointed the deputy administrator of OIRA, which became known as a "black hole"[47] for regulations. It was during this time that environmentalists and others formed their first, unfavorable impressions of centralized review and cost-benefit analysis. In Tozzi's words: "Under the Reagan administration, every environmental regulation had to come to me. I was heavily criticized by the environmental groups and we were frequently called up to [congressional] committee hearings. It was bloody. I loved it."[48]

The battle over Reagan's new order, including the new, more prominent role for cost-benefit analysis, began almost immediately. Proregulatory interests, clearly fearful of what the Reagan administration intended, took a position against cost-benefit analysis. When Weidenbaum published his first study of regulatory costs in the mid-1970s, the consumer advocate Ralph Nader responded with a study of his own, attempting to show that the benefits of federal regulation outweighed its costs.[49] Nevertheless, as the visions of Weidenbaum, Miller, and others were implemented by the Reagan administration, proregulatory groups clearly felt backed into an anti-cost-benefit corner: Saul Miller, spokesman for the AFL-CIO, said at the time of the order, "Our position has always been . . . that we don't like anything that prices out human life."[50]

The new regime had many critics. Many feared that cost-benefit analysis was a code for deregulation, and this concern was not misplaced. Agencies received OMB's inputs so late in the rulemaking process that it was "virtually impossible to do anything productive about them."[51] The size of OIRA's staff, which was tiny relative to the number of regulations it was meant to review, gave rise to costly and lengthy delays.[52] Furthermore, the opacity of the new OMB review process led to fears that industries would be able to kill regulations contrary to their interests under cover of night.[53] In short, critics worried that agencies would have less incentive to incur the large costs of promulgating regulations, and that the administrative state would grind to a halt.

These fears were largely vindicated. Writing in 1986, Alan Morrison, who at the time represented the proregulatory organization Public Citizen, summarized the concerns of many proregulatory groups about how OMB operated.[54] Morrison argued that the OMB review process resulted in "costly delays that are paid for through the decreased health and safety of the American public,"[55] and "operates in an atmosphere of secrecy,"[56] thereby making "a mockery of the system of open participation."[57] He focused his attack on the delays associated with OMB review and cost-benefit analysis: "[T]he vast amount of additional resources spent in justifying proposed regulations to OMB . . . are all burdens on the federal treasury, yet there is no indication that these costs have been balanced against the benefits to be derived from this complex labyrinth of OMB overlay."[58] Morrison was not alone in his concerns. In a statement entered into the 1987 Congressional Record by Representative Henry Waxman of California, Dr. Samuel Epstein, a cancer researcher, placed blame for undiminished cancer rates in part on cost-benefit analysis, accusing President Reagan of "insisting on formal cost-benefit analysis which focus on industry costs . . . and making regulation dependent on the Office of Management and Budget with its subservience to the White House."[59]

During a 1982 congressional hearing on the subject of OMB review of environmental regulation, Representative John Dingell, Chairman of the House Committee on Energy and Commerce expressed serious concerns:

> OMB acts as a conduit for promoting the views of industry affected by proposed regulations through secret, undisclosed, and unreviewable contacts . . . . Moreover, we have received information that the Office of Management and Budget has attempted to influence agency rulemaking on philosophical or political ground without regard for the cost and, more importantly, the benefits of regulations.[60]

At the same hearing, Representative Al Gore questioned a former chief of staff to the EPA administrator under Reagan about the relationship between OMB review and agency decisions.

Mr. GORE: We have had a number of concerns about the regulatory review process established by Executive Order 12,291, and it has been suggested that this executive order and the regulatory review process it establishes often act as a conduit for the expression of views on the part of industry affected by a proposed regulation. Did your experience as EPA Administrator Burford's Chief of Staff show this suggestion to be true?

Mr. DANIEL: Yes, sir, Mr. Gore. There were a number of instances when regulations that we sent to OMB were the subject of communications with OMB, in which it seemed that the feedback we were getting from them was more analysis from the intended regulatee than from OMB staff.

Mr. GORE: Could you give examples of that?

Mr. DANIEL: During the consideration of [Clean Water Act] regulations, we got a number of comments from OMB . . . that were of such a particularized technical nature, and I am talking about in an engineering sense, that they would have had to have come from someone other than the staff of OMB itself.

Mr. GORE: So, you had the strong impression that the Office of Management and Budget was communicating through a back channel with the industry intended to be affected by the regulations . . . and then allowing themselves to be used as a conduit to EPA for comments by the affected industry. Is that correct?

Mr. DANIEL: That is correct, sir.

Mr. GORE: Another problem that this subcommittee has long had with the OMB procedure involves the application of cost-benefit analysis. Several people have suggested to us that when OMB applies a cost-benefit analysis under the procedure, it really doesn't look at the benefits. Principally, it looks at the costs, and ignores the benefits. Have you had any experiences which suggest to you that that is their approach?

Mr. DANIEL: Well . . . when we were deregulating . . . the [Regulatory Impact Assessments] and other types of analyses that ordinarily would be required . . . were not imposed.

Mr. GORE: But in your experience, they looked principally at the costs and not at the benefits, correct?

Mr. DANIEL: That is correct.

Mr. GORE: In those cases in which EPA took some action contrary to the wishes of OMB, what were the consequences?

Mr. DANIEL: Well, usually there were veiled threats of what would happen next. On one occasion, Mr. Gore, I was a participant with the Administrator in issuing some regulations over OMB's objections. These were regulations that had been ordered by court. The Agency—the Administrator was under court order to issue by a certain deadline. When they had not received the requisite OMB approval under the Executive order, she nonetheless signed the regulations and issued them. Late that evening I received a call from an OMB official in which—

Mr. GORE: Who?

Mr. DANIEL: —Mr. Jim Tozzi, who worked with Mr. DeMuth at OMB at that time. But he said to me words to this effect that there was a price to pay for doing what we had done, and that we hadn't begun to pay.[61]

Cost-benefit analysis, then, became closely associated both with conservative antiregulation advocates,[62] and an OMB process that was secretive and tilted toward industry interests. This union of behind-closed-doors decisionmaking and an antiregulatory administrative bias indicated to environmentalist and other proregulatory groups that cost-benefit analysis was a pretext for deregulation, rather than a legitimate analytic tool. Especially in the early days, when cost-benefit techniques were much less fully developed, a large number of judgment calls were made, and those calls tended to be made against regulation. Pragmatically, given the political context, proregulatory groups had little choice but to fight against the use of cost-benefit analysis.

PRESIDENT GEORGE H. W. BUSH AND THE COUNCIL ON COMPETITIVENESS

The developments of the early years of the presidency of George H. W. Bush provide further insight into the antagonistic relationship between proregulatory interests and centralized review of agency decisionmaking. In 1989, Congress, at the urging of environmental groups, among others, refused to reauthorize funding for OIRA or confirm the president's nominee to head the agency.[63] The response was an increase in the prominence of the Council on

Competitiveness, a group headed by Vice President Dan Quayle. Quayle was "a self-proclaimed 'zealot when it comes to deregulation,'"[64] and the council was sharply critical of any regulation and deeply solicitous of business interests.[65]

The council was staffed by free-market enthusiasts with an open contempt for regulatory agencies. The council's executive director, Allan Hubbard, asserted that policy should not be set by "some green eye-shade type in the bowels of the bureaucracy."[66] With the reduced role of OIRA, the council soon "stepped in to fill the political void and set the tone of regulatory review,"[67] plunging into efforts to water down or kill a wide array of regulations. Although separate from OIRA and not part of the regular channels of presidential review of rulemaking, the council accumulated increasing oversight power over contentious regulations.[68]

The council's approach was to persuade or coerce agencies to relax regulatory burdens on American business while "leaving . . . 'no fingerprints' on the results of its interventions."[69] The secrecy was necessary, reasoned Quayle's aides, because many of the issues were "political loser[s]."[70] More disturbing were reports like the following: "In almost every city he visits as a campaigner, Quayle holds closed-door roundtables with businesspeople who have made sizable contributions to the local or national GOP. Hubbard . . . often travels with Quayle and sits in on these sessions."[71] The implication that the council routinely parlayed deregulatory initiatives in exchange for campaign contributions is difficult to ignore.

It is no wonder, then, that environmental groups did not believe they would get fair treatment in a centralized review process that they viewed as a mechanism for insiders to kill regulation by using the access purchased with donations to political campaigns. During the Bush/Quayle administration, the Democratic Congress attempted to place OIRA within the control of less politically motivated civil servants, raising the hope that cost-benefit analysis could be used as a neutral tool. Instead, cost-benefit analysis became further associated with a movement that was biased against regulation and all too eager to capitulate to the demands of industry at the expense of the environment, and the health and safety of the American people.

Missed Opportunities

Although the hostility of proregulatory groups toward cost-benefit analysis is understandable, it has led to some extremely negative consequences. Chief among these is the failure of these groups to develop a positive vision of cost-benefit analysis, so that when they regained access to the White House, they had little to contribute to the reform of cost-benefit analysis that was needed. The result is that an important opportunity to counter the antiregulatory point of view was lost and many of the antiregulatory biases adopted during the Reagan and Bush administrations were left in place. Meanwhile, conservative antiregulatory thinkers did not suffer the same paralysis. They continued to produce a steady stream of theoretical and empirical work about cost-benefit analysis and federal regulation. They also took advantage of the alternative power base that came into Congress in the 1994 elections and were well positioned to immediately move forward with their agenda when George W. Bush walked into the White House in 2001.

THE CLINTON PRESIDENCY

When President Clinton was elected in 1992, many observers hoped, if not expected, that he would abandon the Reagan-era executive review process.[72] Recognizing, however, that Reagan's innovation provided him with an opportunity to exercise substantial control over an ever-more-important regulatory state, Clinton instead co-opted the Reagan orders and made them his own. Executive Order 12,866, issued in 1993, maintained the existing structure of the regulatory review process, continuing Office of Information and Regulatory Affairs (OIRA) review of "significant regulatory action."[73] In response to criticisms of how OIRA review had been practiced in the prior Republican administrations, however, the Clinton order imposed more robust disclosure requirements,[74] emphasized that agencies should weigh "qualitative measures," including "distributive impacts" and "equity" when engaging in cost-benefit analysis,[75] and set deadlines on OIRA review that prevented the agency from permanently stalling the implementation of a regulation.[76]

The message from the Clinton White House was that centralized review and cost-benefit analysis could serve as a neutral tool.[77] Yet that message received a chilly reception from environmental groups and other proregulatory interests. Environmental groups failed to meet on a regular basis with the Office of Management and Budget (OMB), to participate and comment on cost-benefit analyses, to develop their own versions of cost-benefit analysis, or to engage in the development of cost-benefit methodologies.[78] Sally Katzen, who was the administrator of OIRA, notes that the Clinton administration was "receptive to environmentalists"[79] over a range of issues, including about how to conduct cost-benefit analysis. Having observed that industry and other antiregulatory interests were consistently lobbying OMB on methodological issues, she expressed frustration with the environmentalist position, which she characterized as: "We don't like cost-benefit analysis, full stop." Katzen recalls trying to convince environmental groups that cost-benefit analysis could be a "neutral stadium," and encouraging groups to "play in that game."[80] Her efforts were not generally rewarded. When environmentalists did meet with OMB during the Clinton administration, it was not to discuss overall methodology, but was rather more focused on individual rules, either when groups felt the rule proposed by an agency was not stringent enough, or to counter antiregulatory lobbying to bolster an agency proposal. After spending time prodding groups to participate in the discussion over how to conduct cost-benefit analysis, she became sufficiently frustrated that she "gave up in trying to entice them to devote energies to it."[81]

A particularly telling example of the failure of environmental groups to participate in the cost-benefit debate came in the late 1990s, when the Environmental Protection Agency (EPA) was revising its guidelines over how to conduct cost-benefit analysis.[82] It is important to keep in mind that in the administrative apparatus of Washington, D.C., major decisions are often made through accumulation. Big decisions are subdivided into smaller decisions, which are then further subdivided until each is manageable. Information is gathered and processed, formal and informal meetings are held, and the views and perspectives of various actors are vetted and considered. These small decisions—made in hallways, by the authors of agency white papers, by analysts reviewing the testimony of agency officials to be given before empty congressional hearings—accumulate over time, until, sometimes before anybody realizes it, the big decision emerges. It is often then, after the weight of all of those little decisions has piled up, that the public gets involved. At that point, the inertia can be impossible to overcome.

Interest groups successfully influence the bureaucratic process by being present when the little decisions are made. A watchful eye at a public hearing, an impressive and well-researched written comment, meetings and intra-agency information trading, a well-timed letter from a senior staffer at a congressional committee—all are important weapons in the lobbyist's arsenal. These weapons are deployed silently and steadily, and ultimately with great effect. By applying low doses of pressure throughout the administrative process, interest groups can have big effects on ultimate regulatory outcomes.

As little bureaucratic decisions go, the EPA's decision to revise the guidelines was important and its impact would be broad because all major regulations undergo cost-benefit analysis. The guidelines would structure how analysts approached the cost-benefit analysis, what information they considered, and what standards they applied. The methodological choices that go into cost-benefit analysis can have a major impact on outcomes; regulations that are justified under one set of assumptions may be entirely unjustified under another. The biases toward or against regulation that are built into the methodology of cost-benefit analysis play out over and over again in the administrative process, significantly shaping our regulatory regimes.

The revision of the guidelines was broken down into smaller decisions concerning the various methodological questions that arise in cost-benefit analysis. One of these was the value for a statistical life that would be adopted in agency cost-benefit analysis. The value of a statistical life is a crucial concept in cost-benefit analysis, and is particularly important for environmental regulation. Many environmental measures aim to reduce the mortality risks posed by certain contaminants. How we value mortality risk reductions is a key component of the estimated benefits delivered by environmental programs. The idea behind a statistical life is that even minuscule reductions in individual risks, applied to large populations, result in an expected number of lives saved. The individual risk reduction of a particular regulation is multiplied by the population affected by the regulation in order to generate an estimate of saved "statistical lives."

To compare the regulatory benefit with the economic costs of a regulation, the life-saving value of the regulation must be translated into dollars. Traditionally, this is done by looking at the marketplace, where people make dollar-denominated decisions about risk all the time—when they purchase a vehicle, decide where to live and what kinds of products to buy, or what kind of job to take. For instance, people choose between spending on a safety feature on a car, or forgoing the safety feature in order to spend money elsewhere. Or, in comparing jobs, people will typically demand a higher income for work that entails a higher risk of injury. Using statistical tools, economists examine these market-based risk decisions to determine how much people are willing to pay to reduce small risks. The number of statistical lives saved is multiplied by the value of a statistical life to estimate the regulatory benefit delivered by mortality risk reductions, in dollars. This benefit can, therefore, be compared to the economic costs of the regulation, to determine whether the net effect of the regulation is wealth maximizing.

The particular value of a statistical life selected in EPA cost-benefit analysis is enormously significant because much of the benefit of many environmental programs is the reduction of mortality risks. Thus, this value determines, among other things, how much will be spent scrubbing pollutants from industrial emissions, the kinds of measures that will be taken to reduce effluents discharged into waterways, and how many carcinogens will be allowed at hazardous waste sites.

When faced with difficult and politically charged decisions, agencies sometimes convene expert panels. The EPA has a standing Science Advisory Board, which advises the EPA on technical and scientific issues. The EPA charged a committee of the Science Advisory Board to comment on the EPA's draft of its cost-benefit analysis guidelines. Although the views of such committees do not bind the EPA, they are accorded great weight. But a funny thing happened when the committee began to hold meetings: The chairs reserved for the environmentalists stood empty.

The members of the committee attended. And, as with every major (and most minor) governmental decisionmaking processes, the views of industry were well represented. But the environmentalists stayed away.[83]

Environmental groups could not have believed the meetings were unimportant. It is widely known that cost-benefit analysis plays a large role in regulation. Moreover, even though the resources of environmental groups are small compared to the resources of industry groups,[84] such groups have still been able to effect changes in the regulatory process.

It is also difficult to argue that the committee would not have been responsive to the views of environmental groups for political reasons. The EPA revision of the guidelines was taking place when Bill Clinton was president and his people were in charge of the EPA. If there has been a time in the last twenty-five years when environmentalists held influence in the executive branch, the late 1990s was that time. At other times, such as during the George W. Bush administration, environmental groups have felt frozen out for political reasons,[85] but the Clinton years represented a thaw, an opportunity to have their voices heard.

Wesley Warren, the director of programs at the Natural Resources Defense Council (NRDC), and a former associate director for natural resources, energy, and science at OMB, explains his group's decision to avoid the committee meetings: "NRDC isn't going to change anyone's opinion in there. Environmentalists without PhDs in economics from MIT aren't going to make headway in a room full of neoclassical economists."[86] Eric Haxthausen, a former Environmental Defense economist and staffer at OMB, makes a similar point in explaining his interactions with environmental groups when he worked in government: "Groups don't communicate in a way that appeals to OIRA. Often, they would come in with messages geared more to the public. They'd show up with pictures of kids holding inhalers and things like that. Environmental groups are accustomed to making more emotional arguments that resonate on the Hill and with the public but don't necessarily resonate with OIRA."[87]

So environmentalists feel (and to some extent are) ill-equipped to contribute to the technical decisions that go into cost-benefit analysis. This, however, cannot be the whole answer, because environmental groups have been able to effect change in forums where they might be thought to have a competitive disadvantage. They have hired lawyers to influence courts, public relations specialists to wrangle the media, and scientists to lobby regulatory agencies. But they have chosen not to hire the kind of experts that could have influenced the committee and cost-benefit analysis more generally.

Being inadequately prepared to affect the cost-benefit analysis process was not the only problem. Attending the EPA Science Advisory Board committee meetings and advocating for specific methodological changes—like increasing the value of a statistical life—would have violated the general position of environmental groups against cost-benefit analysis. Even arguing in the alternative—"We don't like cost-benefit analysis, but if you are going to do it, this is how it should be done"—might be seen as a tacit endorsement of cost-benefit analysis. Environmental groups had joined other proregulatory interests in fighting the use of cost-benefit analysis across the board, and therefore found it difficult to participate in a process that endorsed cost-benefit analysis, even when there was an opportunity to improve the methodology.

Another important barrier to participating in the methodological debate over cost-benefit analysis is that a number of proregulatory groups have cast their opposition in strictly moral terms. Some environmental groups find that the "moral issues are paramount; they don't want the valuation of human life."[88] Others are more pragmatic, for example, recognizing that it is a "fact of life" that "you can't spend all of society's capital on preventing premature mortality."[89] But the existence of groups that have taken a strong position against cost-benefit analysis, defended in moral terms, makes it more difficult for the more pragmatic groups to become involved in cost-benefit analysis.

The result is that, even when environmental groups were welcomed to give their input, they voluntarily shut themselves out of the process. Because cost-benefit analysis has been recognized by almost every institutional actor as a valid and useful tool, proregulatory groups were never going to be able to abolish the technique altogether. Proregulatory groups have been unable to shape cost-benefit analysis more to their liking as a result of their strong rhetoric and well-ingrained aversion to the technique. They see it as a "warped tool in terms of design and application"[90]—but have found themselves unable and unwilling to reform it.

FIGHTING REGULATION DURING THE CLINTON YEARS

Early in the Clinton administration, the Republican Congress, elected in 1994, was adding strength to the association of cost-benefit analysis with the antiregulatory agenda. Given the Contract with America and the antiregulation rhetoric that accompanied the Republican takeover of Congress, regulatory reform legislation became a hot topic, ushering in what law professor Cass Sunstein (a rare progressive proponent of cost-benefit analysis) has referred to as the "cost-benefit state."[91] Comprehensive regulatory reform initially proposed in 1994 would have required the implementation of cost-benefit analysis for all environmental, health and safety regulations. Efforts to pass legislation requiring federal agencies to consider the efficacy and cost-effectiveness of regulations had begun with the 103d Congress in 1992.[92] But it was with the Contract with America in 1994 that Congress first revealed an appetite for comprehensive regulatory reform legislation.[93] The 104th, 105th, and 106th Congresses all considered legislation that would have required administrative agencies to subject proposed regulations to risk assessment and cost-benefit analysis, going beyond the scope of the Executive Order.[94]

The Contract with America Congress was also deeply skeptical about the benefits of regulation, and attempted to scale back regulatory efforts on a variety of fronts.[95] Here, environmental groups won some victories, defeating some cost-benefit bills. These victories caused proregulatory groups to bunker into their position against cost-benefit analysis. At a time when environmental victories in Congress were hard to achieve, they had struck a blow against a methodology associated with conservative, antiregulatory forces.

Still, while proregulatory groups were mounting rear-guard efforts to fight a general weakening of environmental, health and safety laws, the antiregulatory scholars were hard at work making the case against regulation, and for their version of cost-benefit analysis as the correct cure for the ailing regulatory state. One particularly important example was the "regulatory scorecard" movement.[96] These scorecards were an effort by antiregulatory figures to use cost-benefit analysis techniques to argue that many governmental regulations were staggering wastes of money. To the casual reader, they are a persuasive account of a regulatory state run amok. Despite more recent (generally successful) attempts to discredit the methodology of these scorecards,[97] their main finding—that regulation is often extraordinarily wasteful, with costs orders of magnitude greater than their benefits—has become lodged in the public's mind.[98]

The first scorecard came out before the Reagan administration was out the door. It helped conjure the specter of the intrusive and money-sucking administrative state just in time for the 1988 elections. Authored by John F. Morrall III, an OMB economist, and published in *Regulation* magazine, his piece, "A Review of the Record,"[99] included a table comparing the estimated costs of a set of federal regulations with his monetization of the expected benefits of the regulation. His results were striking—several regulations cost over $100 million per life saved, with one regulation costing almost $70 billion per life. The Morrall piece has been strongly criticized for, among other things, including regulatory proposals that were never adopted as regulations. Many of the most egregious examples of excessively expensive regulations fall into this category. Morrall also employed several controversial assumptions about discounting that led to some outlandish results.[100] Nevertheless, Morrall's table was widely reported, and had a big impact in the public policy arena, stirring debate over regulatory costs and cost-benefit analysis just in time for a presidential election.

During the Clinton administration, other important actors joined the regulatory scorecard game. Professor John Graham, then of Harvard University, writing with Tammy Tengs, released two large studies, which attempted to calculate the net benefits of several regulations. Both studies found that the government was wasting staggering sums. In their first study, *Five-Hundred Life-Saving Interventions and Their Cost Effectiveness*, Graham and Tengs found gross disparities in the amount of money spent to save statistical lives under different regulatory programs, claiming that certain regulations were costing a trillion dollars per mortality avoided.[101] In their second report, *The Opportunity Costs of Haphazard Social Investments in Life-Saving*, Graham and Tengs argued that certain governmental regulations were so costly that by shifting resources from the more costly to less costly programs, tens of thousands of lives could be saved.[102] Testifying before Congress in 1995, John Graham coined the phrase "statistical murder" to describe what he saw as wasteful regulatory programs.[103]

Another important antiregulatory figure, Robert Hahn, also joined in the scorecard game. His contributions came in 1996 and 2000, with separate studies finding that most federal regulation failed cost-benefit tests, and therefore were a net drag on the economy and aggregate wealth. These studies, like the Morall, and Graham and Tengs studies, received widespread attention, placed increased negative scrutiny on the regulatory process, and helped bolster conservative antiregulatory claims.

As suggested earlier, many of the conclusions of these regulatory score-cards are controversial. Critics of these studies have noted that they involve highly contestable and debatable assumptions, and, sometimes, questionable data. A healthy debate about the merits of these scorecards has taken place, both in academic circles and, to a lesser extent, in public policy arenas. The point, however, is not whether these scorecards gave an accurate picture of the regulatory landscape. Rather, the regulatory scorecard movement shows how deregulatory activists and intellectuals were busy at work, pushing their agenda into the public spotlight at a time when they were having little success in making their voices heard in the White House. Whenever one lever of power became less available, they wasted little time in turning to another.

Robert Hahn and John Graham were busy not just with regulatory scorecards. Joined by individuals like W. Kip Viscusi, a Harvard colleague of Graham who has worked in the field of cost-benefit analysis for decades, Hahn and Graham began to research for ways to "improve" cost-benefit analysis.[104] Once they found methodological changes to cost-benefit analysis that they favored, they pushed for these changes with vigor, arguing for different techniques and approaches in scholarly publications and public policy circles. Many of the substantive biases that have found their way into cost-benefit analysis—which are dissected in later chapters—were incubated during this time period.

The original cast of characters had not yet exited the stage. Under the leadership of Christopher DeMuth and Robert Niskanen, respectively, both the American Enterprise Institute and the Cato Institute continued to generate antiregulatory scholarship. Another center of antiregulatory effort, whose leader, Susan Dudley, reappears in this story, was the Mercatus Institute at George Mason University. Mercatus pumped out congressional testimony on a range of regulatory issues, including the negative effects of regulations on small business[105] and how to improve regulatory accountability through more cost-benefit analysis.[106]

The Clinton years were a partial respite for proregulatory interests. With a divided government, the conservatives in Congress were unable to push through any kind of strong antiregulatory agenda, and the White House and federal agencies were directed by individuals largely sympathetic to the concerns of environmentalists, labor interests, and consumers. Although proregulatory groups mobilized on particular issues, attempting to move various regulations and stop particular rollbacks, they failed to develop and articulate an overarching vision of the regulatory state, and specifically failed to advocate in a meaningful way for a more balanced approach to cost-benefit analysis. The result is that little was accomplished during these precious eight years, which could have been used to achieve major reforms in cost-benefit analysis. Meanwhile, conservative activists and intellectuals sharpened their arguments, continued to prime the pump of antiregulatory sentiment, and fostered their base of power in the Republican-controlled Congress, waiting for the opportunities that would present themselves when a leader more congenial to the deregulatory agenda occupied the White House.

GEORGE W. BUSH

Although it would be difficult to claim that President Bush had an electoral mandate for a deregulatory agenda in his first term, having failed to gain the popular vote and having campaigned on a "compassionate conservative" platform that was not strictly deregulatory in focus, his administration has not been friendly toward environmental protection. A refusal to put forward any meaningful policy on climate change, a concerted effort to open up the Alaskan Wildlife Refugee to oil drilling, and a general perceived hostility towards environmental causes all led to strong criticism of the Bush administration by environmental groups in his first term. While the nation's attention has focused more acutely on the war in Iraq rather than domestic issues in Bush's second term, there has been criticism of the president's handling of environmental matters, especially with respect to energy policy and climate change.

The conflict-laden relationship between environmental groups and the Bush administration includes choices that have been made concerning OMB and cost-benefit analysis. Rather than revising the pertinent executive order put in place by President Clinton, President Bush kept it for the first six years of his presidency. His own executive order, issued in 2007, did not eliminate the important changes made by President Clinton concerning transparency, distributional impacts, and delay. Environmental groups were less pleased with the president's staffing choices for OIRA, choices that intensified the feeling among environmentalists that cost-benefit analysis was antiregulatory in nature.

Looking to the set of scholars that nursed the antiregulatory agenda during the Clinton presidency, Bush tapped John Graham to be his first OIRA chief. Environmental groups strongly opposed his nomination. The League of Conservation Voters, the National Environmental Trust, NRDC, and the federation of United State Public Interest Research Groups (U.S. PIRG) all took strong positions against Graham's nomination.[107] NRDC characterized his nomination as a "nightmare for anyone who cares about children's health and the environment."[108] Dr. Linda Greer, an NRDC senior scientist, expressed fears that, at OIRA, Graham would apply "pro-industry, anti-consumer, and anti-environment cost-benefit analyses to regulations."[109] Public Citizen published a report titled *Safeguards At Risk: John Graham and Corporate America's Back Door to the Bush White House*, which argued strenuously that Graham was "unfit to serve at OMB."[110] Several of the most important labor unions opposed Graham as well, including the AFL-CIO, the American Federation of State, County, and Municipal Employees (AFSCME), and the United Auto Workers.[111]

Congressional Democrats were also critical of Dr. Graham. Senator Richard Durbin said during debate over Graham's nomination that "Dr. Graham opposes virtually all environmental regulations. He believes that many environmental regulations do more harm than good."[112] Because Graham was so closely associated with cost-benefit analysis, acting as one of its primary intellectual supporters and helping to shape the methodology of the technique over many years, criticism of his nomination as OIRA director was often closely linked with criticism of the use of cost-benefit analysis in the regulatory apparatus. In the words of Senator Durbin, "Graham favors endless study of environmental issues over taking actions and making decisions—a classic case of paralysis by analysis."[113] Graham's opponents also noted the strong link between his Center for Risk Analysis and several corporate sponsors that could be expected to oppose strict regulation.[114]

Likewise, antiregulatory supporters of cost-benefit analysis tended to favor Graham's nomination. Members of the Senate who favored deregulation and increased use of cost-benefit analysis were Graham's strongest supporters. For example, Senator Phil Gramm—whose wife was an OIRA director during the latter part of the Reagan administration—endorsed Graham's nomination, portraying opponents of the nomination as "unseemly . . . self-appointed public interests groups."[115] It is useful to note that, because proregulatory groups have often opposed the use of cost-benefit analysis, Senator Gramm was able to paint opposition to Graham's nomination as "opposition to rationality in setting public policy, because there are some people who believe . . . that there are some areas where rationality does not apply, that rationality should not apply in areas such as the environment and public safety."[116]

Environmental and other proregulatory groups often had an antagonistic relationship with Graham's OIRA. Wesley Warren of NRDC describes a feeling of deep frustration stemming from OIRA's unwillingness to make modifications based on NRDC's comments: "NRDC kept making comments, and OIRA did not listen. They say that crazy is repeating an action over and over and expecting a different result. After a while, you stop."[117] However, environmentalists did have some victories. During one episode, environmentalists, supported by senior citizens and groups such as the American Association of Retired Persons (AARP), conducted a large public campaign to discredit a technique—dubbed the *senior death discount*—that reduced the calculation of regulatory benefits for elderly Americans.[118] The ability to make this change in how cost-benefit analysis was conducted was a major victory for groups, and shows the potential of proregulatory forces to wield influence when they actively engage in the methodological debate.

It is important to note that during the Graham years, OIRA maintained—and indeed strengthened—its transparency rules. Likewise, Graham's OIRA did not participate in the "paralysis through analysis" that characterized the earlier days of OIRA, maintaining a robust practice of arriving at timely conclusions. E. Donald Elliott, a law professor, a partner at the powerful law firm Willkie Farr & Gallagher LLP, and a former EPA General Counsel in the George H. W. Bush administration, who maintains strong contacts to the George W. Bush administration, credits Graham, and the cost-benefit analyses he oversaw, with convincing the administration to adopt two significant environmental regulations: the Clean Air Interstate Rule and the off-road diesel rule.[119] Nevertheless, proregulatory groups remain strongly convinced that the Bush administration—which Graham served—is hostile toward their interests.

When Graham left his OIRA post, President Bush turned to Susan Dudley, head of the Mercatus Center, to become his replacement. The nomination fight over Dudley followed a familiar course, with traditional proregulatory interests fighting vehemently against her confirmation. If anything, proregulatory groups upped the rhetorical ante during Dudley's nomination process. The Republican Congress failed to move on Dudley's nomination, and the prospect of her nomination dimmed significantly in the wake of the sweeping Democratic victories in 2006. President Bush, however, was not to be thwarted by Congress in his choice, so his office installed Dudley as a senior consultant at OIRA in the fall of 2006. When Congress went into recess at the beginning of 2007, President Bush circumvented congressional review, appointed Dudley, and triggered considerable outrage among proregulatory groups and commentators.[120]

Perhaps the most important recent policy decision involving OIRA came in January 2007, when President Bush announced revisions to Executive Order 12,866, further centralizing control of administrative agencies. There were several key provisions, some of which Dudley had advocated prior to her appointment, including a new requirement that agencies identify a market failure before moving forward with proposed regulations.[121] The revised order also expands the role of centralized review by subjecting guidance documents, in addition to actual regulations, to the OMB review process. Moreover, it places political appointees in the agencies as Regulatory Policy Review Officers, further cementing presidential control over the bureaucracy, and likely reducing the role of nonpolitical career civil servants.

Under President George W. Bush, the link between the deregulatory agenda and cost-benefit analysis has become nearly complete. The period under President Clinton did little to warm the attitude of proregulatory interests toward cost-benefit analysis. During the Clinton administration, many of the key proregulatory players were entrenched in the positions they had taken during the struggles under Presidents Reagan and George H. W. Bush. The Contract with America Congress also placed cost-benefit analysis at the center of its deregulatory agenda, causing environmentalist and other proregulatory interests to come out strongly against that particular version of cost-benefit analysis. By the 1990s, these groups had spent decades justifiably fighting the specific manifestations of cost-benefit analysis in two presidential administrations and in Congress.

One indicator of the current hostility shown towards cost-benefit analysis is the recent book by Frank Ackerman and Lisa Heinzerling titled *Priceless: On Knowing the Price of Everything and the Value of Nothing*. This work passionately advocates abandoning the technique altogether. Lauded by environmental organizations, it provides an important snapshot of the current view of proregulatory interests towards cost-benefit analysis.[122]

In *Priceless*, Professors Ackerman and Heinzerling argue that cost-benefit analysis is flawed, biased against regulation, and incapable of reform. They claim that placing a value on human life is inherently immoral, that the techniques used in cost-benefit analysis for determining the value of avoiding diseases give meaningless results, and that cost-benefit analysis will remain biased against regulation because it is always easier to measure the (relatively more tangible) costs of regulation than the (generally less tangible) benefits of regulation.

Attacks on Ackerman and Heinzerling have come from traditional supporters of cost-benefit analysis,[123] who also tend to have a deregulatory world view. The proregulatory supporters of cost-benefit analysis are very few and far between. The result is that that the Ackerman and Heinzerling position—strongly against cost-benefit analysis in the regulatory context, and advocating rejection rather than reform of the technique—has become the de facto position of the proregulatory community with respect to cost-benefit analysis.

STRANGE BEDFELLOWS

If the rejection of cost-benefit analysis by progressive proregulatory interests, and the embrace of the technique by conservative antiregulatory interests were a matter of diehard ideological commitment rather than political expediency, we would expect these groups to line up on the same side of the fight, no matter the issue. Events have not always borne out that expectation, however. When the sands shift a bit under this particular political alignment—progressives against cost-benefit analysis; conservatives in favor—the alignment shifts as well. This would seem to indicate that the current entrenched positions are the result of specific political fights, rather that immutable worldviews, and are therefore capable of change.

Perhaps the most striking example of shifting sands in the regulatory context—in recent memory, at least—occurred in the context of homeland security regulation. In that case, instead of the traditional alignment of proregulatory progressives and antiregulatory conservatives, the opposite occurred: Progressive groups were wary of governmental intrusion while many conservative interests supported the government's efforts. When the federal government went into the business of regulating terrorism risks, progressive groups were not pleased, and cost-benefit analysis was one of their tools in arguing against these regulations. For example, several supporters of civil liberties who opposed the president's sweeping policies under the "war on terror," including Ralph Nader and the American Civil Liberties Union (ACLU), have supported OMB review of antiterror regulations according to cost-benefit analysis criteria.[124] Graham, when he was still the chief of OIRA, took steps to measure the indirect costs, such as intrusions on privacy, associated with antiterror regulation.[125] At the same time, conservative groups, which generally favor cost-benefit analysis, argued against it in this context as "a waste of time and resources."[126]

In a similar vein, on March 14, 2003, just under a week before the invasion of Iraq, the *New York Times* published a letter to the editor from Professor James Hammitt, director of the Harvard Center for Risk Analysis (founded by Graham), suggesting that "[c]ost-benefit analysis should . . . be used to evaluate the potential war in Iraq. The benefits of ousting Saddam Hussein should be measured against the costs of casualties, waging war, reconstruction, retaliatory terrorism, and increased anti-Americanism."[127] Critics of the war in Iraq have also used cost-benefit criteria to condemn what they see as a costly adventure with little benefit for the American people.[128]

Graham and Hammitt should be commended for their consistency across issues, which shows a genuine commitment to the cost-benefit methodology, despite their commitment to a version of the methodology rejected in this book. Neither progressive nor conservative groups should be faulted for their flexibility; on the contrary, it may be a good thing to be able to react pragmatically to political circumstances. Blind commitment to cost-benefit analysis, damn the consequences, would hardly be a reasonable position for an interest group with a specific agenda. By the same token, proregulatory groups have been foolish to believe that they serve their deeply held commitment to the environment by rejecting cost-benefit analysis because of the way the technique has been applied. Cost-benefit analysis should not be viewed as bad on principle, but good or bad depending on how it is used.

In an interesting twist, in *Priceless*, Heinzerling and Ackerman hold out military spending as the paradigm for rational decisionmaking, comparing the logic of proposed programs like the Star Wars missile defense—which was unencumbered by cost-benefit analysis—as the model for how environmental, health and safety programs should be run.[129] Thus, while some progressives hope that cost-benefit analysis can be used to rein in the perceived abuses of regulation in the war on terror, others see the war on terror as an appropriate example for regulatory programs. However, both Ralph Nader and the ACLU, and Ackerman and Heinzerling, are falling prey to conventional ideas about cost-benefit analysis. The supporters of a cost-benefit analysis of the war on terror encourage this analysis not out of loyalty to the methodology,[130] but because they hope that it can put the brakes on bad regulation. And Ackerman and Heinzerling want environmental programs to look more like the war on terror in the sense that they want those programs *set free* from cost-benefit analysis. Both of these responses stem from the perception that cost-benefit analysis is inherently biased against government action.

Yet cost-benefit analysis is only inherently antiregulatory if proregulatory groups are gulled into passivity by that belief. Proregulatory groups must shake off their torpor. Their opposition to cost-benefit analysis, even if it was understandable at the outset, has become very counterproductive. Their position is now hindering their goals more than it is helping them. They must recognize that cost-benefit analysis can—with work—become a goad as well as a brake on government. As soon as they reach this realization, cost-benefit analysis will cease to be inherently antiregulatory and will become a tool that is exactly as good as we can make it.

Winning the Good Fight (Sometimes)

Although proregulatory interests outside the government have largely abandoned the task of shaping cost-benefit analysis, certain actors within government have taken steps to remove the antiregulatory bias from cost-benefit analysis. One of the most important of these efforts was undertaken by the Environmental Protection Agency (EPA) during the Clinton administration, with the development of its own in-house cost-benefit analysis capability, in response to the traditional antagonism between the EPA and the Office of Information and Regulatory Affairs (OIRA). With its own cost-benefit tools, the EPA had the analytic firepower needed to struggle effectively with OIRA over environmental regulations. The efforts culminated in the EPA Cost-Benefit Guidelines, which provide the EPA with an independent source of justification for its cost-benefit decisions. One of the most important of those decisions was the value placed on a human life, and the methodology for arriving at that value.

THE VALUE OF STATISTICAL LIFE

As previously discussed, the most significant benefit delivered by many federal environmental, health and safety regulations is saving human lives. Reducing mortality risks is the primary goal of many regulatory programs. In order for cost-benefit analysis to function properly, assigning a value to reductions in mortality risks is of the highest importance. It has also proven to be a difficult and contentious process.

Early efforts to assign a value to lives saved were very crude. One common methodology was to estimate the lost earnings that would be produced by regulatory beneficiaries, so that the value of life was equated with potential income. Therefore, the life of a thirty-five year old with an estimated continued earning period of thirty years and an estimated yearly income of $40,000 would be valued at $1.2 million.

The lost-earnings method fails to provide a realistic picture of the benefit of life-saving regulation. As an initial matter, it provides what is sure to be the lowest possible value that a rational person might assign to mortality risk reduction. A person should be willing to pay *at least* .01% of their lifetime earnings to avoid a .01% chance of death. But most people will likely be willing to pay more, because to pay only .01% of anticipated earnings assumes risk-neutrality, and that the utility that they derive from living is fully captured in earnings. People are not risk-neutral. In fact, the entire insurance market, accounting for billions of dollars of revenue, is premised on the shifting of risk between nonrisk-neutral parties. Further, we derive all kinds of utility from life above and beyond our earnings, such as from our relationships, or from leisurely introspection. Reducing the value of life to earnings, then, is surely an underestimation.

Recognizing the inadequacies of the lost earnings method, economists developed the concept of the value of a statistical life. Any method that seeks to quantify the value of life for cost-benefit analysis must first recognize that regulations primarily reduce risks. The small probability that the risk will occur for any individual does not mean the risk can be ignored. If an environmental pollutant causes cancer in 1 of the 100,000 people exposed to it, and 2.5 million people are exposed, we expect it to cause 25 cases of cancer. If a regulation were to ban that pollutant, then the expected direct benefit is 25 saved lives. When a small risk is spread over a huge population, ignoring the risk sacrifices many lives. Economists realized that the appropriate inquiry was how much people were willing to pay to avoid these small risks—the amount could then be applied to the affected population to value the lives saved by the regulation.

There are two accepted techniques for measuring how much people are willing to pay to avoid small risks. The *stated preferences* technique—sometimes called the contingent valuation technique—surveys respondents about their willingness to pay to avoid risk. The survey questions take a variety of forms. For example, surveys have measured the effects of water contamination on the values assigned to residential property,[131] as well as how much people are willing to pay for risk-reduction features in consumer products.[132]

The *revealed preferences* technique, in contrast, works with decisions people have actually made, often relying on labor-market studies. This method has the advantage of being based on actual market transactions, as opposed to responses to hypothetical questions. Typically, revealed preference studies are statistical analyses of wages that measure the additional compensation paid to workers in riskier jobs, when other features of the job—such as the necessary education and skills, work conditions, and prestige—are held constant. This wage premium is sometimes called *hazard pay*. The additional risk factor of the job is compared to the amount of hazard pay demanded by workers to determine the amount that workers must be paid in order to take on additional risk.

The concept of statistical life bears a few more words of explanation, as it is somewhat misleading. The value of a statistical life is an aggregate number. If the average person receives $800 in hazard pay for a 1 in 10,000 chance of death, we say that the value of a statistical life is $800 times 10,000, or $8 million. The EPA, using 26 value-of-life studies, including both labor market and contingent valuation surveys, determined that the value of a statistical life is $6.3 million, in year 2000 dollars. This is not the value of a particular human life. Nor is it the value we would expect a person to pay to avoid a 100 percent probability of death—that number will be different for every person. Indeed, it will likely be close to the value of all of their assets, and any assets they are willing to beg, borrow, or steal. Instead, the value of a statistical life represents the sum of the amounts of money people are willing to pay to avoid *very small* risks to their life. The value of a statistical life might be more accurately called "10,000 times the value of eliminating a 1 in 10,000 risk." This book uses the term "statistical life" only in deference to standard parlance.

EPA AND OIRA

The EPA has always had an especially antagonistic relationship with OIRA. Although there are scores of federal agencies covering many disparate subject matters and promulgating regulations on a wide range of subjects, OIRA has devoted its energies to only a handful of agencies, most notably the EPA and the Occupational Safety and Health Administration (OSHA). There are several reasons for this. Because the EPA and OSHA govern issues that cut across economic sectors, their regulations tend to have high economic costs—triggering OIRA review. In addition, during the early years of OIRA review, presidential administrations were hostile to the environmental and workplace safety agendas promoted by the EPA and OSHA. The EPA has traditionally been seen as particularly regulation friendly, leading OIRA to attempt to counteract this perceived bias towards overregulation.[133]

Because of this antagonistic relationship, over time, the EPA began to build up its cost-benefit analysis capacity. This made good sense. In order to argue with OIRA, the EPA needed to stand on firm ground. Because OIRA argued in cost-benefit terms, the EPA needed to be able to counterargue in the same language. By hiring its own experts and conducting thorough and defensible cost-benefit analyses, the EPA was in a better position to defend its choices during OIRA review.

As part of this process, the Clinton administration's EPA began to establish its cost-benefit guidelines. This process was discussed in earlier chapters, which noted that environmental groups, though they were welcome to participate, sat out the decisionmaking process, largely ceding the advocacy role to proindustry interests.

But it is also important to note that even without environmental groups present, the EPA was able to adopt several measures during the formulation of its guidelines that had the effect of increasing the stringency of regulation. One of the most important advances was the use of willingness-to-pay to measure the value of a statistical life, and specifically, the use of a set of revealed and stated preference studies that estimated the value of a statistical life at just over $6 million. This figure was markedly different from the one used by OIRA at the time, which was sometimes as low as $1 million.[134] But because the EPA had made the effort to justify its decision on strong grounds, OIRA largely accepted EPA's decision.

It was not always clear that EPA would arrive at this conclusion. During meetings of the Science Advisory Board committee looking into the value of statistical lives, staffers at OIRA testified before the committee "in their individual capacity," arguing for a much lower value of statistical life.[135] If a $1-million value had won the day, the estimates of regulatory benefits would have been erroneously reduced by over 80 percent.

It is worth mentioning that during this episode, it was the EPA—the "proregulatory agency," presumably more hostile to cost-benefit analysis— that had the empirical data and economic studies to back up its decision. The EPA derived its value of a statistical life by looking to the median value of over two dozen empirical studies that had been published in peer-reviewed journals—the state of the science at that time. By contrast, it was OIRA officials, supposedly the protectors of cost-benefit analysis and economic efficiency, who were arguing against the use of the latest and most sound economic research. This example shows that when cost-benefit analysis is faithfully adhered to, it can point toward higher levels of protection and more regulation. It always points to less regulation only when the methodology of cost-benefit analysis is subverted to an overarching antiregulatory bias.

As EPA's experience with the value of a statistical life shows, it is possible for proregulatory interests to benefit from cost-benefit analysis. However, in order for the benefit to be realized, the technique cannot simply be turned over to the other side. Proregulatory interests must engage in the nitty-gritty of the technique, ferreting out subtle sources of antiregulatory bias and removing them.

This is the work of American citizens as well. In our democratic system, it is everyone's individual responsibility to participate in the exercise of governmental authority. There is, naturally, a place for expertise in our administrative system, but there also remains an important place for over-sight and accountability of these experts. If the language of expertise is allowed to mask simple partisan decisionmaking—against the interests of the American public—it is our responsibility to go behind the veil and figure out what is really going on.

In order for proregulatory interests to participate in the development of cost-benefit analysis, and for American citizens to perform their essential oversight roles, a basic understanding of the technique and some of the contentious methodological issues is vital. We must take responsibility for our own basic literacy. If cost-benefit analysis is the official language of poli-cymaking, then, as citizens in a democracy, we must learn to understand it.

The following chapters lay out eight fallacies of cost-benefit analysis. These fallacies have become entrenched because the people developing the methodology over the past several decades have tilted strongly against regulation. Although some of these fallacies are appealing on the surface, their falsity can be perceived by looking more closely. The list is not exhaus-tive. There are many more fallacies and sources of potential bias within cost-benefit analysis. But presented here are some of the major topics that have engaged those developing the methodology of cost-benefit analysis in the past decades.

Understanding these eight fallacies is an important first step. The second step is to use the arguments presented here to reform the practice of cost-benefit analysis. This is the responsibility of proregulatory interests groups, as well as citizens and voters participating in democratic politics. By holding our leaders to a restored vision of cost-benefit analysis, we can make up for the damage that has been done to the technique, and allow it to serve a useful role in improving regulatory decisionmaking—and therefore our environment, our public health, and our economic prosperity.

PART II | Eight Fallacies
of Cost-Benefit
Analysis

Fallacy 1: All Unintended Consequences Are Bad

The first fallacy of current cost-benefit analysis is that all unintended consequences are bad. In the past few decades, cost-benefit analysis has become more sophisticated, taking the collateral consequences of regulatory decisions into account. Theoretically, this is a good thing—if a particular regulation would save an endangered species but would have the collateral effect of wiping out another, that collateral cost should be included in the initial analysis. But proponents of current cost-benefit analysis tend to look only at negative collateral consequences. In order to be balanced, cost-benefit analysis must acknowledge the ancillary benefits of regulations as well.

The consideration of the collateral consequences of regulation is called *risk tradeoff analysis*. Its core idea is simple. In seeking to minimize certain risks, regulations can exacerbate others. A serious analysis of a regulation's impact should pay attention not only to how it reduces the target risk, but also to how it raises these countervailing risks. In this way, risk tradeoff analysis promises a more comprehensive evaluation of regulation.

Risk tradeoff analysis garnered attention in the late 1980s and early 1990s through the work of commentators like John Graham, W. Kip Viscusi, and Cass Sunstein. In 1995, John Graham, then the director of the Harvard Center for Risk Analysis, and Jonathan Wiener published a book titled *Risk versus Risk: Tradeoffs in Protecting Health and the Environment*.[136] In that book, Professors Graham and Wiener called attention to a problem they described as "risk tradeoffs." Using vivid examples, they argued that governmental risk regulation often created countervailing risks that were not, but should be, considered.

A countervailing risk is in the nature of a harmful side effect. A pharmaceutical drug may have a variety of effects on the body: some good, some bad. Aspirin might be taken to alleviate a headache, but it can also lead to a stomach ache. In order to justify the use of a medication, the beneficial effects must outweigh the negative side effects. Risk tradeoff analysis asks us to focus on the negative side effects of regulation when undertaking cost-benefit analysis.

Soon after the Graham and Wiener book was published, several other prominent academic commentators of the administrative state, including the methodologically inclined like Professor W. Kip Viscusi of Harvard,[137] and prominent progressive figures like Cass Sunstein[138] at the University of Chicago School of Law, embraced risk tradeoff analysis. Public policy think tanks, most importantly the respected AEI–Brookings Joint Center for Regulatory Studies (a collaboration of the more conservative AEI and more liberal Brookings) are staffed and directed by fans of the technique.[139]

Congress soon took note of risk tradeoff analysis. Several comprehensive regulatory reform bills included provisions requiring agencies to consider countervailing risks.[140] These bills were prominent mostly during the 104th, 105th, and 106th Congresses, when the regulatory reform wing of the Gingrich revolution played an important role in setting the congressional agenda. These bills would have required agencies to consider countervailing risks—or in the words of the bills, *substitution risks*—which might result from major regulations.

Although none of these comprehensive initiatives became law, some bills containing language about countervailing risks have been enacted. The Clean Air Act amendments of 1990 have provisions relating to dirty fuels that require the Environmental Protection Agency (EPA) to report on "any negative health or environmental consequences to the community of efforts to reduce such risks."[141] Similarly, the 1996 amendments to the Safe Drinking Water Act mandate the analysis of "[a]ny increased health risk that may occur as the result of compliance, including risks associated with co-occurring contaminates."[142]

The Office of Management and Budget (OMB) has also incorporated risk tradeoff logic into its regulatory approach. In a 2003 report to Congress, in the chapter discussing "U.S. Approaches to Managing Emerging Risks" OMB notes that "decreasing one risk may increase a countervailing risk."[143] To illustrate its point about the importance of countervailing risks, OMB uses hypothetical examples: "[R]egulations that reduce the level of disinfection byproducts in the water ... may also reduce the effectiveness of disinfection and thereby increase the health risk from microorganisms" and "restricting latex use to prevent allergic reaction in health care workers may increase the risk of infections."[144]

Conservative groups have successfully used the logic of risk tradeoff analysis to convince courts to overturn environmental rules. In 1992, the Competitive Enterprise Institute (CEI), a group "dedicated to advancing the principles of free enterprise and limited government"[145] brought a lawsuit in the U.S. Court of Appeals for the D.C. Circuit, seeking to overturn a decision by the National Highway Traffic Safety Administration (NHTSA) not to weaken fuel-efficiency standards. CEI argued that NHTSA had acted arbitrarily and capriciously by failing to consider that stricter fuel-efficiency standards might lead to less-safe vehicles, by delaying the replacement of old cars or inducing consumers to buy smaller cars. The D.C. Circuit agreed. In *CEI v. National Highway Traffic Safety Administration*,[146] Judge Stephen Williams—a noted administrative law scholar and perhaps the federal judiciary's most outspoken proponent of risk-tradeoff analysis—wrote: "By making it harder for consumers to buy large cars, the 27.5 miles per gallon (mpg) standard will increase traffic fatalities if, as a general matter, small cars are less safe than big ones."[147] NHTSA was forced to reconsider the 1990 standard, and in subsequent cases, was required to explicitly consider these countervailing risks when setting fuel safety standards. Since then, NHTSA has not raised fuel efficiency standards for cars,[148] and Americans continue to consume gasoline at the highest per capita rate in the world.[149]

The nation's highest courts have referred to risk-tradeoff analysis in other important decisions as well. In the United States Supreme Court case *American Trucking v. EPA*[150] the plaintiffs sued the EPA to overturn a rule setting allowable levels of air pollution. In a concurrence, Justice Stephen Breyer maintained that risk-tradeoff analysis should be used by the EPA, finding that: "The statute also permits the Administrator to take account of comparative health risks."[151] In a similar vein, Judge Williams reviewed several regulations and found agency inattention to countervailing risks unacceptable. In addition to the fuel-efficiency case just discussed, in a part of his decision in *American Trucking* that was not appealed by the EPA to the Supreme Court, Judge Williams decided the EPA had a duty to analyze the negative health impacts of its proposal to lower ozone levels, such as increases in skin cancer.

The academic supporters of risk-tradeoff analysis would like to see the administrative state adopt the technique even more comprehensively. Graham and Wiener advocate a statute requiring risk-tradeoff analysis in all future legislative initiatives,[152] and the amendment of many environmental, health and safety laws to change their central mission from goals like "protect the public health" to ones like "reduce overall risk."[153] They also favor an executive order requiring agencies to undertake risk-tradeoff analysis[154] and argue that courts should ascertain whether administrative agencies adequately considered countervailing risks.[155] When countervailing risks outweigh the direct benefits of the regulation, they would have courts strike down the regulation as "arbitrary and capricious."[156]

Sunstein likewise thinks that risk-tradeoff analysis ought to be incorporated into every branch of government. He recommends that a new congressional committee study propose legislation and initiate revisions where new laws would increase risk.[157] Sunstein also favors an amendment to the Administrative Procedure Act requiring that "[a]gencies shall ensure, to the extent feasible, that regulations do not create countervailing risks that are greater than those of regulated risks."[158] He would have courts defer to agency decisions to carry out risk-tradeoff analysis (unless it is explicitly forbidden by statute)[159] as well as take a "hard look" at agency decisions lacking such analysis.

Regardless of how these policy proposals fare, risk-tradeoff analysis is already an important feature of the administrative state. Like the cost-benefit analysis of which it is a part, considering countervailing risks is a staple of governmental decisionmaking.

IGNORING ANCILLARY BENEFITS

Although the consideration of countervailing risks is appropriate, the systematic tendency of academics and policymakers to look only at unintended risks, without also looking at unintended benefits, is not. There is no reason to believe that ancillary benefits are less common than countervailing risks. Aspirin has the unanticipated side effect of upsetting stomachs, but it also has the unanticipated benefit of preventing heart attacks and strokes.[160] Indeed, the ancillary benefit associated with aspirin is probably greater than its target benefit of reducing pain.

This chapter examines three major countervailing-risk categories: direct risk tradeoffs, substitution effects, and lulling effects.[161] It shows that each can have an ancillary benefit counter-part. The clearest category of countervailing risk analysis involves direct risk tradeoffs. These tradeoffs occur when regulating the target risk brings about countervailing risks. Treating children's pajamas with Tris (2,3-dibromopropyl phosphate) protects the children from fire but increases their risk of developing certain cancers.[162] Reducing chlorine in water may decrease cancer but increase microbial disease.[163] Sodium nitrite is both a carcinogen and an important protection against botulism.[164]

But there is no reason to believe that ancillary benefits are not just as common as countervailing risks in this context. To comply with the Clean Water Act, municipalities have constructed wetlands as an alternative to conventional wastewater treatment facilities.[165] These wetlands have generated a wealth of ancillary benefits, including habitat creation and preservation, carbon sequestration, erosion control, and recreational and research opportunities.[166] Similarly, under the Kyoto Protocol, carbon sinks are one mechanism to comply with requirements to reduce greenhouse gases. These carbon sinks also preserve forests in developing countries, thereby maintaining vital habitats and biodiversity, retarding erosion, and securing the long-term welfare of local human populations.[167] Finally, regulations limiting carbon monoxide (CO) emissions from motor vehicles to reduce the long-term risks associated with air pollution have the ancillary benefit of reducing the short-term risk of CO fatalities resulting from accidents and suicides.[168] One study found that the CO regulations had the "unanticipated benefit" of saving an average of twenty-five thousand lives per year. By contrast, the regulations are only expected to save 212 to 551 lives annually from reduced air pollution.[169] In this instance, the ancillary benefit is greater than the direct benefit.

A substitution effect occurs if a regulation causes a shift toward a product or process that carries risks of its own. For instance, banning cyclamate, a type of artificial sweetener, because of its carcinogenic properties led consumers to turn to saccharin, which has also been shown to cause cancer.[170] Regulations aimed at making nuclear-power generation safer might, by imposing large costs, encourage reliance on methods of energy production with other risks—such as contributing to climate change.

But ancillary benefits accrue here too. Recent studies show that reductions of greenhouse gas would be accompanied by reductions in conventional pollutants as well.[171] To reduce carbon dioxide (CO_2) emissions, electricity producers might burn less fuel or burn cleaner fuel. These transformations, designed to reduce greenhouse gas emissions, would also reduce other air pollutants such as ozone, nitrogen oxide, and sulfur dioxide—already the target of clean air regulation because of their negative health and environmental effects. Studies have found a wide range of estimated ancillary benefits associated with carbon reduction;[172] a relatively recent study found benefits in the range of $13 to $14 per ton of averted carbon dioxide production.[173] As in the example of CO described above, reductions in CO_2 have both direct and ancillary benefits.

Under the banner of lulling effects, Professor Viscusi speculates that certain regulations may "lull" consumers into destructive complacency. The introduction of a safety measure, he argues, can cause consumers to overestimate a product's safety and therefore act less carefully.[174]

Yet a beneficial analog to the lulling effect might be an *attentiveness effect*, whereby the promulgation of a health or safety regulation makes people more sensitive to the need for safety beyond the circumstances expressly covered by the regulation. For example, attention to climate change might make individuals more concerned about the use of nonrenewable resources, even ones that do not have an impact on climate change. Or, the introduction of the "organic" label may spur consumers to consider the general healthiness of their food choices, such as fat or sugar content.[175] The best-developed account of lulling effects is presented in Professor Viscusi's study[176] finding that child-resistant caps did not reduce risk, apparently as a result of "increased parental irresponsibility," such as leaving off the caps of bottles.[177] But the fact that the net ancillary effects were negative in that instance does not imply that they would also be negative for different types of risks.

Inattention to ancillary benefits is a hallmark of the leading academic and judicial writing on risk-tradeoff analysis. For example, Viscusi endorses the application of risk-tradeoff analysis to the regulatory process, but refers only to the nontarget harm brought about by the regulation, not the ancillary benefits.[178] Sunstein also fails to address the possibility that regulation might have ancillary benefits.[179]

Like the academic commentators, the courts have ignored ancillary benefits. Judge Williams makes no reference to ancillary benefits in his opinions discussing countervailing risks.[180] In his *American Trucking* concurrence, Justice Breyer refers approvingly to Judge Williams's risk-tradeoff analysis but does not suggest that regulations might bring about ancillary benefits as well as harm.[181]

The legislative branch has fared no better. Legislative initiatives to reform the regulatory process advocate risk-tradeoff analysis, but are silent on ancillary benefits.[182] Likewise, the statutes that Congress has passed that explicitly require risk-tradeoff analysis make no mention of ancillary benefits.

The executive branch has also focused considerably more on countervailing risks than on ancillary benefits. EPA does sometimes consider "co-benefits" in undertaking regulatory impact analyses, for example to justify regulations in the face of OMB opposition to EPA's preferred regulatory outcome.[183] The analysis of ancillary benefits, a voluntary undertaking for executive agencies such as EPA, appears to be spotty.[184]

After risk-tradeoff analysis became established—prodded in large part by Professors Graham and Viscusi—its methodological bias against the consideration of ancillary benefits followed. That bias persists today, even as risk-tradeoff analysis is invoked by academics and judges across a broad range of the ideological spectrum, including Professor Sunstein and Justice Breyer, and is explicitly regarded by some of its staunchest supporters as a means of achieving more efficient though not necessarily less regulation.

Although ancillary benefits have been largely ignored by the academics and policymakers that support risk-tradeoff analysis, there is no reason to think they are any less common than countervailing risks.

CHALLENGING THE CLAIM THAT
ANCILLARY BENEFITS ARE RARE

Proponents of risk-tradeoff analysis generally do not reject the possibility of significant ancillary benefits; they simply do not consider it. This blind spot may be the result of ideological orientation and path dependency. If one is inclined to see regulation as bad, then the problem of countervailing risks seems intuitive, while ancillary benefits seem unlikely. And once risk-tradeoff analysis gained momentum, it simply barreled along without any significant critical analysis.

Graham and Wiener are outliers in considering the possibility that regulatory interventions will produce ancillary benefits. To their credit, they at least fashion an argument for why such benefits should be discounted. First, they argue that our political system is more likely to give rise to countervailing risks than to ancillary benefits. Second, they claim that decisionmakers can be expected to remove such benefits should they nevertheless arise. Neither point is compelling.

Graham and Wiener draw on the modern political science theory of public choice to explain why regulatory interventions produce countervailing risks as a result of omitted voices in the political process.[185] They maintain that regulatory decisions will often have a large impact on certain discrete groups. These groups have a strong incentive to make their voices heard in the regulatory process. By contrast, the incentives for ordinary citizens will be smaller, because any individual regulation is unlikely to affect them much. Because of the disparity in incentives, organized interest groups will play a prominent role in the regulatory process, while the majority of citizens will not.

The political story underlying Graham's and Wiener's prediction assumes that a single interest group will be able to capture the regulatory process and successfully impose its views on the captured agency.[186] In practice, regulatory decisions are typically contested, with groups representing a variety of actors—industry groups, public-interest organizations, labor unions—all jockeying for superiority.[187] Each class of actors also has its own internal diversity. The business community is not monolithic; some firms will be helped by regulations that will hurt their peers disproportionately. Advocacy groups and labor unions also represent a broad array of interests.

The diversity of these interests keeps them from being able to coordinate effectively to transfer risk onto an unsuspecting population. For example, the stringent environmental regulation of new sources of pollution favors existing sources.[188] Stringent fuel economy standards help the manufacturers of smaller cars. There will typically be some powerful interests with an incentive to combat a potential shift of risk to unorganized groups.

Moreover, interest groups are mostly interested in reducing their own risk and are indifferent toward risk increases or decreases for others. If anything, regulations with ancillary benefits will be easier to advocate, because they may be attractive to broader political coalitions. Take, for example, the effort of Eastern dirty coal manufacturers to expand their markets by imposing disproportionate costs on users of clean coal in the late 1970s. As is documented in an important book by Bruce Ackerman and William Hassler,[189] the resulting legislation was crafted in a way that also benefited supporters of increased visibility in national parks in the West. The argument that can be made for systematic forces generating ancillary benefits is at least as strong as the one for countervailing risks.

The Graham and Wiener story simply lacks empirical grounding. It is possible that banning asbestos reduces the safety of car brakes. But this countervailing risk does not help the asbestos industry. Similarly, the reduction of ozone concentrations in ambient air may cause skin cancer, but that does not help the industrial plants that emit the pollutant. One would be hard pressed to find a realistic example in which the countervailing risk was caused by interest group pathologies.

Finally, Graham and Wiener put forth the unconvincing argument that regulators have an incentive to eliminate ancillary benefits in order to avoid distributing politically unearned rewards.[190] They argue that the same regulators who are too indolent or inattentive to notice countervailing risks will diligently determine whether there are ancillary benefits to a regulation. Moreover, if regulators find such benefits, they will either extract a political price from the recipients or excise the benefits.

But it will not always be technically feasible to remove an ancillary benefit and still retain the regulation. It would be impossible, for example, to reduce the CO output of cars for the purpose of reducing air pollution without at the same time reducing the risk of deaths caused by idling cars. Even more importantly, there is absolutely no incentive for decisionmakers to spend time and effort simply to harm a group—if anything, regulators might benefit from positive publicity related to ancillary benefits. The vindictive regulator is both normatively unappealing and descriptively unconvincing as a model of bureaucratic conduct.

INCLUDING ANCILLARY BENEFITS

Risk-tradeoff analysis has important antiregulatory consequences. It leads to rejecting regulations that would have been approved under a cost-benefit analysis that did not take countervailing risks into account. Because risk-tradeoff analysis directs regulators to investigate only countervailing risks, but not ancillary benefits, it systematically biases cost-benefit analysis against regulation.

The solution is simple. Decisionmakers should consider the positive side effects brought about by regulation, not merely the negative side effects. This recommendation is not utopian: If the causal chain between benefit and rule is too attenuated, regulators need not expend resources to track all the positive effects. However, there should be parity between ancillary benefits and countervailing risks. To the extent that either an ancillary benefit or countervailing risk is studied, the other should be as well. Ancillary benefits should be put on the same theoretical and practical footing as countervailing risks.

To show how this might work in practice, consider controls on conventional air pollutants, which deliver the ancillary benefit of reducing greenhouse gases—the converse of the CO_2 example discussed earlier. Everyone is familiar with the process of climate change in which greenhouse gases—mainly CO_2, methane, and nitrous oxide—trap energy given off by the earth, thereby leading to increases in temperature.[191] The environmental implications of global warming are vast and potentially profound, from sea-level rise, beach erosion, coastal flooding, to the wholesale disappearance of coastal wetlands.[192] Agricultural production will be affected, and climate change is also projected to increase the variability and severity of weather patterns, possibly leading to a greater incidence of catastrophic weather. Climate change may increase human mortality and morbidity in a number of ways, including aggravated cardio-vascular problems, increased heat exhaustion, respiratory problems, and increases in occurrences of infectious diseases.[193] All of these risks are very severe, and their reduction is a significant benefit that should not be overlooked.

Coal-fired power plants, which produce about half the electricity in the United States, are a very significant contributor to the nation's CO_2 output, accounting for 40 percent of the country's total emissions.[194] Policies that expressly target reductions in conventional pollutants will also lead to a decrease in CO_2 emissions from the electricity sector. That is because in addition to being the most carbon-intensive fossil fuel, coal is also the dirtiest in terms of the amount of conventional pollutants released into the atmosphere. At the same time, natural gas, in addition to being a less carbon-intensive fossil fuel, is also significantly cleaner-burning than coal. Because electricity producers responded to limits on conventional pollutants by switching from coal to natural gas, they also reduced their CO_2 emissions—an ancillary benefit that, if taken into consideration, significantly bolsters the case for regulation.

For example, the 1990 amendments to the Clean Air Act established a federal regulatory regime for reducing acid rain,[195] principally by capping the emissions of sulfur dioxide—a conventional pollutant—by electric utilities.[196] This cap led many energy producers to switch from coal to cleaner-burning fuels like natural gas. An ancillary benefit of that transition has been a reduction in greenhouse gas emissions relative to what they would have been without the sulfur dioxide cap.

Or, consider a case that has recently received considerable attention: the National Highway Traffic Safety Administration's fuel economy standards for light trucks. In its analysis of the costs and benefits of the standard, NHTSA took into account its negative consequences on employment and sales. But NHTSA failed to take into account the benefit that would result from the decrease in carbon emissions. In a rare example of a court taking ancillary benefit analysis seriously, the Ninth Circuit struck down the regulation, saying that "NHTSA could not put a thumb on the scale by undervaluing the benefits."[197]

Critics of ancillary benefit analysis might complain that the ancillary benefits of a regulation could be too remotely connected to the regulation's primary effects. It is true that the link between the two should not be excessively attenuated. However, there should be parity in the treatment of countervailing risks and ancillary benefits. A link might be too attenuated for certain ancillary benefits to be considered. But the same could be true for certain countervailing risks.

If an agency were to ignore the ancillary effects of a regulation altogether, its understanding of the regulation and its impact on society might thereby be impoverished, but it would not be systematically biased. Such a state of affairs prevailed in the regulatory state until the recent emergence of risk-tradeoff analysis. It was as though the agency had decided to draw a small circle— defined by reference to a tight causal link—around the regulation's primary effects and to consider only the effects that took place within the circle.

With the emergence of risk-tradeoff analysis, the agencies' attention has been drawn to the countervailing risks of regulation. Thus, with respect to some of the secondary effects of regulation, the radius of the circle has been increased—reflecting a looser causal link—to include a wider range of regulatory impacts. In order to maintain parity, it is incumbent upon the agency to consider ancillary benefits as well. There is simply no defensible argument for proceeding otherwise.

It will not always be desirable to consider the ancillary effects of regulation. Sometimes the costs of those studies will be exorbitant and the potential improvements too slight. That is fine. However, the standards applied to determine whether it is worth undertaking risk-tradeoff analysis should be the same as those applied in deciding to undertake ancillary-benefit analysis. For cost-benefit analysis to be fair, and for it to give us an accurate picture of the economic value of regulations, we must not privilege the investigation of adverse effects. If we look under the rug to find costs, we have to look between the couch cushions for the benefits.

Fallacy 2: Wealth Equals Health

Every college student who studies statistics is told that correlation is not causation. In other words, just because Y and Z correlate with each other, we cannot assume that Y causes Z or that Z causes Y. Both are possibilities, but it is also possible that the correlation is random, or that some third agent, X, is causing both Y and Z. For instance, the weather correlates with the seasons, but no one would say that the weather causes the seasons.

The rookie error of confusing correlation with causation is the root of the second fallacy of cost-benefit analysis: Wealth equals health. This fallacy is the basis for the so-called health-wealth tradeoff. Proponents of health-wealth tradeoff analysis observe that there is a correlation between more wealth and more health. Wealthy people do in fact live longer. But then these proponents assume that correlation is causation, asserting that more wealth causes more health. Under this pseudo logic, they assert that because any regulation will impose costs on people, thereby decreasing their wealth, such regulations will also create the countervailing risk of diminishing people's health. In other words, health regulations should be abolished because they kill people.

A statistics teacher would give that reasoning an *F* and move on. Unfortunately, that is impossible here, and the health-wealth argument has gained significant traction. It has been heard in the halls of the White House and in the chambers of the U.S. Supreme Court. If anything, its popularity continues to grow.

In the early 1990s, the Occupational Safety and Health Administration (OSHA) proposed the Air Contaminants Standard in the Construction, Maritime, Agriculture, and General Industries. The proposed rule set the permissible level of exposure for six hundred chemicals in the agricultural sector, set several new general contaminant levels, and lowered the permissible levels of exposure to these chemicals in the construction and maritime industries.

OMB tried to use health-wealth tradeoff analysis to kill it. In a letter dated March 10, 1992, James McRae, acting administrator of the Office of Information and Regulatory Affairs (OIRA), wrote to Nancy Risque-Rohrbach at the Department of Labor, stating that he had "suspend[ed] review of the draft proposed rule"—effectively sending OSHA back to the drawing table.[198] Arguing that "richer workers on average buy more leisure time, more nutritious food, more preventive health care, and smoke and drink less than poorer workers," MacRae maintained that the rule to reduce workplace contaminants might have the perverse effect of increasing worker risk. MacRae reasoned, "If government regulations force firms out of business or into overseas production, employment of American workers will be reduced, making workers less healthy by reducing their incomes." He estimated that "the $163 million annual cost of the [proposed] rule would result in approximately 22 additional deaths per year." Based on these estimations, he suggested that the rule might result in a "net increase of about eight to fourteen fatalities per year."

The reaction from Congress was negative and swift. An outraged Senator Edward M. Kennedy deplored OMB's use of "Alice in Wonderland economics."[199] Two negative stories about the OMB action written in the *Washington Post* and the *New York Times* were read on the Senate floor.[200] Senator John Glenn, then chairman of the Government Affairs Committee, called for an investigation of OMB's reasoning by the General Accounting Office (GAO).[201] The GAO investigation found that OIRA had improperly relied on health-wealth tradeoff analysis as a means of circumventing the statutory ban on carrying out cost-benefit analysis, that the agency did not use the methodology correctly, and that the methodology was, in the words of Senator Glenn, "a pipe dream."[202]

OMB backed down from its position that time.[203] Nonetheless, it has never disavowed health-wealth tradeoff analysis. Because most of OMB's review of agency decisionmaking occurs through informal processes, it is difficult to know how much health-wealth thinking continues to exert an antiregulatory influence. We do know that health-wealth tradeoff analysis has not disappeared from the public debate.

IS WEALTH HEALTH?

Proponents of health-wealth tradeoff analysis begin with the premise that wealthier people and societies are also healthier.[204] They argue that because environmental, health and safety regulations impose large economic costs on society, they have negative health consequences.[205] In the words of Professor Viscusi, "[R]egulatory expenditures represent opportunity costs to society that divert resources from other uses. These funds could have provided for greater healthcare, food, housing, and other goods and services that promote individual longevity."[206] This negative effect must be weighed against the benefits of reducing target risks.

Supporters of the idea of health-wealth tradeoffs rely on a few empirical studies. One of the more influential, entitled *Mortality Risks Induced by Economic Expenditures*, by Professor Ralph L. Keeney,[207] used data from a 1973 study by Evelyn Kitagawa and Philip Hauser, which showed a correlation between income and health. Keeney employed a relatively straightforward mathematical model to determine how general social costs imposed on the population as a whole might be translated into increased risks to health. From that analysis, he gave several estimates for how much social cost will result in one "induced fatality," the most cited of which was $7.25 million in 1980 dollars.[208] Converted to 2006 dollars, this amount is equivalent to $17.7 million.[209] Thus, the argument goes, a regulation that costs more than $17.7 million to save a life kills more people than it saves.

Another influential study was conducted by Randall Lutter, John Morrall, and W. Kip Viscusi, entitled *The Cost-Per-Life-Saved Cutoff for Safety-Enhancing Regulations*.[210] It used a mathematical model that took into account a broader set of variables than Keeney's, notably the correlations between income and various health-related individual choices like drinking, smoking, and exercise. The study estimated that regulatory expenditures of over $15 million per human life saved ($18.15 million in 2006 dollars) will have net counterproductive effects.[211] Other prominent academics like Cass Sunstein have also embraced the idea of health-wealth tradeoffs.[212]

HEALTH-WEALTH TRADEOFFS AND REGULATION

Health-wealth tradeoffs have several antiregulatory uses. The first, and the use that its proponents most favor, is as a substitute for cost-benefit analysis when such analysis is statutorily prohibited. Certain environmental, health and safety statutes, as interpreted by the courts, prohibit agencies from taking costs into account when setting certain standards. For example, as already noted, in *American Trucking*, the Supreme Court interpreted the Clean Air Act as prohibiting the Environmental Protection Agency (EPA) from considering costs when setting ambient air quality standards. Health-wealth tradeoffs, however, offer the potential to reinterpret all costs in terms of health risks, allowing (or forcing) the EPA to circumvent the statutory prohibition.

Second, health-wealth tradeoffs can be used to set an upper bound on the value of a statistical life.[213] A variety of tools have been used to measure the value of risk reduction to Americans, including statistical analysis of the wages paid for risky jobs and surveys. Those tools have generated a set of estimations of the value of a statistical life. The current value used by the EPA, based on the midpoint of a number of studies, is $6.3 million dollars per statistical life (year 2000 dollars). Advocates of the health-wealth tradeoff argue that a number derived from health-wealth analysis should trump any higher number derived from a different analysis because the use of the higher value will result in death. Health-wealth analysis then acts as an antiregulatory "emergency switch" that activates if people are willing to pay "too much" to reduce risk.

Finally, the health-wealth tradeoff allows proponents of deregulation to seize the rhetorical high ground by framing arguments about regulatory costs in terms of health risks. John Graham coined the inflammatory phrase *statistical murder*[214] to characterize regulations that impose large economic costs. Instead of arguing that society is unwilling to pay a certain amount of money to reduce health risks, advocates of deregulation have attempted to recast the debate as one of competing health claims, rather than as the true choice—economic costs versus health and safety risks. Even television pundits have gotten into this act. For example, John Stossel, coanchor of ABC's *20/20* and a strong opponent of governmental intervention in the marketplace, has used a health-wealth tradeoff argument in broad attacks against regulation, stating, "Wealthier is healthier, and regulations make the country poorer. Maybe the motto of OSHA should be: 'To save four, kill ten.'"[215]

HEALTH-WEALTH IN ACTION

The idea of health-wealth tradeoffs has been influential well beyond its academic origins and has been used by courts, OMB, and Congress to overturn regulation, circumvent statutory prohibitions against taking costs into account, and recast regulatory costs in terms of health risks.

In *Lockout/Tagout*,[216] plaintiffs challenged an OSHA rule designed to reduce instances in which industrial equipment can "suddenly move and cut or crush or otherwise injure a worker."[217] In a concurring opinion to the judgment remanding the rule to OSHA for further consideration, Judge Williams rejected the union's contention that less stringent regulation was necessarily adverse to worker safety, saying:

> More regulation means some combination of reduced value of firms, higher product prices, fewer jobs in the regulated industry, and lower cash wages. All the latter three stretch workers' budgets tighter (as

does the first to the extent that the firms' stock is held in workers' pension trusts). And larger incomes enable people to lead safer lives.[218]

This opinion was cited in the MacRae letter discussed above.

Other distinguished judges, including Frank Easterbrook[219] and Richard Posner,[220] have supported the concept of health-wealth tradeoffs. Most importantly, Justice Breyer embraced health-wealth analysis in his concurring opinion in *American Trucking*. In that case, industry groups opposed to new clean air standards challenged the constitutionality of the Clean Air Act, and argued that the EPA had to consider costs when setting ambient air quality standards. The majority rejected both of those challenges, holding that the Clean Air Act prohibited the consideration of costs in this context. In his concurrence, Justice Breyer used the logic of health-wealth tradeoff to argue that since excessively expensive regulation not only violates canons of cost-benefit analysis but also reduces overall health, such regulation therefore violates the statutory requirement to promote public health. He stated, "Nor need regulation lead to deindustrialization. Preindustrial society was not a very healthy society; hence a standard demanding the return of the Stone Age would not prove 'requisite to protect the public health.'"[221]

We have already seen the use of health-wealth tradeoff in the OMB letter that temporarily shut down OSHA workplace contaminant regulations. John Graham's reference to statistical murder was quoted by Congressman John Mica of Florida in support of a regulatory reform bill that was viewed by many as deeply antiregulatory.[222] The idea that regulations, by lowering economic productivity, can result in increased mortality has found its way deep within the antiregulatory Washington, D.C., culture, and has even influenced more progressive actors like Justice Breyer.

CAUSATION: THE QUESTIONABLE ASSUMPTION

So, we must all retake Statistics 101: Correlation is not causation. The data used by Keeney showed a *correlation* between income and health. Correlation is a statistics term used when two variables tend to vary together. In the Kitagawa and Hauser study, on which Keeney relied, the healthier people tended to be wealthier people (and vice versa). As discussed earlier, a correlation between two variables does not tell us anything about causation.

It might be that increased wealth leads to increased health. This might happen if greater wealth tends to *cause* people to act more carefully, or spend more money on effective health care. Alternatively, it might also be that increased health leads to increased wealth. Healthier people can work more hours, can be more effective at their jobs, and have higher productivity than less healthy people. Finally, some other factor, which leads to both increased health and increased wealth, might explain the data. For example, education increases earning power; it might also lead to the abandonment of risky behavior such as smoking.

Keeney is quite explicit about his causal assumptions. Even though he acknowledges that Kitigawa and Hauser "suggest that it may be poor health that leads both to less income and greater mortality,"[223] he "assume[s] that the relationship between higher incomes and lower mortality risks is induced, meaning that higher incomes will lead to lower mortality risks."[224] In Keeney's work, this relationship is just an assumption, not a conclusion. When Keeney's work becomes incorporated into the public policy debate, however, this nuance gets lost.

The Lutter study makes the same assumption. In that study, the authors review a set of other studies showing that income *correlates* with risky behavior like smoking. The authors then proceed as though this data showed that low-income *causes* risky behavior. This study has exactly the same problem as Keeney's—it assumes, but does not defend, a causal relationship between wealth and risky behavior; nothing more than a correlation has been shown. Although it is *possible* that low income causes risky behavior, it is also possible that risky behavior causes low income, or that a third factor—like education—explains both income and health. We just don't know.

Recent research has used sophisticated estimation techniques and more robust data to understand the causal relationship between health and wealth.[225] James P. Smith, a senior economist at RAND, published a major study in 2005 entitled *Unraveling the SES-Health Connection*. (SES stands for socioeconomic status.)[226] Smith wrestled with the issue that is merely an assumption in prior studies, ultimately casting serious doubt on their conclusions.

First, Smith asked the *reverse causation* question—whether reduced health leads to reduced wealth. The hypothesis is intuitive. Sick people work less, incur more health-related expenses, and may save less. Using survey data from the Health and Retirement Study (of households with at least one person aged 51 to 61) Smith found significant effects on income that were attributable to health shocks. He was able to make this causal claim because he based it on data collected over time, not just once. Smith estimated the average aggregate wealth impact from a major health shock (cancer, heart disease, and lung disease) to be almost $50,000 over time. He then tested his findings against a larger portion of the life cycle using data from the Panel Study of Income Dynamics (PSID), a large data set covering over thirty years and 35,000 individuals. He again found that health shocks predict wealth effects; the strongest effect is for the age group 50 to 60, perhaps because this group is close to retirement, but the effect remains important for other age groups as well. So, at least in part, the causal link between health and wealth means that health problems can reduce wealth.

Second, Smith sought to decouple several features of socioeconomic status, which is based on a number of related aspects, including financial elements such as income and wealth, and nonfinancial factors such as education. Because the elements of socioeconomic status correlate with each other, they also correlate with health. This means that the health-wealth effect could also be called the health-education effect, because an analysis that plots health and wealth will look similar to one that plots health and education. Health-education effects do not translate into an argument against regulation, however, and so they have not been as prominent in the public policy debate. Still, there is no obvious reason to assume that income or wealth, rather than education, is driving the correlation.

Smith investigated this question and found interesting results. Most notably, once wealth, income, and education are disentangled, neither wealth nor income is a particularly powerful predictor of health.[227] This bears repeating: Smith disproved the fundamental assumption underlying health-wealth analysis. The reason that both income and wealth seem to have a relationship with health is that education has a significant relationship to health—the more educated you are, the healthier you tend to be. As Smith says, "additional schooling is strongly and statistically significantly predictive" of better health.[228] He offered several theories to explain this, but acknowledged that more work needs to be done to understand the health-education relationship. He also undertook an investigation of the relationship between health, education, and income by looking at the group of individuals with the lowest education levels. Within that group, the relationship between income and health disappears for all but the poorest respondents. Smith provided a tentative explanation: Respondents in the lowest income bracket tend not to be working and individuals in poor health also tend not to be working.

Smith's study is not the last word on the subject. But it does show that the assumption that wealth causes health is debatable, and that any policy that just assumes such causation is irresponsible. Because current health-wealth analysis makes that assumption, it is ready for the recycling bin.

WOULD LESS REGULATION BE THE RIGHT ANSWER?

Let's now assume the Smith study turned out to be wrong. Let's also assume that proponents of the idea of health-wealth tradeoff could produce valid studies showing a causal relationship between income, or wealth, and health. Even then, it is not clear that less regulation would be the appropriate solution to health-wealth tradeoffs.

Imagine lower income did cause worse health. We would expect that if such a relationship existed, there would be a diminishing marginal effect of income on health—that is, the more money you had, the less the loss of a few dollars would affect your health. If Bill Gates lost $1,000, or even $10 million, it is unlikely that his health would be affected at all (he might not even blink). If, however, a person living at the poverty line, without access to health insurance, were to suffer a $1,000 loss of income, we would expect a significant effect. Thus, the health-wealth effect is both a matter of regulatory costs, and a matter of how, and by whom, those costs are borne.

Keeney understood this important feature of health-wealth tradeoffs. In his model, the risk-reduction benefit of an additional dollar of income quickly diminishes to zero with increasing income. He predicts health-wealth effects mostly at the bottom end of the income scale. In his model, those that make over $68,000 in family income (year 2006 dollars)[229] see *no* additional health benefit from *any* amount of additional income. Keeney creates different models depending on how regulatory costs are distributed throughout society, arriving at different predictions about the health-wealth tradeoff depending on who bears regulatory costs.

Thus, if a health-wealth tradeoff existed, there would be two general solutions. The one advocated by the deregulatory crowd is to reduce regulation. The other is to change the distribution of regulatory costs. The deregulatory solution has been well vetted. The distribution arguments, however, have gotten very little airtime even though there is no reason to focus on the regulatory rather than the redistributive side of the question.

If the health-wealth effect exists, it would primarily affect people on the lower end of the income scale. Agencies could therefore revise regulations so that regulatory costs were not borne by that group. The regulations would have various effects on the economy, all of which are considered costs. Job losses are a possibility, as are decreased land values and higher prices for consumer goods; plants and technologies may be rendered obsolete. These costs affect different populations differently—increases in the costs of luxury goods, job losses in a profession, or reductions in shareholder value are unlikely to affect the poorest Americans much. Job losses for less-skilled labor or price increases for basic necessities such as electricity or heating oil, however, would impact the poor significantly. Agencies could take these considerations into account when designing regulations in order to minimize the health-wealth impact of regulations.

Alternatively, it is possible to compensate low-income Americans who bear regulatory costs. Job retraining programs, transitional health insurance, relocation subsidies, tax incentives for economic development—all could be used to soften the blow of regulatory costs on low-income people. Transfer payments are also a mechanism to compensate for regulatory costs. All of these, by providing increased economic opportunity or resources, would reduce or eliminate any health-wealth effect from a regulation.

Unfortunately, the distribution side of the equation has been largely ignored. Individuals and interest groups who oppose regulation tend to also dislike redistribution. When antiregulatory groups seized on the issue of health-wealth tradeoffs, they also quickly seized on "less regulation" as the answer. Instead, they could have asked how to minimize the impact of regulation on the poor. While commentators were calling for less regulation, more economically efficient solutions lay on the ground, waiting to be picked up.

HEALTH AND ECONOMIC PRODUCTIVITY

This chapter has debunked the health-wealth myth. First, the core assumption underlying the health-wealth tradeoff—declines in wealth cause health problems—is not justified. Alternative explanations for the health-wealth correlation are not only plausible, but are supported by solid empirical analysis. Second, even if the causal relationship existed, the redistribution of regulatory costs (or compensation for regulatory losses) would be at least as plausible a solution to the problem as deregulation. If the proponents of the health-wealth tradeoff really believed their own arguments, they would be calling for a large-scale redistribution of society's resources from the rich to the poor. No one has heard this from them recently.

The question now is whether the idea of health-wealth tradeoffs has a useful place in the regulatory debate. Treated properly, it does. Once we drop the unhelpful and incorrect notion that there is a simple and straightforward causal relationship between wealth and health, we can look at the health-wealth data with fresh eyes and find an additional justification for health and safety regulation, rather than an argument against it.

Environmental, health and safety regulation is designed to increase health. By reducing exposure to toxic chemicals, preventing workplaces accidents, and reducing highway fatalities, regulations make Americans healthier and safer. If, as seems likely, health shocks reduce economic productivity, then environmental, health and safety regulation can be expected to increase economic productivity. This boost is an ancillary regulatory benefit, which should be included in determining the value of a regulation.

The idea that health problems lead to losses in productivity is not new. Early estimations of the value of a statistical life saved relied heavily on this idea, going so far as to equate lost productivity with the value of a statistical life, a position not advocated here. However, losses in economic activity due to poor health and mortality that can be reduced through regulation are an important reason for regulatory interventions. Gains in economic productivity can be expected to offset some of the economic costs that regulations impose.

To a certain extent, current cost-benefit analysis takes into account the economic productivity gains resulting from health and safety regulation. Some regulations reduce the number of "workdays" lost due to illness, a reduction that has sometimes been taken into account by cost-benefit analyses.[230] In addition, the willingness to pay to avoid risk—the standard value that is given to risk-reducing regulation—likely includes some of the lost productivity that would result from a health or safety emergency. In order to eliminate such a risk, a person should be willing to pay at least as much as the value of the lost productivity anticipated from a risk. In addition to anticipated health care costs and the value of being healthy and safe, lost productivity can be expected to be a component of an individual's willingness to pay to reduce risk.

The health-productivity link shows that placing health benefits on one side of the ledger and economic costs on the other leads to a misperception about the project of cost-benefit analysis. The idea is not that society is buying better health and paying for it with lost economic productivity. Rather, the purpose of cost-benefit analysis is to identify regulations that increase aggregate wealth. An important component of increasing wealth is increasing economic productivity, something that efficient regulations, by improving health, can at least sometimes be expected to do. Health-wealth tradeoffs, then, turn out not to be arguments against regulation. Rather, the concept is a reminder that regulations can have a positive effect on economic activity by making people healthier and safer, and therefore more productive.

Fallacy 3: Older People Are Less Valuable

Regulations save lives. When decisionmakers ask whether a particular regulation is justified, they are often swayed by the number of lives it saves. How they measure the benefit of a saved life, then, is critical. The standard way to measure the benefit of a saved life is to look at people's willingness to pay to avoid health and safety risks, which is then used to estimate the value of a statistical life. Recently there have been efforts to substitute the value of *life-years* for the value of statistical life. Use of life-years, however, leads to the third fallacy in cost-benefit analysis—that older people are less valuable than younger people, in proportion to their life expectancies. Under the life-years methodology, because younger people will on average lose more life years when they die, their lives are assigned a much greater value—the life of a 40-year-old is seven times more valuable than that of a 70-year-old. This outcome is both inconsistent with economic theory and flatly contradicted by empirical data on how people value risk.

The origin of the life-years approach is typically traced to an article by Michael J. Moore and W. Kip Viscusi entitled *The Quantity-Adjusted Value of Life*.[231] In that study, Moore and Viscusi introduced the idea that the value of a statistical life "cannot be divorced from the duration of life involved since lives are extended, not permanently saved."[232] They argued that "in the case of fatalities, a young person loses a much greater amount of lifetime utility than does an older person."[233]

Compared with the average subject of a wage-risk study, who is roughly 40 years old with a 35-year life expectancy,[234] a beneficiary of a regulation might be 70 years old and in poor health, with a life expectancy of around five years. Proponents of the life-years method argue that it is inappropriate to apply a value of statistical life estimate derived from studies of 40-year-old workers to elderly individuals who have significantly fewer remaining life years.

Proponents of the life-years method use a constant per life-year value, so that all life-years are valued equally no matter when they occur during the life cycle. They derive that number by taking the value of a statistical life and dividing it by the average life expectancy of the subjects of wage-risk studies. The application of a constant per life-year value across the life cycle results in smaller values being assigned to the elderly or the unhealthy. For example, using a $180,000 life-year value, the life of an elderly (or unhealthy) individual with a remaining life expectancy of five years would be valued at $900,000. Therefore, under the life-years approach, the value assigned to the life of the elderly individual would be only one-seventh the $6.3 million valued assigned to an individual of average age.

WHY IT'S BAD: THE CASE OF SMOG

To illustrate the contrast between the statistical life and the life-years methods, consider it in the context of ground-level ozone regulation. Ground-level ozone, commonly known as smog, leads to many terrible respiratory conditions, including asthma, permanent lung damage, and death. Besides these health effects, it also has negative environmental effects, including harm to plant life and decreased visibility. For these reasons, ozone levels have been regulated since 1970.

Under the Clean Air Act, the Environmental Protection Agency (EPA) sets permissible ozone levels. The agency is required to review these levels on a periodic basis to keep them current with developing science. At this writing, the EPA is conducting such a review. Several studies since the last review in 1996 have shown that the harm of short-term exposure to ozone has been underestimated. New data on the effects of ozone exposure on, in the jargon of the EPA, "additional respiratory-related endpoints, newly identified cardiovascular-related health endpoints, and mortality," have caused the staff of EPA to recommend consideration of a stricter standard that would require a lower level of ozone.[235]

Regulating ozone has not been easy. Ground-level ozone is generally created through a chemical reaction in which volatile organic compounds and nitrogen oxides mix in the presence of sunlight. These compounds have myriad sources, including motor vehicle exhaust and gasoline vapors. Controlling the pollution associated with automobiles is famously difficult. Although pollution per mile driven has fallen in the last thirty years, the number of miles driven has risen,[236] leaving ozone levels dangerously high in many parts of the country.[237] Engineering solutions to these problems have been scarce and costly.[238]

A more stringent regulation from the EPA, then, would be an enormous headache for the affected industry. But how can industry complain about a headache that saves lives? One answer is that the benefit of the headache is less than it might seem to be, because "saving lives" should be understood not as saving individual lives but as saving life-years.

Use of this method could scuttle or weaken new ozone standards. Individuals with existing respiratory problems will likely be the chief beneficiaries of a stricter regulation. As a population, these individuals will have a lower life expectancy than the average American worker, either because of advanced age or ill health. Adopting a life-years methodology would prevent some of the most vulnerable people in our society from being counted the same as everyone else, potentially blocking regulations that can save their lives.

If short-term exposure to elevated ozone levels results in the deaths of individuals with an average life expectancy of five years, then the benefit of the regulation, calculated by the life-years method, will be one-seventh that of the benefit calculated with the value of a statistical life estimate: $900,000 per life. A half-billion-dollar benefit is transformed into a $70 million benefit with a wave of the life-years wand. Compared to the statistical life method, the estimated regulatory benefit is reduced by as much as 85 percent. Thus, life-years, used in this and similar contexts, can have extremely important consequences—the difference between smog-induced deaths and cleaner air.

LIFE-YEARS ANALYSIS IN THE REGULATORY STATE

Life-years analysis has become an important part of several recent cost-benefit analyses conducted under the George W. Bush administration. John Graham was its main advocate, and with coauthor Tammy Tengs, had previously championed the life-years method in an influential criticism of federal regulations.[239] As Office of Information and Regulatory Affairs (OIRA) director, Graham prodded the EPA to use "alternative benefit calculations" placing the life-years calculations alongside calculations based on the value of statistical lives. As a result, the EPA incorporated this technique in several important cost-benefit analyses.[240]

The use of life-years analysis became the subject of significant public debate when critics in the media and in the environmental and senior citizen communities charged that the valuation techniques used by the EPA for the Clear Skies Act cost-benefit analysis amounted to a "senior death discount."[241] Highly unfavorable stories ran in the *New York Times*, the *Wall Street Journal*, and the *Washington Post*. The criticism eventually forced the Bush administration to drop some of the more controversial techniques. Even during the political hoopla over the senior death discount, however, John Graham only somewhat revised his views on the life-years methodology, conceding that it needed to be improved, but disagreeing with the idea that it needed to be scrapped altogether.[242]

Despite the outcry, the life-years method has not been abandoned by the Bush administration. It remains an important and influential way of thinking about cost-benefit analysis both at the Office of Management and Budget (OMB) and within administrative agencies. As recently as September 2006, members of the EPA Science Advisory Board's Committee on Environmental Economics discussed the utility of life-years analysis for EPA cost-benefit analysis, failing to come to a consensus conclusion.[243]

WHY IT'S WRONG

The life-years method does not flow from either sound economic theory or good facts. The approach is fundamentally inconsistent with the important tenet of economic theory in which value is determined by the willingness to pay.[244] Under that tenet, the economic value of mortality risk reductions should be determined by how much an individual would voluntarily exchange for the reduction. It would only be economically defensible to decrease the value assigned to mortality risk reduction to account for age if one's willingness to pay decreases as one ages.

But the life-years method ignores willingness to pay as a proxy for value, and instead assumes a downward linear relationship between a person's age and the value of that person's life. This assumption is inconsistent with the standard economic observation that individuals generally assign greater value to goods that are more limited in supply. The technique uses a constant per life-year value, so that all life years are valued equally no matter when they occur during the life cycle.

As people age, they can anticipate fewer future life years. Because of this scarcity, we might expect that they would value their future life years more highly than younger people would. By assuming that no difference exists between the values a 40-year-old and a 70-year-old would attribute to an additional year of life, the life-years method overlooks the effect of scarcity on valuation.[245] By ignoring the effect of scarcity and focusing regulatory efforts on reducing risk for young and healthy people, the life-years method delivers regulatory benefit to those who value it least. This approach takes the standard economic logic of "willingness to pay" and stands it on its head. Generally, the most efficient system is the one that moves resources to the people that value them most. The life-years method accomplishes exactly the opposite. Moreover, across a certain age range of their lives, as people grow older, they have more income and wealth. It is well established that the willingness to pay to avoid risk is highly correlated with income. The greater affluence of middle-aged individuals (at least preretirement) thus suggests an increase in the willingness to pay, contrary to the prediction of the life-years method.

Various models—all ignored by life-years advocates—seek to determine how the value of risk reduction might change with age. No clear answer has emerged.[246] Some models predict that as the probability of death increases, so does the willingness to pay to avoid risk,[247] because people cannot take money to their graves. In other models, increases in background risk, which occur as people age, decrease the willingness to pay for a specified risk.[248] Other models are simply ambiguous.[249] It is possible that none of these models captures the whole story. What is important, however, is that no plausible economic model offers even lukewarm support for the diminishing linear relationship between life expectancy and willingness to pay that under-girds the life-years method. The life-years method, then, is entirely without theoretical justification.

Second, this method is devoid of empirical support and inconsistent with existing empirical work. Relevant studies have found that the willingness to pay does not resemble the constant age-dependant discount postulated by proponents of the life-years method. The results of these studies have varied somewhat. Some studies have found that the willingness to pay for risk reduction is independent of age. A 2002 stated preference study by Anna Alberini, Maureen Cropper, Alan Krupnick, and Nathalie Simon[250] found no statistically significant decline, with age, in the willingness to pay for risk reduction in the U.S. population.[251] Furthermore, the study found that the willingness to pay did not decline among people with lower life expectancy attributable to diagnoses of cancer, or heart or lung disease. On the contrary, people with these conditions tended to be willing to pay more for risk reduction. Other studies have found that the willingness to pay increases with age. A revealed preferences study done by V. Kerry Smith, Mary Evans, Hyun Kim, and Donald Taylor Jr., using data from the Health and Retirement Study found that the oldest and most risk-averse individuals required "significantly higher, not lower" compensation in order to take on greater risk.

Still other studies have found an inverted-U-shaped relationship between the willingness to pay and age, in which the willingness to pay increases early in life, levels off in the middle, and then drops off near the end.[252] One of these studies, by Thomas Kniesner, W. Kip Viscusi, and James Ziliak[253] found that the inverted-U-shape was lopsided, with willingness to pay shooting up during the younger years, peaking at around age fifty, and then declining at a much slower rate.

In a large review of value-of-statistical-life estimates from over sixty studies in ten countries, Viscusi and Joseph Aldy looked at how age tended to impact the willingness to pay. They found ambiguous results, with some studies showing no significant relationship between age and the willingness to pay, while others suggested that age tended to decrease the willingness to pay. The studies that showed the willingness to pay decreasing with age, however, are suspect because of the deeply unintuitive finding that people are risk-loving, meaning that they were willing to pay to take on risk rather than demanding a premium.[254]

Although the empirical work on the relationship between age and willingness to pay has yet to provide a clear explanation about how age affects the willingness to pay to reduce risk, it clearly disproves the life-years hypothesis. All studies show that the life-years method is empirically unjustified and will lead to the systematic underestimation of the regulatory benefits of important programs. Even the estimates showing a relationship between age and willingness to pay do not support as steep and constant a decline as is assumed by the life-years method. All of the empirical evidence shows that this method produces extremely significant underestimates of the value of risk reduction to elderly individuals and individuals with low life expectancies due to poor health.

Use of the life-years technique, then, divorces cost-benefit analysis from its economic foundations. Because cost-benefit analysis claims to identify economically efficient regulation, its methodologies must be economically coherent—which the life-years technique is not. Use of this technique, or some other alternative valuation that is not grounded in economic theory and reality, amounts to smuggling noneconomic conclusions about how people "should" value risk into cost-benefit analysis. This perverts the meaning of the technique and ultimately renders its conclusions confused and useless.

WILLINGNESS TO PAY AND THE USE OF AVERAGE VALUES

The correlation among willingness to pay, age, wealth, and other individual characteristics raises important questions about how to calculate the benefits of life-saving regulations. Even if empirical work revealed a rock-solid relationship among certain individual characteristics, including age and willingness to pay, the question of whether regulators *should* take those differences into account, rather than using average values, would remain open.

For example, as just discussed, income can be expected to correlate quite closely with a willingness to pay for risk reduction.[255] Ethnicity and race may correlate as well.[256] It is not clear, however, that dividing the beneficiaries of regulations through categorization according to income or race would be ethically defensible—or, for that matter, legal. The same holds true for age; it is not clearly morally acceptable to target a specific subpopulation and reduce its estimated value of risk reductions without doing the same for other demographic factors.

The standard willingness-to-pay methodology uses average values for risk reductions, and does not break down these values according to demographic subpopulations. This practice, however, is also open to criticism. Because it is unwilling to allow the valuation of a statistical life to reflect people's actual preferences, a cost-benefit analysis using an average value of a statistical life is unmoored from its economic justification.

In the aggregate, however, using the average value of a statistical life can produce reasonably efficient levels of regulation. More finely tuned valuations might result in less error if the population affected by a regulation had markedly different valuations. Nevertheless, those errors will occur on "both sides"— i.e., over- and under-estimations—so that, overall, regulation should be neither too strict nor too weak. Although some inefficiently weak or strong regulations will pass a cost-benefit analysis test, using the average value of a statistical life does not create a systematic bias, either in favor of or against regulation.

If the average is used for the value of a statistical life, people with high willingness to pay receive "too little" regulation, people with low willingness to pay receive "too much" regulation, and the average person gets a "just right" level of regulation. In many cases, it will not be possible to finely calibrate regulation, so this phenomenon is simply a byproduct of the inability to individually tailor regulations.

Even if regulations do affect subpopulations rather than the population as a whole, the use of an average value allows us to avoid making troubling race-gender-income-age-based categorizations. Furthermore, the use of average values tends to result in a form of regulatory wealth transfer whereby those with less wealth (who, therefore, have less willingness to pay) get more regulatory benefit than they might bargain for, and those with more wealth get somewhat less than they would prefer. So long as the costs of the regulation are not borne by the direct beneficiaries—as they almost never are—the result is a progressive distribution of social goods—in this case regulatory benefits—that is not normatively troubling. Although redistribution through regulation is generally not the most efficient means of achieving egalitarian results,[257] it can be justified if reliance on average values avoids morally troubling categorizations. Thus, even if there were support for the relationship between willingness to pay and age contained in the life-years approach, which there is not, it might still not be appropriate to use life-years valuations for regulatory purposes because these valuations single out the elderly over other groups for negative treatment.

CONCLUSION

The life-years method, which leads to the fallacy that older people are less valuable than younger people, should be abandoned. The current state of the science is the value of a statistical life, based on revealed-preference studies. The effects on age of the willingness to pay are interesting, and deserve future study. Even if age can be shown to have consistent effects on the willingness to pay to avoid risk, however, many thorny issues remain. Those issues include the fundamental unfairness of treating lives differently, or how to treat children (who, because they have no assets, have little willingness to pay). We currently avoid these problems by using average values. Before we abandon that strategy, proponents of new methodologies have the burden to show that their new techniques address these issues at least as well as the current method.

There is another important lesson to be learned from life years. With their campaign against the "senior death discount," environmentalists actively confronted a methodological issue within cost-benefit analysis with very significant success. They forced the George W. Bush administration to revise its position, illustrating that if progressive groups get involved in the conversation over how cost-benefit analysis is conducted, they can prevail, especially if they stand on the moral and rational high ground, as they did on this issue. The debate over life years, while far from over, shows that proregulatory interests can win important victories by fighting these fallacies in the trenches.

Fallacy 4: People Cannot Adapt

The fourth fallacy of cost-benefit analysis is that people cannot adapt. This fallacy underlies a relatively new technique for valuing regulation that has been gathering steam over the past decade, and may soon become a prominent fixture of cost-benefit analysis—quality adjusted life-years (QALYs). QALYs are used as an alternative to statistical lives saved. However, QALYs systematically overestimate the quality of life losses from less-than-perfect health because they fail to account for how people adapt to health setbacks. In addition, there is a conceptual flaw that limits the usefulness of QALYs: They cannot be incorporated into cost-benefit analysis because a constant dollar-per-QALY exchange rate does not exist.

In the late 1980s, the state of Oregon engaged in a heated debate over the provision of health insurance, spurred in part by the plight of a seven-year-old boy, Coby Howard, who was diagnosed with leukemia and was in need of a bone marrow transplant.[258] Oregon struggled, like many state governments in the United States, with the high cost of health care and the growing uninsured population. As part of its attempt to reduce the costs that the state was bearing under the federal Medicaid system, the Oregon legislature determined that the state would not cover the medical procedures that Coby needed. When his case came to light, there was significant media coverage, public consternation, and even private fundraising to pay for his transplant.[259]

Unfortunately, Coby died before private donations could fund his treatment. The debate about how the state should pay for health care costs, however, continued. The discussion of Coby's case centered on the perceived tradeoff between covering many kinds of procedures and expanding state-provided health care coverage to include more uninsured people. In 1989, the Oregon legislature made a clear choice by enacting a law intended to achieve universal health care for all Oregon citizens.[260]

Although universal health care was never achieved in Oregon—in part because of conflicts with Medicaid—significant aspects of Oregon's health care regime did go through important changes in the early 1990s. Most important to this chapter, Oregon undertook a concerted effort to ration health care by excluding certain procedures from coverage. It ranked medical procedures according to cost-effectiveness criteria—the most cost-effective procedure was ranked first, and the least cost-effective was ranked last. Oregon's legislature then set a budgetary amount that it was willing to pay for health care. This budget determined a cost-effectiveness cutoff—only procedures above this cutoff would be covered.

Estimating the cost of a particular procedure is fairly straightforward, at least theoretically. However, in order to determine the procedure's cost-effectiveness, one must look at its benefits. In order to quantify the benefits of medical procedures, Oregon used the QALY methodology, which assigns a numerical value to different health states so that these states can then be ranked on a common scale.

These numerical values can be determined in a variety of ways; in Oregon, they were determined using a survey of a sample of the state's population. The Oregon survey asked the following question:

> In the next few minutes, we will describe several health situations. We would like you to tell us how you feel about each one by giving it a score. If you feel the situation describes good health, give it a score of 100. If you feel it is as bad as death, give it a score of 0. If the situation is about halfway between death and good health, give it a score of 50. You can use any numbers from 0 to 100, such as 0, 7, 18, 39, 50, 63, 78, 89, 100, and so forth. Remember, you can use any number between 0 and 100.[261]

Questions described specific health states, such as, "You can be taken anywhere, but have to be in bed or in a wheelchair controlled by someone else, and need help to eat or go to the bathroom, but have no other health problems," and "You can go anywhere and have no limitation or other activity, but wear glasses or contact lenses."[262]

The Oregon method used a survey of the population at large. In other cases, QALY surveys are done of medical professionals with, presumably, more knowledge about the health states described.[263] Either way, QALY surveys target a population that is presumed not to suffer from the conditions described. Respondents derive their familiarity with the health states described through education, exposure to others, or simply through imagination.

QALY surveys sometimes take somewhat different forms than the Oregon study. In addition to simply asking respondents to assign a value to health states, a common survey asks respondents to trade different health states against extensions to life expectancy, thereby attempting to get a clearer picture of the "true" value people assign to the quality of various health states.[264] The general approach, however, is the same: A sample population is surveyed to determine how they feel about various health states, compared to a state of perfect health.

These surveys determine the *quality adjusted* aspect of QALYs. The *life-years* aspect is determined by looking to the additional life expectancy provided by the procedure. The purpose of the Oregon rationing program was to maximize the number of quality-adjusted life-years, given the budget allocated to medical procedures.

The QALY approach was not particularly popular in Oregon. An initial problem was that several of the rankings were counterintuitive—for example, treatments for thumb-sucking received higher cost-effectiveness rankings than treatments for cystic fibrosis.[265] Eventually, Oregon abandoned QALYs and adopted a more subjective method, relying primarily on a panel of experts and a public comment process to determine the rankings. Even with the new methodology, there were concerns that Oregon was violating the Americans with Disabilities Act, and it was only after many revisions that a version of health-care rationing was accepted by the federal government.[266]

QALYs can also be used outside of the medical context in the cost-benefit analysis of regulation.[267] For example, if the life-year value in a revealed preference study is based on perfect health and valued at $180,000, then the QALY method adjusts downward to account for any health problem. If wearing glasses is given a value of 90 percent of perfect health, then the QALY value of a regulation that extends for one year the life of a glasses-wearer would be $162,000.

QALYs ON THE HORIZON

There are important signs that movement towards the use of QALYs in the cost-benefit analysis of regulation may be on the horizon, even though this technique is not yet well entrenched in the administrative state. Important academics, influential judges, and OIRA itself have shown interest in using the methodology to determine the benefits of environmental regulation.

Over the last decade, several academics have endorsed QALYs. Cass Sunstein, the influential scholar at the University of Chicago, argues that QALYs have appeal, especially as an extension of the life-years concept that he also favors. Sunstein does acknowledge some of the shortcomings of QALYs, noting the "serious questions of equity" that could arise in certain contexts. Nonetheless, he "does not mean to suggest that these are fundamental objections to the use of QALYs."[268]

Another important figure who has offered support for the use of QALYs is Susan Dudley, the OIRA head appointed by President Bush in April 2007 during a congressional recess. When she was director of the Mercatus Center, the antiregulatory think tank, Dudley wrote:

> There is a substantial literature extolling the analytic virtues of QALYs. However, in the context of making public decisions about regulations, it will be difficult to persuade the public that it should accept age-based or health-based "quality adjustments." We do not ordinarily make such quality adjustments when using value-of-life as the measure of benefits. A strong case can be made for quality adjustments, particularly when they are empirically derived ... and not provided by "medical experts." But our advice to OMB would be to first begin using simple longevity [i.e. life years] as the measure of benefit, and to leave the question of quality adjustment for another year.[269]

Though this statement acknowledges that there may be serious disadvantages, such as public opposition, to the expanded use of QALYs, it expresses at least cautious support for the methodology.

QALYs have also entered the judicial discourse. Most directly, in its *American Trucking v. EPA* decision, the U.S. Court of Appeals for the District of Columbia Circuit stated that QALYs may be a legitimate tool for regulatory analysis. The holding states that the interpretation of the Clean Air Act given by the Environmental Protection Agency (EPA) violated the U.S. Constitution's nondelegation doctrine—the principle that Congress cannot delegate overly broad authority to an executive agency. Judge Stephen Williams, writing for the majority, suggested that the EPA could look to Oregon's use of QALYs to build a "structure" to cabin its discretion.[270] Judge Williams also devotes a lengthy footnote to describing how concerns that the QALY method discriminates against people with disabilities can be overcome.[271] Because the Supreme Court reversed the D.C. Circuit's finding that EPA had violated the nondelegation doctrine, Judge Williams's discussion of QALYs was not addressed.

Similarly, even before Susan Dudley's arrival, the Office of Management and Budget (OMB) had begun to consider the use of QALYs. In its 2001 report to Congress, OMB discussed how it planned to revise its guidelines on cost-benefit analysis, stating that it wished to concentrate on a few "critical analytic issues."[272] It selected QALYs as one of several "analytic practices [that] seem especially ripe for review in the foreseeable future."[273] The OMB guidelines, eventually released in 2003, included a significant section on QALYs. The discussion was limited to cost-effectiveness analysis—the technique used to determine the least-cost method of achieving a particular regulatory goal. The guidelines state that if a proposed rule "creates a significant impact on both mortality and morbidity," the agency should "consider using at least one integrated measure of effectiveness," such as QALYs.[274] The use of QALYs in cost-benefit analysis is only one small step from where OMB has already taken us. Given Dudley's prior embrace of QALYs, such a step may well be in the offing before George W. Bush vacates the premises.

MEASURING QALYs

One of the most serious problems with the QALY method is that it asks healthy people, *ex ante*, to evaluate various health states. People without disabilities are asked to rate the quality of life of a person living in a wheelchair; people with healthy lungs are asked to rate the quality of life of a person with a chronic respiratory aliment. Even if QALY surveys are given to doctors—who presumably have a better basis for making these determinations—they are asking people who are fundamentally unfamiliar with the daily experience of living with the health conditions described.

People who lack experience with a particular health condition are not in a good position to make judgments about the quality of life of people with that condition.[275] Their second-hand knowledge and their sense of empathy and imagination are not appropriate substitutes. A primary issue that interferes with the accuracy of QALY surveys is the ability of people to adapt to negative health conditions. It is a well-documented phenomenon in the medical literature that people with very serious health conditions nevertheless often do not report major changes in their quality of life.[276] This phenomenon—sometimes called *response shift* or adaptation—has puzzled quality-of-life researchers, because people who suffer very serious diseases—like cancer and HIV/AIDS—often continue to report relatively high qualities of life. Compared with the assessments given in QALY surveys, the *ex post* assessments of quality of life by people with serious negative health conditions are strikingly high.

A variety of theories have been proffered to explain adaptation. Under some theories, people change their definitions of quality of life, by emphasizing certain aspects of well-being and downplaying others, in order to maintain a fairly stable sense of overall quality of life.[277] People may rely on social support networks to cope with illness, and may simply learn to manage certain aspects of their illness. Alternatively, people's frames of reference, and therefore their quality-of-life scales, may change. Current research is attempting to untangle the variety of ways in which people cope and adapt to health setbacks, and to understand why people do not report large quality-of-life losses after experiencing major physical setbacks.

As a result of adaptation, QALY surveys underestimate the quality of life of people with disabilities and health problems. When healthy survey respondents imagine the quality of life of people with negative health conditions, they do not account for their ability to cope with these problems. Significant psychological resources—not fully understood—seem to allow people to maintain high perceptions of their quality of life, even when experiencing difficult health problems.

Another source of inaccuracy in the *ex-ante* evaluation of quality of life stems from the salience bias created by QALY surveys. Individuals tend to pay disproportionate attention to information that is salient. For example, statistics presented in a dry manner may have much more informational content and probative value than one person's story presented in a compelling narrative manner. The story, however, is likely to get more attention.

When conducting QALY surveys, the researcher asks the respondent to focus on one particular aspect of the quality of life of a hypothetical person. For example, the researcher asks the respondent to imagine the quality of life of a person who "can be taken anywhere, but has to be in bed or in a wheelchair controlled by someone else, and need help to eat or go to the bathroom."[278] The respondent is then asked to rate the *overall* quality of life of a person with that health condition. This overall determination is difficult because the respondent has been asked to focus on the health problem, and therefore will tend to overestimate its importance in this hypothetical person's life. As a result, there will be a systematic undervaluation of the quality of life of people with illnesses and disabilities.

CONVERTING QALYs TO DOLLARS

Even if all of these antiregulatory measurement biases were somehow eliminated, for QALYs to be helpful in cost-benefit analysis they must be converted to a dollar scale, with the use of a constant dollar-per-QALY exchange. As in the case of life-years, however, a constant QALY rate requires strong assumptions about people's preferences. Empirical work shows that these assumptions do not hold—people do not have a constant rate at which they are willing to trade dollars for QALYs. The use of QALYs to measure regulatory benefits is therefore inconsistent with economic theory.

In the context of mortality, the use of QALYs could be justified only if people who suffer from negative health conditions are willing to pay less than the average person in order to avoid additional risks. But, it is not intuitively obvious that asthmatics, people with disabilities, or others with lower QALY values would be willing to pay less than healthier people to reduce risks to their well-being. The previous chapter discussed several conflicting theoretical models, some of which show that people with existing risks to their health are willing to pay *more* to avoid additional risks. This observation makes economic sense—a person who has less health may be willing to pay more than a healthy person to avoid further impairments to his health. Reducing the valuation of regulatory benefits because the target population has lower "quality of life" does not make sense.

QALYs can also be used in order to value the benefits of regulations with effects on morbidity. In these cases, benefits are valued by looking to the increase in QALYs created by improving a population's health. In order for the QALY standard to be consistent with economic theory, individuals should all be willing to pay the same amount to increase their QALYs, no matter how those QALYs are increased. But this need not be the case. To cite just a few factors that can divorce QALYs from willingness to pay: People may be willing to pay more to extend life than to increase health, even if the result is the same QALY increase; people may be willing to pay more to avoid some risks instead of others, even if the change in QALYs is the same; and people may be willing to pay different amounts per QALY at different points in their lives.

Empirical work comparing how willingness to pay relates to QALYs confirms that there is no simple dollar-per-QALY conversion rate.[279] For starters, the empirical work that has been done on life-years, finding that there is no steep linear relationship between age and willingness to pay, is relevant. Because the QALY method values mortality risks based on extensions to life expectancy, we would expect older people to have much lower valuations of mortality risk reductions. As discussed in the previous chapter, this is not empirically the case—the relationship between age and willingness to pay to reduce risk is far more complex than the steep linear relationship implied by both the life-years and the QALY method.

A further problems stems from how people with different negative health conditions value risk reduction. In order for the QALY framework to hold, people with all quality-of-life reducing illnesses and disabilities must be willing to pay less to avoid risk than healthy people, and that change must be proportional to the effect of their negative health condition on their quality of life. But this is not necessarily the case. For example, a recent stated-preferences study conducted in Japan found that although people suffering from cancer were willing to pay less than average to avoid mortality risks, people with heart disease were willing to pay more.[280]

More generally, an article by Kevin Haninger and James K. Hammitt of the Harvard Center for Risk Analysis directly studies the relationship between willingness to pay and QALYs.[281] They conducted a stated-preference study of nearly 3,000 respondents in order to test whether the willingness to pay to reduce risk is proportional to changes in expected QALYs—that is, whether there was a constant willingness to pay per QALY. In their study, respondents rated their own health, giving both subjective assessments of their well-being and ranking their health according to the "Health Utilities Index Mark 3"— a standard tool used to measure health-related quality of life.[282] The study then elicited their risk preferences by testing their willingness to pay more for safer but more expensive food. Their results show that the willingness to pay per QALY varies according to both the severity and duration of illness. This relationship means that willingness to pay per QALY is not constant, and the dollar-per-QALY ratio needed to use QALYs in cost-benefit analysis is not consistent with people's actual risk preference. Other empirical studies reach similar findings.[283] As a result, QALYs are not compatible with cost-benefit analysis because they do not provide an alternative to the direct measurement of willingness to pay.

CONCLUSION

Both the life-years method and QALYs are attempts to develop an alternative standard for valuing regulatory benefits. In the case of mortality risks, the standard they seek to replace is the value of a statistical life, in which all mortality risks are valued the same, no matter what the characteristics of the target population. In the case of morbidity risks, QALYs seek to replace a direct willingness-to-pay method that seeks to identify how people actually value risks to their health.

At best, both the life-years method and QALYs seek to draw a more complete picture of people's risk preferences. The development of the life-years method stems in part from the recognition that "life saving" regulations can really only extend life, and that different regulations will affect life expectancy differently. The QALY method also focuses on the health of the individual, evaluating regulations based on their effect on health as well as mortality risks.

The problem with both methods is that they make overly strong assumptions about the nature of people's risk preferences—they fill in the picture with guesses about how people should respond to risk. But those guesses have been shown to be both theoretically unjustified and empirically incorrect. People do not merely respond to life expectancy when valuing mortality-risk reductions, nor do they have a constant willingness to pay to increase their QALYs. Rather, the relationship between life-years, QALYs, and the willingness to pay is far more complex. Even though this relationship is not well understood, we do know that the assumptions about people's preferences in both the life-years and QALY methods are not accurate.

Life-year and QALY techniques are thus divorced from the economic grounding of cost-benefit analysis. The purpose of cost-benefit analysis is to identify wealth-maximizing regulations, namely, those approximating the situation that would arise absent market failures; that people are willing to pay to have in place; and that deliver benefits that are valued more highly by people than their costs. Any methodology that obscures the relationship between willingness to pay and valuation, or ignores it altogether, makes cost-benefit analysis less accurate.

However, the desire to generate a more complete picture about risk preferences is laudable. It is certainly worth studying how a person's willingness to pay to avoid risks changes over the course of her life, and how much people are willing to pay to avoid health risks. There may even be a way to incorporate some of the QALY research that has been done—which is quite extensive—into a willingness-to-pay framework in the context of morbidity risks. It is at least possible that some meaningful relationship between responses to QALY surveys and willingness-to-pay surveys will be found in certain contexts, so that the data from QALY surveys could be used to augment standard revealed- and stated-preference studies.

For now, however, the best estimates of people's risk preferences come from willingness-to-pay studies—with revealed-preference studies being the gold standard. The value of a statistical life, a construct that treats all mortality risks the same, is superior to the alternatives that have been offered, and is closest to how people across a relatively broad range of ages actually respond to risk. It is unclear that the life-years or QALY methods will ever usefully contribute to our current benefit valuations. Further inquiries into the relationships between health, life expectancy, and willingness to pay to avoid risk are warranted, but radical changes to how we conduct cost-benefit analysis in this area are not.

Fallacy 5: People Always Want to Put Off Bad Things

The next two chapters should be considered a pair, in that they both address the issue of *discounting* in cost-benefit analysis. Discounting is a technique that marks down future dollars to translate them into present dollars. It assumes that because people prefer immediate gratification, a dollar today is worth more than a dollar next year (even correcting for inflation). This assumption undergirds the sentiment, "I'd gladly pay you Tuesday for a hamburger today."

Unfortunately, in the environmental, health and safety context, two kinds of discounting are run together—individual discounting and generational discounting. Although individual discounting is defensible—with some important caveats discussed later in this chapter—generational discounting is not, and the next chapter argues for it to be retired altogether.

There are two contexts in which environmental, health and safety benefits occur in the future, rather than at the time of the regulation. In the first, the target risk has a long latency period: decades can pass between the exposure to a contaminant and the manifestation of the related disease. In the second, regulatory benefits accrue to future generations.

Proponents of cost-benefit analysis, including Cass Sunstein,[284] W. Kip Viscusi,[285] and John Graham, both in his academic writing[286] and in his role as head of Office of Information and Regulatory Affairs (OIRA), favor discounting benefits that occur in the future, in both the latency and future generation contexts. The Office of Management and Budget (OMB) strongly endorses discounting—in its guidelines to agencies on how to conduct cost-benefit analysis, it recommends using a seven percent discount rate.[287] The OMB cost-benefit guidelines specifically justify discounting for health- and mortality-related benefits, for both long-latency diseases and regulations affecting future generations. The Environmental Protection Agency (EPA) cost-benefit guidelines also include a lengthy discussion of discounting; in those guidelines, EPA favors discounting in both intra- and inter-generational contexts, but also recommends that regulators analyze the undiscounted costs and benefits as well when regulations affect future generations.[288]

In contrast, environmentalists and others favorably disposed toward regulation oppose discounting. For example, in his book, *Earth in the Balance: Ecology and the Human Spirit*, Al Gore argues that discounting is a "short-sighted and arguably illogical assumption" that "assumes that all resources belong to the present generation."[289]

A great deal turns on the resolution of this issue. A study by Lisa Heinzerling showed that many environmental, health and safety regulations promulgated since the 1970s have acceptable cost-benefit ratios if the value of lives is not discounted, but fail cost-benefit analysis if those values are discounted.[290]

Although they are often treated the same, the two contexts are conceptually different and require different approaches. The long-latency period context raises the question of whether we should discount benefits that accrue to the same individual—*individual discounting*. The future generations context raises the question of whether we should discount benefits that accrue to different individuals (*i.e.*, individuals in different generations)—*generational discounting*.

This chapter addresses individual discounting, arguing that discounting may be appropriate to reflect people's preference for benefits now rather than in the future. However, the conventional wisdom needs a mild corrective: People may generally prefer receiving benefits now rather than later, but they do not always hold that preference. Sometimes people are affected by dread, *i.e.*, they would rather get something bad over with quickly. That factor is certainly likely to be in play in at least some long-latency disease cases, meaning that people's welfare would be significantly diminished by the dread they experienced over the latency periods. Furthermore, long-latency diseases are associated with suffering and involuntary risks. For all these reasons, an upward adjustment of the value of avoiding these risks is necessary to avoid falling prey to the fallacy that people *always* want to put off bad things. The current practice of discounting future benefits at the rate of standard financial instruments is likely to underestimate the value of avoiding long-latency diseases.

ASBESTOS — WHAT HAPPENS TO A BAN DEFERRED?

Consider the case of asbestos. Asbestos is a naturally occurring mineral that has been used for hundreds of years for its fire-resistant properties. In modern times, asbestos has been employed extensively in the construction industry for sound-proofing, insulating, and fire-proofing in materials such as plaster, vinyl floors, caulk, and sheetrock tape. Asbestos is also used in other products, including fire blankets, and car-brake shoes and pads.

Exposure to asbestos causes health problems. When disturbed, asbestos can become airborne and be inhaled. Asbestos fibers are extremely small, making them difficult for the lungs to expel. Exposure to asbestos is associated with significant respiratory ailments. Asbestosis is the result of scarring in the lungs generated by asbestos exposure; it can reduce lung function and, in extreme cases, can lead to respiratory failure. Mesothelioma is a cancer, rare in those not exposed to asbestos, of the lining of the lungs and chest cavity. Diagnosis of mesothelioma is complicated because the early symptoms, such as shortness of breath, coughing, pain in the chest, and abdominal swelling, are associated with other diseases. A history of early exposure to asbestos is often what alerts physicians to the possibility of mesothelioma. Treatment of mesothelioma is difficult and the median survival rate is only 6 to 12 months after diagnosis. Other forms of cancer, such as cancer of the larynx, are also associated with asbestos exposure.

There is a significant lag between the time of exposure to asbestos and when health problems manifest themselves. Ten to twenty years typically elapse between exposure to asbestos and the development of asbestosis. The latency period for mesothelioma is even longer—its peak incidence is 35 to 45 years after exposure to asbestos.

The harmful effects of asbestos have been known for a long time. An early report on the harms of asbestos dust was given to the British Parliament at the end of the nineteenth century.[291] In the early 1970s, asbestos gained the serious attention of U.S. regulatory agencies. In 1972, in light of increasing evidence of asbestos's harmful effects, the Occupational Safety and Health Administration (OSHA) promulgated an occupational rule of progressive stringency.[292] A year later, the EPA promulgated standards governing the emission of asbestos under the Clean Air Act.[293]

In 1976, Congress passed the Toxic Substances Control Act in response to concerns over the large number of industrial chemicals released into the environment. In addition to imposing record-keeping, reporting, and testing requirements, the act gives the EPA the authority to ban chemicals that pose an "unreasonable risk." In 1979, the EPA issued a notice of its intent to regulate asbestos, eventually settling on an asbestos ban as the appropriate regulatory approach.

The issue of discounting was salient during the EPA's consideration of the asbestos ban. After EPA submitted a draft of the rule to OMB for review, which did not undertake any discounting over the latency period,[294] A. James

Barnes, then the EPA's acting Deputy Administrator, received a letter from OMB raising questions about whether the benefits of the rule exceeded its costs.[295] OMB's cost-benefit analysis used a value per-cancer-case-avoided of $1 million and discounted this amount at a rate of 4 percent for the length of the latency period.[296] The effect of this discounting over a forty-year latency period was to reduce the $1 million value of life to $208,000. Using the 10 percent discount rate favored by OMB at the time (but not used in this instance), society would have been willing to spend only $22,000 to save a person's life forty years into the future.

In 1989, EPA issued its final rule. In that rule, it applied a discount rate of 3 percent to the time between the promulgation of the regulation and the anticipated *exposure* to asbestos. It chose, however, not to discount during the latency period following the exposure.

The affected industries challenged the regulation in *Corrosion Proof Fittings v. EPA*.[297] They made a variety of arguments, using what Judge Jerry E. Smith of the Fifth Circuit characterized as a "protest everything" approach[298] in which they challenged, among other things, the failure of the EPA to swear in witnesses who testified at a hearing and the use of a hearing officer rather than administrative law judge to preside over the hearings. The court rejected most of those arguments. But the challengers prevailed on some points, including the claim that the EPA had not appropriately discounted the benefits of the regulation over the latency period. In October 1991, the Fifth Circuit vacated the regulation and sent the EPA back to the drawing board.

In his opinion, Judge Smith took the position that discounting over the course of the latency period was necessary to provide for a fair comparison of costs and benefits at different times:

> Although various commentators dispute whether it ever is appropriate to discount benefits when they are measured in human lives, we note that it would skew the results to discount only costs without according similar treatment to the benefits side of the equation. ... Because the EPA must discount costs to perform its evaluations properly, the EPA also should discount benefits to preserve an apples-to-apples comparison ....[299]

For this proposition, Judge Smith cited an article in the March 23, 1991, issue of the *Economist*—the popular current affairs magazine.[300]

The EPA, under President George H. W. Bush, failed to seek review of the Fifth Circuit opinion in the Supreme Court, allowing the ruling to stand. The asbestos ban has been tabled ever since.

VALUING LIFE SAVING REGULATION —
THE PROBLEM OF TIME

As discussed in an earlier chapter, the value of a statistical life is derived from willingness-to-pay studies, typically wage-risk studies that compare the wages earned by workers in risky jobs to workers in comparable but less risky jobs. These studies have been conducted almost exclusively in the context of industrial accidents, in which the worker either is fatally injured and dies instantly, or does not.[301] They do not address how a worker's willingness to pay for risk reduction would change if the time period between the exposure to the risk and the health impact were lengthened, as is the case in long-latency diseases.

In principle, it is possible to directly determine people's willingness to pay to avoid the risk of long-latency diseases. Workers could be told the additional probability of, say, dying of cancer from a riskier job, and the latency period. They could then be asked how much additional compensation they demand in order to accept the job with the higher risk. The data could then be used to determine the value workers place on risk reductions for long latency threats.

There are, however, several problems with conducting these kinds of studies. First, the data on deaths resulting from latent harms is more limited than that from instantaneous accidents. The federal government has been compiling occupational data for only a few decades—less than the latency period of some of the harms.

Job-related accidents are also much easier to track than latent injuries. During the latency period, people may relocate, causing employers to lose touch with them. Workers also may not remember being exposed to a contaminant. Thus, there are large practical problems for the study of wage differentials for long-latency diseases.

It is also likely that cognitive limitations are much greater with low-probability latency diseases than for industrial accidents—the risks are less salient, and harder to understand and process.[302] Wage differentials, even if they could be ascertained, might reflect people's cognitive limitations rather than their genuine risk preferences.

Moreover, an individual's real risk from exposure to certain contaminants is affected by lifestyle choices such as smoking. Workers would have to understand how exposure interacts with their lifestyles to create their personal risks, and researchers would have to account for these confounding factors. Because of these difficulties, revealed-preference studies generally do not focus on long-latency diseases.

Some attempts have been made to avoid these problems by using stated-preference studies to determine the willingness to pay to avoid exposure to long latency-type risks.[303] Although these studies contribute to our understanding of the willingness to pay to avoid long-latency disease risks, they are subject to the vulnerability that plagues all stated-preference studies: Survey respondents are answering hypothetical questions and not playing with "real money." It is therefore problematic to rely on stated-preference studies because their conclusions are not supported by actual revealed-preference data.

Given the problems of directly measuring willingness to pay to avoid long-latency diseases, discounting is used as a second-best approach used to translate the results from the accident context into the long-latency context. In their simplest forms, economic models compare benefits derived at different times by analogizing those benefits to cash flows and discounting the future stream of benefits by means of a discount rate.

Discounting, in the context of money, reflects the fact that it is more desirable to receive a payment sooner rather than later. This preference is not merely a function of the existence of inflation. In comparing monetary flows occurring at different times, the effects of inflation can be adjusted by converting all amounts to constant dollars. But even in an inflation-free world, it is best to receive a given amount of money as soon as possible. Having the money sooner gives one the option of immediate spending, which is precluded when getting money later.

The fact that valuations of life obtained in industrial accidents could be discounted over the time that elapses between a regulation and the accrual of its benefits, however, does not imply that such discounting is always appropriate.

DISAGGREGATING DISCOUNTING — LATENCY VERSUS BENEFITS TO FUTURE GENERATIONS

As discussed above, the wisdom of discounting human lives often conflates two different issues. In the first, the benefit of environmental protection will accrue to an individual in the future because the harm has a latency period. An individual exposed to a carcinogen, such as asbestos, faces an increased probability of dying perhaps twenty or thirty years after the exposure. An environmental-protection measure implemented today can avoid that future risk—averting a risk of death at the end of the latency period. In the second, the benefits of controls accrue primarily to future generations. Climate change caused by the burning of fossil fuels is a prominent example.

In the first case—long-latency diseases—discounting is used as a tool to account for the fact that people may be willing to pay significantly more to eliminate immediate harm than to eliminate delayed harm. If the person prefers the risk to be delayed, then valuations derived in the context of immediate risks, such as industrial accidents, should be discounted to obtain valuations appropriate to the case of delayed risks. The comparison is between two different kinds of risks faced by the same individual. If the individual prefers the adverse effect to come later, there are no compelling moral or ethical impediments to honoring that choice.

In the second case—harm to future generations—the question is not about how to compare two different risks faced by the same individual. Instead, the choice is between risks faced by *different individuals*. Should we value more highly the preferences of one individual merely because she lives at an earlier time than the other? That question, to which the next chapter is directed, is fundamentally moral and ethical. It implicates the responsibility of current generations for the welfare of future generations. The issues raised are conceptually distinct from those that arise in the case of latent harms.

LATENCY: PREFERRING SAFETY SOONER
RATHER THAN LATER

In the context of long-latency diseases, discounting values of life obtained for instantaneous accidents is appropriate if people prefer the reduction of near-term risks over long-term risks of the same magnitude. For example, given the choice between a 1 in 1,000 risk of immediate death, and a 1 in 1,000 risk of contracting a disease that will remain dormant for ten years and then kill instantly, an individual might prefer the latter. Discounting represents a second-best method of accounting for a preference for safety sooner rather than later.

The magnitude of that preference can be gauged by adjusting the numbers: What about eliminating a 1 in 2,000 risk of immediate mortality versus eliminating a 1 in 1,000 risk of a disease with a ten-year latency? Or more generally, what risk reduction now would be equivalent to a 1 in 1,000 reduction ten years in the future? The point at which the person is indifferent between the two options determines how risk reduction is being traded against time.

Empirical work has been done to estimate the degree to which people discount the value of future risk reductions. As mentioned earlier, there have been attempts to use stated-preference studies—a recent study by Professor Anna Alberini and coauthors found an implicit discount rate of four and a half percent for people in the United States.[304] W. Kip Viscusi has also conducted several studies of discount rates relying on wage data, finding discount rates between two and eleven percent.[305] However, there are important limitations on the empirical work in this area—both revealed- and stated-preference studies are subject to important caveats. Nevertheless, it is important to note that the available empirical evidence generally supports the conclusion that people have some time preferences for health and safety risks.

FUTURE SELVES

Discounting in the context of long-latency diseases might give rise to the concern that the discount rate is based on a common myopia among people to favor the present at the expense of the future. As a result, they might take inadequate care of their future selves, preferring instant gratification instead. If this were the case, discounting the benefit of avoiding long-latency diseases would only respect irrational preferences that reduce the total utility of a person over the course of her lifetime.

According to this perspective, the individual is a succession of "multiple selves."[306] The concern is that the individual's current self will make decisions that undervalue the interest of the individual's future self by choosing a discount rate that is too high. This formulation gives rise to a typical externality problem whereby the person reaping the benefit of the decision— the current self—is different from the person facing the cost—the future self.

The biggest problem with this objection is that it proves too much. Most decisions that we make have future consequences. For example, every time we borrow money, we reduce the resources available to us in the future. To find an externality in each decision with future consequences opens the door to governmental regulation of every financial decision we make. Such an approach would therefore constitute a serious affront to individual autonomy.

Interfering with individual preferences in the name of protecting a future self might be appropriate in the face of fairly egregious myopia. Social Security—which is a forced savings program—is justified as providing protection against insufficient savings for retirement. Even in this instance, however, the government does not try to arrive at an optimal savings rate, instead seeking only "the assurance of a dignified existence in old age."[307] Outside of a small number of fairly extreme examples, however, we respect individual preferences, thinking that a person, rather than a governmental technocrat, is in the best position to plan for her own future welfare. The future-selves argument against discounting should be rejected.

But although this downward adjustment of the value of a statistical life derived in instantaneous industrial accidents is appropriate, certain upward adjustments are necessary as well. Indeed, one must account for the dread factor associated with latency diseases, the involuntary nature of exposure to environmental pollutants, and the suffering associated with certain kinds of latent diseases, particularly cancer.

DREAD

In the May 5, 2006, issue of *Science*, an article entitled *Neurobiological Substrates of Dread*[308] published the results of a neuroimaging study that focused on how the brain responds to the anticipation of an undesired outcome. As the title indicates, the authors were interested in dread—how fear of future outcomes influences our choices now.

The authors of the study sought to understand why, in some contexts, people "prefer to delay gratification and to speed up the occurrence of unpleasant outcomes."[309] This result conflicts with the predictions of standard economic theory that "people should want to expedite desired experiences and delay undesirable experiences for as long as possible."[310] These predictions are the basis for the discounting model in which outcomes occurring at different times are compared with each other by discounting the future occurrence by some rate based on time preference.

In the study, participants were shocked at a low, but painful voltage. Prior to the shock, they were given two choices, to be shocked either sooner or later. When faced with a choice between identical shocks at different times, participants chose to take the shock sooner 78.9 percent of the time. Moreover, some participants were willing to take more painful shocks to reduce the delay. These participants were categorized as "extreme dreaders" because of their willingness to increase the total voltage experienced in order to avoid the period of dread. Thus, the study found that the antidread preferences were sufficiently strong to counteract any time preference—the desire to put off the painful shock. Overall, most participants preferred to reduce the delay.

The authors went on to compare these antidread preferences to neuroimages taken during the study. They found dread responses in a number of regions of the pain matrix of the brain. Based on the imaging data, they theorized that "the subjective experience of dread that ultimately drives an individual's behavior comes from the attention devoted to the expected physical response ... and not simply a fear or anxiety response."[311]

This study contributes to the understanding of discounting in the context of latency diseases. Although rational actors may generally prefer to delay unpleasant risks, they may in specific contexts prefer to hasten them because of an antidread preference. The antidread effect would be especially relevant in the part of the latency period after the detection of a life-threatening disease but prior to mortality—when dread may be extreme.

To be sure, distinctions between this study and the long-latency disease context should be acknowledged. The time periods are significantly different. In the neuroimaging study, delays were measured in seconds rather than years. The harm is different—minor shocks versus life-threatening diseases. And the harm was more salient to the participants during the course of the delay; they knew the shock was coming and their surroundings provided a constant reminder. But the findings of the neuroimaging study indicate that, at least in some contexts, people do not have a preference for delaying negative experiences—quite the opposite. In order to accurately approximate people's actual risk preferences, then, any discounting of the adverse consequences of the risk during the latency period needs to be coupled with an increase in the estimate of these consequences as a result of dread.

INVOLUNTARY RISKS

In addition to dread, long-latency diseases have other characteristics that may justify increases in the value assigned to risk-reducing regulations. Many long-latency-disease risks subject to regulatory intervention are the result of involuntary exposure. There is an extensive literature suggesting that individuals assign greater value to avoiding risks that are thrust upon them involuntarily than to risks they incur voluntarily.[312] Because on-the-job risk is generally thought of as a voluntary risk,[313] in contrast to certain kinds of risks targeted by environmental, health and safety programs, such as toxic air pollution, willingness-to-pay estimates based on labor-market studies will systematically undervalue risk reduction.

For example, some recreational activities are quite risky. During the 2004–2005 ski season, for example, 45 fatalities occurred.[314] Because that risk is undertaken voluntarily, however, there has been no substantial legislative push to make skiing safer by regulating the ski industry—for example, by requiring helmets. Likewise, the voluntary risks associated with smoking, diet, and lack of exercise, which account for hundreds of thousands of deaths per year, are given relatively little in the way of regulatory expenditures. In contrast, involuntary risks, especially environmental risks, have received more attention from federal regulators.

Determining whether a risk is voluntary or involuntary is difficult. Even in the case of smoking—a paradigmatic voluntary risk—a nicotine addict who began smoking as a child, in response to advertising and cultural signals, may not be making a free choice. Similarly, workplace risks might be considered voluntarily undertaken if the employee was aware of the risk, but an employee with inadequate opportunities for other work might not be making a voluntary choice. [315] Assuming that the wage-risks studies are properly conducted, however, the workers in those studies would have had a choice among jobs of different risks, and the voluntary label would therefore be appropriate.

In contrast, one generally thinks of exposure to hazardous air pollution as an involuntary risk. There would be, however, a voluntary element if the exposure could be avoided by, say, changing residences. Nonetheless, information on the aggregate risks at different locations is far less well understood than the data that tracks industrial accidents. For this reason, the risks attached to exposure to air pollution are generally classified as involuntary risks.[316]

Empirical studies show that people attach more value to being free from involuntary risks. In one stated-preference study, for example, the degree to which people viewed a risk as avoidable was directly predictive of whether they would choose to reduce a risk—the vast majority of survey respondents preferred to reduce the involuntary risk at the expense of the voluntary risk.[317] The study found that people preferred programs that reduced risks perceived as unavoidable, even if those programs saved fewer lives than others targeting avoidable risks. In order for people to be indifferent between programs targeting avoidable and unavoidable risks, the program targeting the avoidable risks had to save 28 percent more lives.[318]

SUFFERING

There is an additional important difference between the nature of deaths resulting from industrial accidents and those that occur in the long latency context. The former occur instantly and without warning. The latter often occur following a long and agonizing ordeal. There are clear reasons why people might prefer to reduce risks of long-latency diseases if they are associated with significant amounts of suffering, above and beyond the mortality risks.

Some studies have been undertaken to get a handle on the extent to which people's willingness to pay to reduce mortality risks varies with the kind of health threat involved. One study by George Tolley, Donald Kenkel, and Robert Fabian attempts to quantify the values attached to the avoidance of unforeseen, instantaneous deaths on the one hand, and carcinogenic deaths on the other.[319] They do so by starting with a baseline willingness to pay based on wage studies, and add a component for the period of illness preceding death, based on stated-preference studies. They arrive at a valuation for avoiding cancer deaths that is roughly double the valuation of avoiding instantaneous deaths.[320]

Long latency does not necessarily imply that a risk was placed on an individual involuntarily, or that mortality will be preceded by significant illness and suffering. However, many of the long-latency diseases targeted by environmental, health and safety regulation have these characteristics. This is especially true in the case of cancer risks, which are an important class of long-latency risks targeted by environmental, health and safety programs. In these contexts, it is important to counterbalance any time preference that people have for delaying risk with their preference against involuntary risks and mortality risks that entail illness and suffering.

CONCLUSION

This chapter argues that discounting makes sense in the case of latent harms, but this reduction in the estimate of the benefits of regulating latent harms must be coupled with significant upward adjustments to account for the dread experienced during the latency period, the involuntary nature of environmental harms with latency periods, and the suffering generally associated with death from diseases, particularly cancer, that exhibit latent harms. If these upward adjustments are not made, the benefits attached to programs that reduce long-latency risks will be inappropriately low, and cost-benefit analysis will erroneously discourage the regulation of these risks.

Fallacy 6: We Are Worth More than Our Children

Discounting in the long-latency context is an empirical question of people's time preferences; it does not raise any substantial moral issues. Discounting in the future-generations context, however, is very different. Deciding how much to spend today in order to reduce environmental risks for future generations is not a question of time preferences for any group of people,[321] but is an allocation question between people living at different times. Fundamentally, such allocation decisions are moral.

This chapter argues that the current practice of discounting benefits for future generations at a constant rate consistent with the return on traditional financial instruments is wrongheaded, and leads to the fallacy that we are worth more than our children. Instead, a modified version of the concept of sustainable development can serve as a useful starting point for a moral discussion of our duties to our children, grandchildren, and future inhabitants of the planet.

A CONVENIENT UNTRUTH

In Al Gore's recent documentary film, *An Inconvenient Truth*, the former vice president presents the case that industrial societies are causing climate change. Gore, who has made protection of the environment a core piece of his political agenda, seeks to raise alarm about the severity of climate change and the need for immediate action. He relies on the work of climatologists and other scientists who have spent decades documenting the link between human activities—most importantly, the burning of fossil fuels—and climate change.

However, that need for action has not been universally recognized. The current Bush administration has taken no significant step toward either domestic or international greenhouse gas controls, backing out of the Kyoto

Protocol and allowing the issue to languish.[322] It has done so primarily by questioning the scientific consensus supporting the link between human activities and recent and projected increases in global temperatures. The administration has taken affirmative steps to downplay this link, including the suppression of research emanating from federal agencies.[323]

It is possible that the Bush administration genuinely questions the science of climate change. But uncertainty about climate change cannot justify inaction. As others have pointed out, waiting for absolutely conclusive information before acting is irrational.[324] Whenever the projected gains in decisional quality from an additional unit of information are outweighed by the losses associated with delay, waiting for more information is foolhardy.

The Bush administration's unwillingness to respond to a significant environmental threat can be explained in at least three ways. The first explanation is the time horizon of electoral politics. The costs of climate change mitigation will be borne up front, while the benefits will not accrue until much later. This puts environmental issues out of synch with electoral politics, because the costs would have to be borne by current voters, while the benefits would be reaped by voters who have yet to come into being.

The second possibility is the position of the United States in the global economy. The costs of mitigating climate change—by reducing greenhouse gas emissions—are greater for rich countries, because they are the biggest emitters. Yet the benefits of mitigating climate change are smaller for the United States than for less-developed countries. The least developed countries are likely to be hardest hit, because they rely more heavily on agriculture for income, because they tend to be located in warmer and more severe-weather-prone areas, and because they lack the resources to adapt to such change. Developed countries like the United States have less to lose because they have cooler climates and more abundant social resources to adapt by shifting agricultural practices or addressing the rising sea-level. Again, but this time for geographical rather than temporal reasons, the costs would be disproportionately borne by people who vote in American elections, while the benefits would disproportionately accrue to people who do not.

A third possible explanation lies in the use of discounting. Because the benefits of mitigating climate change will occur in the future, and the costs must be expended now, the popular account of cost-benefit analysis dictates that the benefits in the future should be discounted to their current value. This fact is reflected in financial markets by the interest rate: If you have money now, you can trade it for more money later. The convenient untruth is that discounting is appropriate in the intergenerational context. Through the use of discounting, the failure to act on climate change can be justified in cost-benefit terms.

According to plausible estimates, the global average temperature will rise between 2 and 5 degrees Celsius over the next fifty years.[325] There is a possibility that the increase may be higher, especially if climate change induces "feedback loops" whereby higher temperatures lead to effects like the melting of permafrost, which in turn lead to the release of greenhouse gases, which in turn lead to even higher temperatures.[326] The effects of temperature rises of this magnitude would be extreme, and could include major losses in certain agricultural sectors, flooding and the erosion of coastlines, more extreme weather, drought, the spread of tropical diseases, and the displacement of people. If these events come to pass, they will have a major impact on the global economy and the well-being of the world's population.

The convenient untruth could allow people not to care very much about climate change. Because all of this unpleasant-sounding mayhem will occur in the future, the right thing to do—according to many proponents of cost-benefit analysis—is to discount the benefits of combating climate change using the interest rate on financial instruments. We can then get an accurate picture of what we might, as a society, be willing to pay to avoid these calamities. Using the discount rate of 10 percent—which until recently was the Office of Management and Budget's (OMB's) preferred rate[327]—society should be willing to pay about $8.5 billion now in order to avoid $1 trillion in damages in fifty years, and $72 million to avoid $1 trillion in damages in one hundred years. Stated another way, if the value of a statistical life is $6 million dollars, society should be willing to pay about $50,000 to save a life in fifty years, and $435 dollars to save a life in one hundred years. Because the costs of mitigating climate change are significant,[328] under these assumptions, the best policy appears to be to do nothing at all.

The use of discounting may not be the driving cause of the current Bush administration's inaction on environmental issues. It is, however, at least a powerful means of justifying that inaction. Intergenerational discounting pervades current cost-benefit analysis. As this chapter shows, the convenient untruth hides an important moral decision about intergenerational responsibilities.

DISCOUNTING IN THE FUTURE
GENERATIONS CONTEXT

The practice of discounting future benefits is prevalent throughout the federal administrative system. Although some attention has been given to the distinction between individual and generational discounting, that distinction is often made only to be ignored or minimized. OMB *Circular A-4*, a publication that outlines the official advice of OMB for agencies conducting regulatory review, advises discounting in both contexts. In recognizing that "[s]pecial ethical considerations arise when comparing benefits and costs across generations" the OMB Circular suggests two approaches. The first is to conduct generational discounting in the same way as individual discounting, but to "supplement the analysis with an explicit discussion of the intergenerational concerns." The second is to conduct discounting for future generations at a slightly lower rate than in the latency context.[329] The OMB Circular gives several reasons for favoring the first approach, stating that it would "prevent[] time-inconsistency problems" and referring to a unitary discount rate as "attractive from an ethical standpoint" based on anticipated future economic growth.[330]

Among academic commentators, the discounting of future benefits is the favored approach. For example, in a recent paper, Cass Sunstein, writing with Arden Rowell, argues that the discounting of benefits to future generations is permissible because money rather than lives is being discounted.[331] Recognizing that unacceptable distributional results may come about because of this practice, Sunstein and Rowell argue that these concerns should be addressed at the backend, through a separate analysis of distribution. Specifically, they contend that future generations should be compensated for risks created by current generations.

Unfortunately, these commentators are wrong.

A SIMPLER WORLD

Imagine a very simple world, in which two people with identical utility functions will live subsequent, but not overlapping, lives of fifty years each: person 1 lives between years 1 and 50 and person 2 lives between years 51 and 100. This world contains 100 units of resources in this world, and no possibility of productive economic activity. Each unit of resource that is consumed is completely destroyed.

In this world, giving equal consideration to each inhabitant, resources would be allocated evenly, so that each person would receive 50 units of resources. If a positive discount rate is used, however, even a relatively small one, the bulk of the resources would be allocated to the first inhabitant. It is difficult to see the fairness of such an arrangement.

Indeed, if the two inhabitants were located on separate islands at the same time, it would be manifestly unfair to allocate more resources to one than the other, based on some arbitrary criterion such as who inhabits the more northerly island.

If people are separated in three-dimensional space, but still inhabit the same timeframe, it is clear that fairness requires an equitable distribution of the available resources.

Our intuition should be equally clear in the intergenerational context, in which people share the same three-dimensional space, but inhabit different time frames. In this simple society, in which every allocation to the first person takes something away from the second person, discounting would be fundamentally unfair to the later party.

This simple model should draw out our fundamental moral intuitions in the intergenerational context. What is at stake is an allocation decision between individuals, which is unavoidably a moral decision that should be governed by notions of fairness and equal consideration for all people. It is fundamentally different from the context of individual discounting (which could be modeled as how one individual would allocate the 100 units to herself over time). We are not choosing how to allocate the world to our future selves. We are choosing how much of the world, and in what condition, to leave to our children, grandchildren, and their progeny far into the future.

A WEALTHIER FUTURE

Of course, the real world is more complicated. It may be that our initial intuition is overridden by accounting for more real-world factors. For example, it has been argued that, since future generations can be expected to enjoy higher levels of consumption than present generations, we should discount future benefits to reflect the decreasing marginal utility of consumption.[332] If the current rate of technological development and economic growth continues, inhabitants of the future will enjoy greater productivity and consumption opportunities. Because future generations will be better off— the argument goes—the same benefit will produce less utility than it would if delivered to today's poorer population. Because the costs are imposed on the current, relatively less wealthy, generation, we need to discount future benefits to reflect the fact the beneficiaries of the regulatory program are, in material terms, better off than those who are burdened by it.

This argument assumes that beneficiaries in the future will be better off than the current individuals burdened by regulation. But this will not always be the case, as suggested by the geographical disparities mentioned earlier. Most studies of climate change show that its negative consequences will be suffered disproportionately by individuals in poor, developing countries. Bangladesh, for example, is likely to be particularly affected by sea-level rises.[333] In contrast, the contribution to the global warming problem lies to a large extent with the developed countries, and the financial responsibility for mitigation measures will be borne primarily by these countries.[334] The question is whether the Bangladeshis of the future will be better off than the U.S. residents burdened by environmental regulation today.

The answer would seem to be no. In 2005, the United States and Bangladesh had estimated per capita gross national products (GNP) of $41,768 and $452, respectively.[335] The figures differ by a factor of more than 90. It is quite unlikely that in 100 years Bangladesh will have a higher GNP (in current dollars) than the United States has now. To the extent that the United States is paying for environmental measures and Bangladesh is benefiting from them, discounting to compensate for differential levels of consumption makes no sense. In fact, a negative discount rate would have to be used to reflect the fact that when the benefits of climate change measures begin to accrue, Bangladesh will be poorer than the United States is now. Such a rate would justify spending more now than the benefits in the future, contrary to the position advocated by discounting theorists.

If we begin the project of discounting to account for the marginal utility of consumption, we must see that project to its end. That would entail a holistic analysis of where regulatory costs are borne and where regulatory benefits will accrue, which in turn would require forecasts of the relative consumption levels of those regions. For what it's worth, this analysis has proven so difficult that it is rarely carried out in the context of regulations that benefit and burden different populations of the current generation. The degree of complexity when future generations are involved will be much higher.

APPETITE FOR DESTRUCTION

Another factor that is sometimes used to justify discounting is the chance that a catastrophe could destroy human civilization.[336] If a large asteroid collides with Earth and annihilates all human life, efforts undertaken now to reduce climate change in the future will have come to naught. We should take account of this fact by discounting future benefits by the probability that they will never be enjoyed. Allocating more resources to earlier generations makes sense because they are more likely to be around to enjoy them.

There are several problems with this theory. First, although it makes sense to discount future benefits by the probability of their nonoccurrence, the appropriate discount rate here would be tiny. We cannot catalogue all events that might destroy humankind, but known natural catastrophes of this scale are almost inconceivably rare. To wipe out humankind, an asteroid would have to be about 1 to 10 kilometers in diameter. Asteroids of that size strike the Earth once every half-million years.[337]

Other species-destroying risks are also extremely unlikely. Events such as a black hole wandering into the solar system, attack by extraterrestrials, or the unexpectedly rapid decomposition of the sun have exceedingly low probabilities. These so-called natural disasters are sufficiently unlikely as to make their risk, for the purposes of discounting, insignificant.

Human-caused disasters are more likely. Humans continue to develop vastly powerful technology. If unleashed, some of it could destroy humanity. An all-out nuclear war is one example. Extreme climate change is another—in fact, the "Doomsday Clock" maintained by the Bulletin of the Atomic Scientists was moved two minutes closer to zero in 2007 to reflect climate change risks—as is the "grey-goo" resulting from runaway nanotechnology, or the creation of super-intelligent robots capable of destroying all human life. Although these scenarios are also very unlikely, they represent some risk of species destruction that is nonnegligible from a discounting perspective. But none of these unlikely scenarios would justify discounting at anything close to the rate used for financial instruments.

Furthermore, using the probability of self-destruction to justify the discounting of future benefits is ethically questionable. If we are contributing to the probability of humanity's extinction, should we then invoke this possible outcome as an argument to allocate more resources to ourselves? A plausible answer is that the current generation should not benefit in this manner from its own bad acts.

THE ROLE OF OPPORTUNITY COSTS

The decision not to discount benefits accruing to future generations should not be understood as a decision to ignore opportunity costs in the intergenerational context. Consider a harm that could be addressed immediately or sometime in the future. If we address the environmental problem now, we incur some expense now. Alternatively, if we address the problem in the future, we do not incur the expense until a later time, and can place the money in an alternative investment until then. In order to decide whether the fix the problem now, or wait and invest in the meantime, we must compare the two decisions. One way to account for this is by taking the cost of the project in the future, and discounting it to the current value at the rate of return on the alternative investment. If that cost is less than the cost of fixing the problem now, we should wait. It never makes sense to spend more when we can achieve the same result for less.

This analysis holds true even for irreversible environmental problems. In some contexts, if the environmental harm is not addressed immediately, it cannot be undone. To determine whether we should address the issue, we must compare the benefits of the remedy to the benefits that would be derived from alternative investments. In some cases, it might make sense to allow the environmental harm to persist, if the yield on alternative uses of the funds is greater than the yield to the remediation program. In that case, the future generation would have to face the environmental harm but would enjoy, for example, the fruits of greater investments in technological innovation.

It might appear that taking account of opportunity costs in deciding whether to undertake environmental projects for the benefit of future generations leads to the same results as discounting future benefits. This is true in some cases but not in others, as there is a critical conceptual difference between the two models. The discounting model assumes that funds not invested in a regulatory program will be invested in financial instruments for the benefit of future generations, but that assumption is rarely (if ever) true. In contrast, the opportunity cost model compares actual alternative investments. Under the opportunity-cost framework, we would either consider the return on alternative mutually exclusive projects, or the contribution of the regulatory project to reductions in economic growth. This framework compares actual alternatives, rather than imaginary investments.

INFINITE DEFERRAL

Some commentators have argued that unless future benefits are discounted at the rate of return on other investments, regulatory expenditures will always be deferred into the future and ultimately will never be undertaken. For example, Susan Putnam and John Graham state:

> If a smaller discount rate were to be applied to health than to money, it would always make sense to postpone adoption of public health programs that invest money now for deferred health improvements.[338]

Under this theory, society would choose at its first decision point to forgo the regulatory program in favor of investing the funds, in the expectation that they would grow into a larger pot that could be distributed in the future. But at this future decision point, society would engage in the same calculus and decide to postpone the expenditure again.

This argument is specious. First, regardless of whether environmental benefits are discounted at the market rate, it would always be desirable to undertake regulatory investments that yielded more than a market rate of return. Therefore, the Putnam/Graham hypothesis has to be limited to those cases in which the environmental expenditure returned a benefit at less than the rate of financial instruments—a much narrower claim.

Second, for some environmental threats, the cost of addressing the problem may increase over time. This is a common situation. A leaking Superfund site may be relatively cheap to clean up, until it pollutes an aquifer. Certain climate change impacts may be irreversible, so that no expenditure in the future will be able to undo the damage. Thus, it may make sense to address the problem sooner rather than later, if the increase in the cost of remediation is increasing faster than the return on alternative investments. If there is a risk of catastrophic irreversible damage—such as under certain climate change scenarios—reasonable risk aversion would suggest that we eliminate the threat as much as possible, even if the current benefits are outweighed by the current costs.

Finally, it may be difficult to transfer resources across projects in the future.[339] An investment in education might pay off more in the short run, but an investment in an environmental program might have higher returns over the long term. Yet it might be impossible to transfer money out of education and into the environmental program in the future. Public sentiment, a powerful teacher's union, or the difficulty of converting infrastructure could all serve to obstruct the transfer.

Projects with higher-than-market rates of return, as well as projects that involve catastrophic risks, increasing costs, or problems of transferability, will all be approved in a cost-benefit framework that does not use discounting. The Putnam/Graham argument, then, amounts to a largely theoretical problem dealing with a small (and perhaps empty) set of potential regulations—it is not sufficiently broad to justify intergenerational discounting.

POOR US

A different argument maintains that a failure to discount future benefits will cause us to impoverish the present generation down to subsistence levels for the benefit of future ones. As Tyler Cowen and Derek Parfit describe the argument (to which they do not subscribe): "We clearly need a discount rate for theoretical reasons. Otherwise any small increase in benefits that extends far into the future might demand any amount of sacrifice in the present, because in time the benefits would outweigh the cost."[340] In turn, subsequent generations will face the same problem, and they become impoverished as well. Thus, "failure to discount would leave all generations at a subsistence level of existence, because benefits would be postponed perpetually for the future."[341]

This argument takes a misleadingly narrow view of how one generation affects its successors. The standard of living for future generations will depend on the flourishing of the present ones in areas such as technological knowledge, educational attainment, and productive capacity.[342] A regulated market-based economy is the model that leads to the highest rates of growth of such human-produced capital. Such a system would not survive if consumption levels were limited to subsistence. Thus, a certain level of consumption is justified to continue the economic growth that benefits future generations more than would holding natural resources intact for their use.

In addition, this argument assumes that if we have any solicitude for future generations, that solicitude must be equally distributed across all such generations. If we agreed that each generation should be treated equally to the end of time, then it would make sense to have regulatory projects that generate future benefits to the point at which they deliver fewer future returns than general economic growth. Yet many conceptions of intergenerational responsibility would not require us to treat all future generations the same. Such conceptions might require a present generation to enjoy some of the fruits of its labor, or require that they prefer its children and grandchildren over more remote generations.

SUSTAINABLE DEVELOPMENT AND INTERGENERATIONAL RESPONSIBILITY

If we do not use discounting to define our moral obligations to future generations, we need an alternative. Although it is not possible to fully articulate this alternative here, several theories have been offered that have more intuitive moral appeal than discounting.

The concept of sustainable development has been an influential model of intergenerational responsibility.[343] Sustainable development has been defined as "meet[ing] the needs of the present without compromising the ability of future generations to meet their own needs."[344] Although there are many competing ideas about what a goal of sustainable development would require of the current generation,[345] there are several areas of agreement as well. The primary obligation to future generations is often defined in terms of a constraint that specifies how much must be left to a subsequent generation.[346] Some level of destruction of most natural resources is allowed, as long as future generations are compensated in another way, such as by technological development.[347] However, certain natural resources may be irreplaceable—like lands contained in national parks—and must be protected for subsequent generations.[348]

There are important criticisms of the sustainable development concept. First, sustainable development remains an underspecified obligation—it does not address, on its face, matters such as population growth or whether the current generation must leave sufficient resources to maintain the current levels of growth of living standards. Sustainable development also seems to place too little obligation on the current generation. For example, even if a trivial expenditure of funds today could result in large returns in the future, sustainable development criteria would not require that expenditure if the future beneficiaries are better off than the current generation. Thus, it does not require even minor sacrifices by the current generation for the sake of big gains for future generations, if the future generations will be just a bit better off than we are now.

Two other general approaches to intergenerational responsibility bear mention. The first is a general utilitarian framework. Consistent with such approaches, in an intergenerational context, the social decisionmaker would seek first to undertake all projects that have desirable cost-benefit ratios. Then, if the resulting distribution of resources were unattractive, the social decisionmaker would require redistribution.

Finally, the corrective-justice approach requires those responsible for environmental degradation to mitigate the adverse effects of such degradation. Economically speaking, this obligation acts to internalize environmental behavior, requiring people to remedy their environmental damage. Morally, it recognizes that agents are responsible for the foreseeable negative consequences of their actions, and should be held to account for their harm to others. It reduces the impact of externalities on decisionmaking.

A fully formed intergenerational accountability will likely involve aspects of sustainable development, utilitarianism, and corrective justice. It will not involve the strict discounting of future benefits, nor mechanically discounting for growth in consumption. Though hard choices remain about our obligations to future generations, we cannot avoid them by merely resorting to inapposite economic tools. In the intrapersonal context, discounting is rooted in respect for individual preferences. In the intergenerational context, in contrast, it is the result of our desire to avoid difficult decisions regarding what we owe others, or, worse, of our desire to avoid owing much to others. Shirking a decision is a decision in itself; in this context, it is very much the wrong decision.

Fallacy 7: People Value Only What They Use

This chapter discusses the use of existence value as a technique for assigning value to environmental preservation. *Existence value* is the value people assign to natural resources, such as the Grand Canyon and endangered species, even if they never "use" those resources. Environmentalists tend to favor the use of existence value—equally predictably, their opponents have sought to discredit existence value and the stated-preference surveys usually used to measure it. This chapter argues that it is incorrect to believe that people can value only what they use, and that, therefore, regulatory benefits for important preservation programs will be seriously understated if existence value is not counted.

WHO CARES ABOUT A LITTLE OIL SPILL IN ALASKA?

About 12,000 years ago, a piedmont glacier—a glacier flowing out of a valley onto flat land—located in what is now Alaska, began retreating back into the mountains, leaving Prince William Sound in its wake. The sound is a formation of islands, mountains, and bays with a shoreline made up of numerous large and small bays, inlets, fjords, and freshwater streams. Montague Island and several other smaller islands to the south of the sound shelter it from the Gulf of Alaska. The sound is encircled in the east, west, and north by the Chugach Mountains.

When the glaciers left, creatures emerged. First came plankton, then fish and water mammals like humpback and minke whales, orcas (killer whales), sea otters, and sea lions. Birds—the double-crested cormorant, great blue heron, surf scooter, red-breasted merganser, horned puffin—and land mammals—river otters, short-tailed weasel, Sitka black-tailed deer, wolverine—took their shelter on the shoreline. Black bears fed on the salmon making their yearly upstream swim to their natal streams. The area around the sound includes ecosystems ranging from rainforest to alpine tundra. The Pacific Coast Rainforest dominates, with its "lush, moss, and lichen-draped spruce and hemlock forests."[349]

About 7,000 years ago, the sound was settled by a group of Native Alaskans called the Chugachimuit. English and Spanish explorers arrived in the late eighteenth century. The end of the nineteenth century saw gold-rushers. In 1900, a fort was built at the end of an eleven-mile narrows that extended from the sound into the interior.[350] The town that sprung up around the fort was devastated by an earthquake on March 27, 1964. That earthquake had a magnitude of 9.2 on the Richter scale, the largest in the United States and second largest in the world since 1900.[351] The town was rebuilt. In 1973, Congress approved the Trans-Alaskan Oil Pipeline, with the refounded town of Valdez as its southern terminus. As the town's population swelled, a proper port was constructed, permitting Valdez to boast of having the most northerly ice-free port in the United States.[352] Soon, vast oil tankers transporting millions of barrels of oil were routinely traveling through the Valdez Narrows on their way to Prince William Sound, out into the Gulf of Alaska, and beyond.

Twenty-five years to the day after the earthquake of 1964, a tanker was traveling through the Narrows on a routine voyage. The captain had ordered the crew to take the tanker out of the normal shipping lanes to avoid small icebergs. The vessel did not return to the shipping lanes in time. At 12:04 A.M., it struck Bligh Reef. The tanker ruptured, spilling approximately eleven million gallons[353] of crude oil into the Prince William Sound.

The Exxon Valdez oil spill was an environmental disaster of the first order. Emergency response and cleanup were hampered by the spill's remote location. Hundreds of thousands of sea birds and thousands of sea mammals like otters and seals were killed, in addition to untold numbers of fish and fish eggs. The government and Exxon attempted to clean up the spill, burning some of the oil and using booms and skimmers to mop up the rest.[354] The American public saw images of oil-coated birds struggling along an oil-coated shoreline, and the negative effects ripped through the Alaskan economy.

Numerous legal battles followed. The state of Alaska and the federal government sued Exxon, and a private-class action lawsuit was filed. In preparation for the suit, the state of Alaska conducted a stated-preferences study to estimate the value that the American public placed on keeping the Prince William Sound free of large oil spills. The survey did not target people who had lost recreational opportunities, or for whom the spill had adverse business consequences. It focused instead on Americans who might never visit Alaska, but who derived a benefit from knowing that the Prince William Sound area is preserved—and who were sickened to learn of the environmental damage wrought by the Exxon Valdez oil tanker. The survey made a conservative estimate of $2.8 billion, in 1990 dollars, in "aggregate lost passive use values,"[355] otherwise known as existence value.

With that study as backup, the U.S. Justice Department and the state of Alaska entered tough settlement negotiations with Exxon. On March 13, 1991—just two years after the oil spill, a nanosecond in legal time—the Justice Department announced the settlement agreement. Exxon would pay $1 billion in civil and criminal penalties.[356] Exxon continued to pay for cleanup activities as well, eventually paying roughly $2 billion towards cleanup efforts. The class action case went to trial, resulting in a verdict of $287 million in actual damages and $5 billion for punitive damages. That verdict has been appealed a number of times. In 2007, a panel of the Ninth Circuit upheld $2.5 billion in punitive damages, and Exxon has been granted review in the Supreme Court.[357]

It is impossible to know the importance of the existence value study in the Exxon-Valdez litigation. But, without some idea of existence value, the $3 billion already spent by Exxon would be hard to justify. The Alaskan court found that the tangible economic damages from the spill were roughly one-twelfth of what Exxon has already paid, and one-twentieth of its potential liability. Although some cleanup would have been warranted, Exxon probably could have gotten away with much less than it did by containing the spill and saving money by addressing the problem more slowly. The public, however, demanded a more complete cleanup and a fuller reckoning from the company. That need is hard to explain if the Prince William Sound—a remote place that few Americans will ever see—does not have existence value.

In the past several years, opponents of existence value have embarked on a campaign to erode support for the use of stated-preference studies of existence value in the cost-benefit analysis of environmental preservation regulation. They have had some success; for example, in a 2002 Office of Management and Budget (OMB) report on proposed regulations, the monetized benefits of a forest preservation measure completely omit the existence value of ancient forests, making the measure appear to be economically inefficient.[358] To avoid a significant bias against environmental protection projects, it is extremely important that existence values not be shut out of the cost-benefit calculation. Unless we acknowledge the value that the existence of natural resources has for us, and future generations, we will see less protection for America's remaining unspoiled places.

USELESS OR NONUSE VALUE?

Natural resources have all kinds of uses. They are used as raw inputs into the manufacture of goods: Trees are used to make everything from houses to paper towels; iron ore is used to make cars and frying pans. Natural resources can be used for waste disposal—land is used to dispose of solid wastes, treated sewage is dumped into rivers, and smokestacks pump waste gases into the air. Land is a necessary ingredient in real estate. Natural resources are also necessary for basic human biological functioning—we need clean air to breathe and clean water to drink.

Recreation and enjoyment are also common natural resource uses. People swim in lakes and oceans, and visit national parks to gaze at mountains and rivers. Summer camps introduce children to nature. People go camping and backpacking, ski, ride snowmobiles, hunt, and take meandering walks along local streams.

Natural resources clearly have value in the cases in which they are put to an identifiable use. The iron ore input into steel manufacturing has a market value. Even if the natural resource in question can be used cost-free, as is the case for certain kinds of waste disposal—like air and water pollution—the natural resource has a value. A power plant that is allowed to emit sulfur dioxide for free would be willing to pay for the right to those emissions, if the government were to require it, because that right to emit generates revenue. Many recreational uses of natural resources are free, or very low cost. A week-long pass to Lassen National Park in northern California costs $10. Many visitors to the park, however, would pay much more than that—they enjoy significant surplus value from the recreational experience. Sophisticated techniques have been developed to measure how much value people place on the recreational uses of natural resources. Even if these techniques did not exist, however, it would be clear that natural resources have positive economic value.

In addition to the use value of natural resources, many people assign nonuse value to environmental protection. Nonuse value is typically divided into three categories.[359] The first is called option value. The *option value* of a natural resource is the value a person assigns to the possibility of using that natural resource sometime in the future. Though a person might not have any immediate plans to visit Yosemite National Park, he or she still might not want it strip mined, if only because the option to visit the park sometime in the future—perhaps with children or grandchildren—would be destroyed. Options are familiar from the financial newspapers—the big CEO paydays come from their options to purchase their company's stock. Option value for natural resources is a similar concept—a natural resource can have value to someone, even if that person does not currently plan to use it, because its existence guarantees that person the option to use it at some point in the future.

A related form of nonuse value is bequest value. A person might not assign any value to the option of using a natural resource, but he or she might nevertheless want to preserve the resource for future generations. The resource, then, has *bequest value* as a good to be bequeathed to others. Many people wish to leave valuable things to their beneficiaries; likewise, natural resources, with their potential use values, have value because they can be left to future generations.

The final form of nonuse value—and the one that has gotten the most attention—is existence value. Natural resources have *existence value* not from the option of using them in the future, or leaving them for others to use, but from their mere existence. An endangered species that no one really cares about seeing, and that has no anticipated use value whatsoever, can still have existence value if people prefer to have the species around rather than let it slip into extinction. People may be willing to pay to preserve tracts of rainforest that neither they nor their potential beneficiaries could reasonably expect to visit. The fact that people are willing to make economic sacrifices in order to preserve natural resources that they could not possibly use shows that existence value is motivating their behavior.

It is important to note that existence value is different from the intrinsic value of natural resources. We might think that certain nonhuman life forms, or even nonliving natural structures such as mountains, have an intrinsic value in their own right, above and beyond the value that is placed on them by humans. This intrinsic value would have nothing to do with human valuations, and would exist even if humans placed no existence value (or use value) whatsoever on the continued survival of nonhuman life or nonliving natural structures. By definition, such intrinsic value cannot be accounted for in cost-benefit analysis.

STATED-PREFERENCE SURVEYS

It is widely accepted that people place value on the existence of certain natural resources, and equally accepted that it is difficult to estimate that value. Existence value is not a traditional good openly traded on markets. Without markets for existence value, it is difficult to observe the current price that people are willing to pay for an additional unit of existence value. Without that price, we do not know how to value regulations that preserve the existence of natural resources.

This is not to say that no markets exist for this kind of good. One possible transaction is actual land acquisitions for preservation purposes. For example, the Nature Conservancy, a privately sponsored environmental preservation organization, holds $2.5 billion worth of conservation assets—conservation lands or conservation easements—and raises significant revenue, almost $500 million in contributions in 2005.[360] It is probably safe to assume that some portion of donations to the Nature Conservancy are made by individuals with no clear plans to use the Conservancy lands, indicating that donors assign existence value to the conservation of lands and species.

Private donations, however, are unlikely to serve as a good proxy for the willingness to pay for existence value because existence value is a public good. Public goods are benefits that cannot be effectively cordoned off to those who pay for them. People will rarely pay to produce enough of a public good, because they would prefer to wait for someone else to pay for it, and then "free-ride" off others' contributions. As a result of this free-rider problem, public goods tend to be underproduced. In the existence-value context, a person might value the Amazon rainforest, but also know that others value it as well. This person, then, might wait for other people to donate, and then enjoy the existence of the rainforest even though he or she did not pay for it.

In fact, the market failure that makes private transactions a poor proxy for existence value is what makes governmental intervention necessary. If people's existence valuations could be fully vindicated through donations to private conservation organizations, governmental intervention would be unnecessary. People would purchase all of the natural resources they wished to preserve. Yet because of market failure, governmental interventions can increase overall wealth by mitigating the effects of the free-rider problem.

Economists have turned to stated-preference studies in order to determine people's willingness to pay for the existence of natural resources. Rather than looking to transactions on the marketplace for valuation, stated-preference studies ask participants for their valuations of natural resources. These studies vary widely. Some directly elicit valuations, while others simulate market-type transactions.

The existence-value study conducted after the Exxon-Valdez oil spill interviewed one thousand individuals randomly drawn from the U.S. population.[361] During the interviews, participants were shown photographs of the Prince William Sound area, and given a description of the spill, its consequences, and the cleanup effort. Participants were then given the option of voting for several programs to protect Prince William Sound from future oil spills. The costs of these programs were expressed as a one-time tax on individual tax households. The value of the tax ranged from $10 to $250, depending on the level of protection afforded.[362] Analysis of those votes generated estimates of the interviewees' willingness to pay.

As discussed earlier, economists prefer to use revealed-preference studies because the decisions being studied result from actual market transactions. Stated-preference studies are acknowledged to be a second-best alternative to be used when revealed-preference studies are difficult or impossible to conduct, as they are for existence value.

EXISTENCE VALUES, EXISTENCE VALUES, EVERYWHERE?

Ever since cost-benefit analyses began incorporating existence values, industry groups and other critics have objected strenuously. These challenges to existence value have thus far been mostly unsuccessful, and the technique is now used widely in cost-benefit analysis. Yet, certain signs suggest that future challenges will receive a more sympathetic hearing. The most important signs of change have come from Susan Dudley, former director of the conservative Mercatus Center at George Mason University, and the new Office of Information and Regulatory Affairs (OIRA) administrator.

Dudley has argued that nonuse values exist for a large variety of things, and that regulations will increase existence value for some things, providing a regulatory benefit, and decrease existence value for other things, creating a regulatory cost. In comments concerning a proposed Environmental Protection Agency (EPA) regulation under the Clean Water Act governing how power plants can use fresh-water sources for cooling their facilities, Dudley wrote, in her pregovernmental position at the Mercatus Center, "Some individuals may gain non-use values from the knowledge that forage fish are not caught in cooling water intakes; however, others may derive non-use values from the knowledge that low-income consumers can purchase goods at lower cost."[363] These countervailing existence values would exist for a wide range of regulations—any economic cost could be associated with some theoretical existence value: "Would the rule make electricity production less energy efficient? How do people feel about that? Are we extracting more material—coal, or cement—from mines in order to comply with these regulations? Do people have non-use values related to mining?"[364] Given the complexity and scale of the nonuse values implicated by any regulatory decision, Dudley argues that the EPA is better off ignoring them altogether.

People certainly place existence value on things other than natural resources. So it may well be that they are willing to pay to protect the existence of fishing communities, family farms, and lumberjacks. Certain policies seem to indicate that they do, including subsidies for farms and some fisheries management policies. Steps have even been taken to value these types of cultural goods.[365] To the extent that these preferences do exist, they should be taken into account in the cost-benefit equation.

However, before such offsets can be taken into account, they must be shown to exist. Scores of peer-reviewed studies have been published on the existence value of natural resources. In contrast, the existence values of other goods have not been extensively tested. To take these nonnatural resource existence values into account, we need evidence that they are real and nontrivial.

A critic might respond that there are simply too many kinds of existence values, such that this recommendation would lead to endless research. Yet cost-benefit analysis has never attempted to give a fully accurate picture of the universe. Rather, since conducting cost-benefit analysis is costly, the point is to reach a relatively accurate picture of the costs and benefits, and then stop collecting and analyzing the data when the costs of further analysis outweigh the additional benefits of increased accuracy. For insignificant existence values, the cost of data collection may be greater than the benefit of the data collected.

We should not let the potentially large number of classes of existence value paralyze cost-benefit analysis. Rather, we should focus our analytic energies on the class of existence values we *know* to be important, namely natural resource existence values, and then encourage a research program that seeks to identify other important classes of existence values. If we identify existence values for nonnatural resources that truly are significant, then they should be included in cost-benefit analysis.

THERE ARE NO EXISTENCE VALUES

A second line of argument taken by opponents of existence value is that there is no such thing. These critics contend that stated-preference studies purporting to measure existence value actually measure something else, such as "attitude[s] toward a public good," "a 'warm glow' [received] from expressing support for good causes," and assessments of "what ... is good for the country."[366] Dudley, writing for the Mercatus Center, has characterized existence values as "a normative notion of what should be, divorced from actual behavior or revealed preferences."[367] These criticisms are motivated in part by inconsistencies between the results derived from stated-preferences studies, in addition to skepticism that people have preferences for environmental goods "they have never heard of,"[368] and a feeling that it is "unrealistic to think that individuals would give up more than a small amount of income ... in exchange for a non-use value."[369]

Reports of the nonexistence of existence value have been greatly exaggerated. Some people are clearly willing to pay to preserve natural resources for which they have no use value—donations to preservationist environmental organizations are an important case in point. The protection of distant ecosystems, like the Amazon rainforest, and reclusive and hard-to-find megafauna like polar bears and whales, attest to the fact that people have an economically legitimate preference to preserve the existence of natural resources.

Additionally, society, through its actions, reveals a set of aggregate preferences with respect to its willingness to pay to protect those resources when it sets aside wilderness areas.[370] This process creates one mechanism that can be used to place a value on the existence of particular natural resources: the value that society is willing to pay to protect them.[371] The best stated-preference surveys tend to simulate democratic processes; for example, by asking respondents in a relatively understandable way to "vote" for or against a measure that will cost money, but also protect natural resources. These values are appropriately used in the context of cost-benefit analysis because they reflect real-wealth variables: If people are willing to be taxed to protect a resource, they are willing to pay for it, and protection measures, which cost less than the aggregate willingness to pay, will be wealth-enhancing.

Though the preference to protect existence value may seem implausible to some, there is undeniable economic data showing that it is real.

A SERIOUS LOOK AT STATED-PREFERENCE STUDIES

The final challenge[372] to the use of existence value is based on concerns about the reliability of stated-preference studies.[373] As discussed in earlier chapters, stated-preference studies contain a number of problems, all of which are variations on the fact that respondents are not "playing with real money." Because participants are not subject to budget constraints, they may overestimate their willingness to pay for a particular good. In addition, participants may enter "protest" values, either very large or very small valuations, or may act strategically to influence survey results by recording very large valuations for policies with which they agree, even if those valuations exceed their actual willingness to pay. Respondents may give what they perceive to be the "right" answer, rather than their own valuations, or may give the answers they expect the person administering the survey wants to hear. These problems are compounded in the existence-value context because participants are being asked to place values on goods that are not normally valued, and with which they may be unfamiliar.

Critics of the stated-preferences methodology have some empirical support for their position. Indeed, some survey results seem to contradict economic theory and basic rationality. Perhaps the most important of these results is the failure, in some surveys, of participants to respond to the scope of the good being protected. One oft-quoted study found that people were not willing to pay substantially more to save 200,000 birds rather than 2,000 birds.[374] This result casts doubt on the survey technique, because it is unlikely that people's willingness to pay for a bird-saving project would be unresponsive to the number of birds saved. If stated-preference studies are so flawed as to be meaningless, there might be no choice but to abandon them. That would mean neglecting existence values—or allowing experts to make best guesses about existence values—until superior measurement techniques are developed.

In the early 1990s, significant public debate erupted about existence values and the use of stated-preference studies. Congress reacted to the Exxon-Valdez oil spill with the Oil Pollution Act of 1990, which, among other things, provided for liability for the destruction of natural resources by an oil spill. At roughly the same time, the D.C. Circuit denied a challenge to the Department of the Interior's regulations concerning natural resource damages under the Superfund toxic site cleanup program, generally supporting the consideration of nonuse (or existence) value.[375] These events led to significant backlash, including a raft of reports and high-profile conferences attacking stated-preferences studies of existence value.[376]

The National Oceanic and Atmospheric Administration (NOAA), which was charged with implementing provisions of the Oil Pollution Act, found itself in the middle of a political maelstrom. To deliberate over disparate views, it established a panel of economic experts, chaired by Nobel prize-winning economists Kenneth Arrow and Robert Solow, to assess the reliability of stated-preference studies in estimating existence value.

The panel reviewed a number of the major criticisms of stated-preference studies, some of which they found "particularly compelling."[377] It discussed evidence that the findings of stated-preference studies were sometimes inconsistent with rational choice, responses were implausible, respondents acted without any meaningful budget constraint, and participants were potentially ill informed about the nature of the studies. The panel was troubled by all of these problems, and set forth guidelines on how to conduct stated-preference studies, as well as a set of recommendations for further research into the design and implementation of these studies.

The panel did not, however, condemn stated-preference studies wholesale. In fact, the panel found that stated-preference studies ultimately "convey useful information"[378] and "can produce estimates reliable enough to be the starting point of a judicial process of damage assessment, including lost passive-use value."[379] Though the panel was concerned that "hypothetical markets tend to overstate willingness to pay," it believed that both the design of stated-preference studies, as well as the judicial process, could help correct this flaw. The panel recommended that stated-preference studies continue to be used to estimate existence value, provided that they were designed properly and were understood to be the result of an imperfect measuring process. The panel's recommendations for study design included the use of proper sampling methods, the minimization of nonresponses from study participants, the use of face-to-face interviews rather than telephone surveys, testing for potential interviewer biases, and better reporting and screening of potential questions. The panel also set out a list of best practices, which included a generally conservative design—a preference for underestimation rather than overestimation, a willingness-to-pay rather than a willingness-to-accept standard, and the use of a referendum vote format.

Opposition to stated preference studies from some corners may stem more from the studies' results than from genuine concerns over the methodology. For example, under the current Bush administration, the EPA changed from the standard mix of revealed- and stated-preference studies, and based its value-of-life estimates exclusively on stated-preference studies in several important cost-benefit analyses.[380] These stated-preference studies generally showed a lower value of a statistical life, and therefore could be used to justify less stringent environmental standards. Complaints against the use of stated-preference studies in this context were not heard from the same actors who oppose their use for existence value.

In the end, the criticisms of existence value are not sufficiently strong to justify abandoning this significant set of preferences. Existence-value studies should follow best practices, and those studies that have fundamental flaws should not be used in cost-benefit analysis. Further, analysts can recognize the limits of stated-preference studies, and use their best judgment when applying these numbers to real-world examples. If these studies are done following state-of-the-art techniques, however, they are a legitimate input into the decisionmaking process. In order for the benefits of environmental preservation to be properly valued, we must take into account the preferences that people have to protect these resources, even if they have no plans to use them. If we do not take existence values into consideration, we will impoverish ourselves by overdeveloping wilderness areas, threatening endangered species, and destroying places of natural beauty that people hold dear.

Fallacy 8: Industry Cannot Adapt

Earlier chapters focused largely on how regulatory benefits should be measured—whether life-years rather than lives should be used; whether benefits to future generations should be discounted or not. This, the final of the eight chapters discussing the fallacies of cost-benefit analysis, turns from the benefit side of the equation to the cost side and argues against the idea that industry cannot adapt to new regulations. Cost-benefit analysis, by assuming that industry does not respond to regulations by finding the cheapest possible way to comply, has traditionally overestimated the cost of compliance—in some cases quite significantly.

AN OZONE LAYER, ON THE CHEAP

In September 1987, the Montreal Protocol on Substances that Deplete the Ozone Layer was signed, creating what many believe to be the most successful international environmental regime in existence.[381] Environmental governance at the international level is extraordinarily difficult, as efforts to combat climate change, among other environmental problems, have shown. The Montreal Protocol is considered a resounding success for several reasons. It tackled a major environmental threat: the depletion of the ozone layer caused by atmospheric emissions of industrial chemicals. It managed to overcome the coordination problems that occur whenever a group of nations tries to accomplish anything. Most importantly, it actually worked. The production and release of ozone-depleting chlorofluorocarbons (CFCs) has been cut dramatically and in advance of the schedule set forth in 1987. The ozone layer has begun to heal. Though the threat that human activity poses to the ozone layer has not been completely eliminated, we have made a great deal of progress, and many believe that the Montreal Protocol provides us with the tools we need to tackle additional threats. It stands as the model for how environmental diplomacy can be carried out.

The Montreal Protocol came about after more than a decade of organizing on the part of scientists and environmentalists in favor of intergovernmental action to limit CFCs. In late 1973, Mario Molina and F. Sherwood Rowland at the University of California at Irvine began researching the fate of CFCs released into the atmosphere. Within three months, Rowland and Molina realized they had stumbled upon, in Rowland's words, a "potentially grave environmental problem involving substantial depletion of the stratospheric ozone layer."[382]

In 1974, they coauthored a paper on the threat of CFCs to the ozone layer published in *Nature*.[383] On September 26, 1974, the *New York Times* published a front-page story about the dangers posed by CFCs,[384] calling public attention to this pressing environmental problem.

Before long, the nascent environmental movement had seized upon the ozone layer as a major issue. In addition, the scientific community took up the task of confirming the work of Rowland, Molina, and the other scientists that had made claims connecting CFC release to ozone depletion. The National Academy of Sciences produced several studies, which consistently found that CFCs were implicated in ozone depletion.[385] By 1978, both the Environmental Protection Agency (EPA) and the Food and Drug Administration (FDA) had issued regulations essentially banning all nonessential uses of CFCs in aerosol.[386] With these moves in the United States and other countries, CFC emissions from aerosol uses dropped dramatically. CFCs however, also have several nonaerosol uses, including use as a solvent and in coolants. Before long, the growth in nonaerosol uses had made up for any gains from the aerosol ban, and CFC emissions were again on the rise.[387]

It became increasingly clear that further steps would be needed to cut back on CFCs. The science linking CFCs to ozone depletion was strong.[388] The risks associated with a weakened ozone layer—which would allow higher levels of dangerous ultraviolet rays to penetrate the atmosphere and reach the earth's surface—included increased levels of skin cancer and significant damage to vegetation. International coordination was needed to ensure an effective CFC regime, because the production and release of CFCs anywhere across the globe threatened the ozone layer. With these facts in mind, negotiations to phase out the use of CFCs began.

As these negotiations were heating up, the EPA commissioned a report from RAND to determine the costs associated with CFC reductions. The report, titled *Social Cost of Technical Control Options to Reduce Emissions of Potential Ozone Depleters in the United States*, was released in 1986[389] and was used by negotiators during the bargaining prior to adoption of the Montreal Protocol. The RAND study was based in part on information provided by industry, but also included independent analysis. RAND was not a representative of industry, but rather was paid by the EPA to provide a fully independent assessment. However, the RAND study was based on technologies developed prior to the Montreal Protocol, when industry had little incentive to develop alternatives to CFC use.

A recent study, comparing the *ex ante* estimates of compliance costs and the actual costs, found that the RAND study substantially overestimated compliance costs.[390] In fact, the reduction of CFCs per increase in price was two to three times higher in certain cases than that predicted by the RAND study.

An EPA study, produced after the Montreal Protocol was signed, gave a more accurate picture of the cost of compliance. At this point, the EPA was preparing a regulatory impact statement for its regulations pursuant to its obligations under the protocol. However, after the adoption of the protocol, it became clear that there would be CFC regulation in the United States, and industry had stepped into high gear, developing ways to reduce their costs. Between the RAND study and the EPA estimates, "one of the most important changes appears to have been the development of much greater optimism about the potential for new chemicals that could substitute for CFCs in major applications."[391] The two-year difference produced a much greater degree of accuracy, because information about the direction of technological development had become clearer. Although the RAND study was based on the implementation of the old technology available prior to the signing of the Montreal Protocol, that international agreement changed the landscape by creating a significant incentive for firms to develop new technologies. At that point, the innovativeness of the American economy kicked in, and ways to achieve compliance at lower costs were found. By the time of the EPA study, these new technologies were on the table, and EPA was able to get a clearer idea of what CFC regulations were going to cost.

Fortunately, one of the many virtues of the Montreal Protocol is flexibility— a rare gift in an international regime. Compliance was so much cheaper than anticipated that regulators were able to set more ambitious targets several times. If the Montreal Protocol had not included a provision to update its emissions targets, the more difficult and time-consuming process of renegotiating the entire treaty would have been needed to reflect the relatively small cost of compliance.

We are not always so lucky. Many times, once a regulation has been finalized, it is somewhat set in stone. If cost estimates are too high, we will tend to regulate too weakly, or worse, not regulate at all. Though the second fate was avoided in Montreal, and the first was tempered by the flexible structure of the Montreal Protocol, we could easily have ended up with a very cheap regime that bought us too little in the way of ozone protection.

INDUSTRY NUMBERS

The first and clearest source of bias in favor of overestimating costs is the reliance of cost-benefit analysts on industry sources for data about the cost of complying with new regulations. Because industry has a clear incentive to overstate the cost of complying with regulations they do not like, and because they definitely do not have an incentive to put time into forecasting the direction and pace of technological development for the sake of more accurate cost-benefit analysis, we can expect industry numbers to be systematically overstated.

As Sally Katzen, head of OIRA under President Clinton, has written, regulators responsible for the issues that affect large portions of the economy—like environmental, health and safety regulation—"cannot be expected to be as familiar with the actual operations of the varied factories, construction sites, or farmlands that might be affected by the regulations."[392] They, therefore, have no choice but to rely, to some extent, on data provided by industry sources. However, as is clear to any habitual observer of the regulatory process, industry is rarely pleased to find out that EPA or Occupational Safety and Health Administration (OSHA) is looking in their direction. They fear, often correctly, that regulations will be a burden in both time and resources and will cut into firms' value. At the same time that EPA and OSHA are threatening industry with proposed regulation, they look to the same actors to generate the cost data that will be used to determine whether that disfavored regulation will go through. This places industry representatives, even ones acting in good faith, in a very difficult position. As Katzen notes, "if you do not want to do something, you inflate the amount of time, inconvenience, and cost you estimate it would take."[393]

This process does not necessarily have to be intentional. The easiest course of action for an industry representative who needs to generate cost data is to look at what the cost of compliance would be with existing technologies and production processes. Data about costs of existing technologies is readily accessible. The number of engineers and other experts is reduced when their task is to estimate the costs of complying with proposed regulations using the means at hand, rather than trying to determine new techniques that could be used to achieve compliance more cheaply. Thus, the course of least resistance for an industry representative dovetails with the course that overstates costs.

Cases of industry overestimating the costs of regulatory compliance are not hard to find. In the 1970s, the chemical industry predicted that the cost of complying with a benzene emissions rule would run in the hundreds of thousands of dollars per plant. It turned out that by substituting another chemical for benzene, compliance could be attained at virtually no cost.[394] The cost of phasing out leaded gasoline in the United States was 95 percent lower than industry expected.[395] In a similar vein, Lee Iacocca, then vice president of the Ford Motor Company, predicted in 1970 that the Clean Air Act "could prevent continued production of automobiles ... [and] is a threat to the entire American economy and to every person in America."[396] More recently, industry overestimated compliance with 1996 tailpipe regulations by several orders of magnitude.[397] These instances are not limited to the United States. In a report prepared by the Stockholm Environmental Institute for the Swedish Ministry of the Environment, the authors examined several European-level regulations and found that industries opposed to regulation had often significantly overstated the negative economic impacts prior to implementation.[398]

Industry representatives have a clear advocacy role when approaching the EPA or another regulatory body about prospective regulations. As part of that advocacy, they forward their institutional interests best when they can convince regulators that the proposed regulation will be expensive. If costs are thought to be very high, the likelihood of regulation decreases, as does the probable level of stringency of any regulation adopted. This advocacy role conflicts with the real need of the regulator to get an accurate picture of regulatory costs. Industry has the ability to artificially inflate estimates of regulatory costs, to their own narrow benefit but to the detriment of the accuracy of cost-benefit analyses, and ultimately to the American economy and people.

"END-OF-PIPE" VERSUS PRODUCTION PROCESS CHANGES

Even predictions by central regulators or independent analysts about the anticipated costs of environmental programs carry a significant risk of overestimation. As previously discussed, one source of bias is that it is easier for analysts to look at the application of available technology to the problem, rather than to anticipate the direction of technological development. A particular case of this occurs when cost-assessors look to the use of "end-of-pipe" technology rather than changes in production processes.

Both end-of-pipe methods and production process changes have the potential to reduce emissions. End-of-pipe methods attempt to capture some of the emissions before they escape the plant and are released into the atmosphere or water. Paradigmatic examples of an end-of-pipe technology would be catalytic converters on cars, or scrubbers on power plants. A simple screen that prevents debris from escaping is a low-tech version of the end-of-pipe method.

Production process changes seek to reduce the amount of harmful pollution that is created in the first place. Changes in production processes are often much cheaper per unit of pollution reduction than end-of-pipe technologies. Switching from high-sulfur coal to low-sulfur coal reduces the amount of pollution that is produced by coal-fired power plants. Switching from coal to natural gas reduces pollution even more. In the manufacture of goods, toxic solvents can be replaced by nontoxic alternatives. As an everyday example, traditional drycleaners have used the chemical perchloroethylene (or PERC), exposure to which can cause both acute and long-term health problems.[399] Switching to a non-PERC alternative is a production process change that reduces exposure to this harmful chemical.

A major component of the Clean Air Act Amendments of 1990 was the Acid Rain Program directed at cutting down on emission of sulfur dioxide and nitrogen oxides from power plants. Sulfur dioxide and nitrogen oxides are major contributors to acid rain, and the Acid Rain Program was an innovative and ambitious effort on the part of federal government to tackle this long-standing environmental threat.

One of the most important innovations of the Acid Rain Program was the use of tradable permits in sulfur dioxide to build flexibility in the program and allow firms to pursue the most cost-effective means of cutting down on sulfur-dioxide emissions. Under tradable permit schemes, regulators determine the total allowable amount of pollution under the regime and establish an initial allocation of permits. They then rely on participants in the marketplace to trade permits, depending on how cheaply they can reduce emissions. Firms that can easily cut emissions do not have to buy many permits, while permits can be purchased by facilities that need them. If things work out, emissions are kept below the total cap at the lowest cost.

The sulfur-dioxide trading program, then, allowed firms a variety of ways to comply with the regime. They could pay for the permits, or they could find ways to reduce their emissions. There was, therefore, an important incentive for market actors to identify and develop new and cheaper ways of reducing emissions. It turns out that they did, and they did so largely by changing their production processes rather than adopting end-of-pipe technologies.

Switching production processes turned out to be cheaper than expected for a variety of reasons—railway deregulation made the transport of low-sulfur coal cheaper, better coal production lead to lower prices, and new plants were designed to handle different types of fuel.[400] Further, there was a "large increase in natural gas-generating capacity"[401] brought about by change in federal rules allowing new natural gas plants, in addition to relatively low natural gas prices and "the availability of increasingly efficient natural gas technology."[402] Although the cost of end-of-pipe scrubbers has also been found to be cheaper than expected, much of the cost-savings in compliance with the sulfur-dioxide trading program have come from production changes. All in all, technology changes and favorable market conditions resulted in a large disparity between the predicted costs of compliance and the actual costs. In 1991, an interagency task force created by statute to provide information for policy and regulatory decisions on acid rain—the National Acid Precipitation Assessment Program (NAPAP)—estimated that the cost of reducing sulfur-dioxide emissions would range from $370 to $800 per ton, with an average estimate of about $550 per ton. Recent NAPAP and EPA estimates have found that the true cost is closer to $250 per ton[403]—less than half the average estimate and a third less than the lower bound estimate.

Because the difference in compliance costs between end-of-pipe technology and production process changes is often significant, it is vital that cost estimators look to both when making cost estimates. Though it may seem that basing cost estimates on known pollution-control technology is a safer way to estimate costs, this method will tend to overestimate costs. It is possible that some production process changes will not come about, but that is to be expected. It is even desirable that costs are sometimes underestimated if they are also sometimes overestimated. It is unlikely that we will ever be perfect at predicting how regulations will affect the economy, and how economic actors will adjust to address new regulatory mandates. Changes in production processes may be harder to anticipate than the use of end-of-pipe technology, but we know from past experience that production changes are possible, and are a likely response to regulatory action. Cost-benefit analysts that depend too much on end-of-pipe technologies when deriving cost estimates are likely to systematically overstate costs, leading to flawed cost-benefit analyses that are of little value to decisionmakers.

THE DYNAMIC MARKET

The production process changes versus end-of-pipe technology problem is a subset of a larger problem in cost estimation: taking too little account of the dynamic nature of economic growth. When cost estimates are based on static models of the economy, with fixed levels of technological development and no room for innovation, it is unsurprising that cost estimates are inflated. Thankfully, the American economy is a dynamic system that adapts to changes in the game.[404] Firms that fail to adapt in the marketplace are at a competitive disadvantage relative to firms that can make changes, innovate, cut costs, and ultimately deliver superior products at lower prices with greater profits. With our relatively efficient capital markets, investment can be expected to flow toward the firms that adapt and away from firms that do not. The ability to predict, adapt to, and take advantage of new regulation is a major component of success in the contemporary marketplace.

Some have even argued that regulations can even lead to higher levels of productivity by spurring innovation. This argument has been propounded by, among others, Professor Michael E. Porter of the Harvard Business School. Porter has developed the idea of an "innovation offset," a benefit that firms get when a regulatory necessity becomes the mother of invention. If these innovation offsets are high, they can make up for the cost of compliance, meaning that environmental goals are achieved at zero cost. Even if full offset is rare, the ability of regulation to spur technological developments and other forms of innovation that ultimately produce value means that overall compliance costs are less than they would be in a static system.

The argument presented in this chapter is more limited than Porter's offset theory, which is controversial.[405] Even if technological development spurred by regulation does not lead to overall productivity gains, innovation and adaptation can cut down on the overall cost of complying with regulation. When firms have the flexibility to choose how to meet regulatory goals, they have both the information and the incentive to find the lowest cost alternatives.

The design of the regulatory program seems to matter a great deal. Researchers testing Porter's hypothesis have found that when environmental regulations are very specific and inflexible, giving little choice to industry and managers about how environmental goals are met, there is little productivity gain from environmental compliance. However, when rules are more flexible, give greater discretion to managers and owners, and yet are stringent in the level of overall environmental compliance that is demanded, productivity gains have been found.[406]

Especially as market-based regulatory regimes become more common, the effects of innovation and market dynamics on the costs of regulation have to be taken into account. Even under traditional command-and-control regulation, performance standards, rather than design standards, are generally preferred. Under performance-standard regimes, the government sets allowable emissions based on the best-available technology and firms can choose how to achieve those emission levels. Under design-standard regimes, the government specifies the technology that must be used. Performance standards are widely believed to be superior because firms can achieve similar pollution levels at lower cost.

The purpose of regulating through economic incentives is to give even greater flexibility to regulated firms to develop least-cost means of achieving regulatory goals. If we do not take account of this effect when doing cost-benefit analysis, market-oriented approaches will appear to have cost-benefit profiles similar to those of traditional-style regulation. This is harmful in two respects. First, it is possible that market-based regulation at the same stringency level would pass a fair cost-benefit analysis whereas a command-and-control measure would not. If the effects of economic incentives on regulatory costs are not taken into account, then the market-based system may also fail cost-benefit analysis, leading to underregulation. Second, failure to account for the innovation brought on by economic-incentive-based programs may tilt future regulation in favor of command-and-control even though cheaper alternatives may be available.

Some might argue that dynamic-market effects are too speculative, and therefore do not have a place in cost-benefit analysis. However, consideration of how industry will respond to regulation is little different from analyzing the countervailing risks or ancillary benefits of regulation. Both require analysts to look at the secondary effects of regulation—the variety of ways in which regulations affect individuals and firms and how people react to new regulations. In order for cost-benefit analysis to give a fuller picture, looking to these consequences is necessary. Though some market dynamics will be too far removed and unforeseeable for cost-benefit analysis to realistically take them into account, it is not too much to ask regulators to anticipate some of the major and predictable responses of industry to regulation in order to more accurately estimate the true economic costs of regulation.

EMPIRICAL EVIDENCE: IS THERE SYSTEMATIC BIAS?

Given the strong theoretical reasons to believe that cost overestimation is prevalent, and the empirical evidence pointing to systematic cost overestimation, there is good reason to believe that overestimating costs is a serious problem within cost-benefit analysis. Unfortunately, the empirical literature on cost estimation is not sufficiently well developed to generate clear conclusions about the extent of systematic bias and the conditions under which overestimation is most likely to occur. Much of the literature on the subject targets specific regulations or environmental issues and takes the form of anecdotal case studies documenting instances in which costs have been initially overestimated. Relatively few studies have attempted to estimate the systematic bias, and they have not generated strong conclusions. Nevertheless, the empirical evidence certainly raises legitimate concerns that costs are overestimated, raising the need for both increased research in this area and reforms designed to more accurately assess the true costs of regulatory compliance.

There is ample anecdotal evidence that regulatory costs have been overestimated in the past. As discussed in the sections above, both CFC regulation and the Acid Rain Program provide stark examples of seriously overestimated costs of complying with environmental programs. Other examples of cost overestimation by regulators cited by commentators include regulations governing asbestos, coke-oven emissions, and vinyl chloride.[407] In some cases, overestimation reached extremely high proportions, with estimates equal to several times the actual cost of compliance. As William Reilly, EPA administrator under President George H. W. Bush, has stated, "A review of some of the major regulatory initiatives overseen by the EPA since its creation in 1970 reveals a pattern of consistent, often substantial, overestimates of their economic costs."[408]

Studies of particular regulatory areas have also found instances of cost overestimation. The costs of complying with regulation of chlorinated substances were found to be overestimated in both U.S. and foreign contexts.[409] Estimations of the price impacts of efficiency standards for appliances made by the Department of Energy were higher than actual price increases,[410] and firms complying with OSHA regulations often deployed newer technology, at lower costs, than regulators anticipated.[411] Studies have also found underestimation in some cases. For example, one study found an underestimation of costs in specific air pollution regulations in Arizona.[412] But studies looking at similar pollution measures in other states have found the overestimation of compliance costs.[413]

A few more general studies have been done to examine whether there is systematic under- or overestimation of costs. In 2005, the Office of Management and Budget (OMB) conducted an informal survey of past cost-benefit analyses to determine the degree of accuracy of the cost and benefit estimates; they found that costs tended to be overestimated.[414] To conduct that study, they looked at forty-seven rules "for which some post-regulation information was published by academics or government agencies."[415] OMB recognized that this was a "convenience sample" and therefore "not necessarily representative" of the body of federal rules.[416] In that study, they also considered cost or benefit estimates to be "accurate" if they were within 25 percent of *ex post* reported cost, a determination they admitted was "arbitrary."[417] Within the group of regulations that OMB considered, however, there was a greater tendency for costs to be overestimated than underestimated.

Other studies have also been done. One of the larger studies, which is frequently cited, also found that costs were overestimated.[418] It discovered that for regulations utilizing market-based incentives, overestimated costs were consistently attributable to unanticipated technological development.[419] In that study too, the sample was somewhat biased, because the authors chose regulations where there already existed "a relatively detailed ex-post estimate"[420] The authors acknowledge that their sample was biased toward "larger, more controversial regulations"[421] and ones for which "results can be readily measured in observed prices."[422] The sample was also tilted towards rules that use market-based incentives. Though the OMB and independent studies were imperfect, as the authors acknowledge, they both point in the same direction of cost overestimation.

GETTING SERIOUS ABOUT GETTING BETTER AT COST-BENEFIT ANALYSIS

As has been pointed out by commentators who generally favor cost-benefit analysis, "there is currently very little incentive for governments to conduct or support *ex-post* reviews of regulations."[423] There is even less incentive for government to evaluate the accuracy of cost-benefit analysis. If cost-benefit analysis is going to improve, however, these evaluations are indispensable. Agencies and OIRA cannot identify errors and make corrections if there is no evaluation process after the cost-benefit analysis is conducted.

OMB has recognized the importance of conducting *ex post* evaluation of cost-benefit analysis, and in a response to public comments, found that the "vast majority of comments were enthusiastic" about greater *ex post* scrutiny with a "remarkable" level of shared sentiment "even among commentators who historically have disagreed on a wide range of regulatory policy issues."[424] Given the importance of cost-benefit analysis in the federal apparatus, regular evaluation of past analyses will give both the agencies and central reviewers the opportunity to learn from past errors, improve their estimation techniques, and increase the quality and accuracy of cost-benefit analysis moving forward.

Agencies and OMB should not wait for conclusive empirical evidence about the degree to which costs are overestimated to make needed improvements in how costs are counted. There are many potential sources of errors in developing regulatory cost estimates. Often, these errors will tend to generate estimates that are too high. To reduce the prevalence and importance of these errors, serious steps should be taken now to improve both cost-estimation methodology and the capacity of agencies and central reviewers to compile and analyze cost information.

Finally, it is important that agencies and analysts themselves engage in innovation in the area of cost-benefit analysis and cost-estimation. The techniques for predicting how the marketplace will react to regulations should be continually improved and updated—research and development in this area should be an important priority for regulators and central executive review. Innovation can take a variety of forms, from the strengthening of institutional bases of knowledge, to finding creative ways to elicit information from industry sources. One potential direction that innovation might take us in the future is the use of "information markets" to generate information about potential compliance costs.[425] Information markets have gained prominence in recent years as their ability to predict future events with high degrees of accuracy has become clearer.[426] Several corporations have used information markets internally to estimate a wide variety of future events. For example, Hewlett-Packard has set up markets where employees can trade over events like future sales and revenue.[427] In the information market, employees can use the information they have to buy and sell based on their personal predictions, free from fear of antagonizing a superior and without respect to their location on the corporate ladder. In this way, information from sources that might be ignored in typical firm bureaucracy can percolate back up to high-level executives.

In the cost-estimation context, participants could trade on the *ex post* costs of a regulatory program, making predictions about what those costs would be. This would be easiest if there is a clear measure of *ex post* costs, such as the price of an emissions permit. If access to the information market was broad, then engineers and others who work for affected industry would be able to participate, aggregating their personal information in a way that maximizes their incentive to accurately predict future costs. Information from "the ground"—essential to central regulators impacting broad industries—would be able to work its way to the agency without having to pass through official corporate channels. Further, participants would have incentives not to make worst-case scenario predictions, but rather to make estimates as accurate as their information allows.

This chapter does not propose that information markets replace traditional cost estimation in cost-benefit analysis. The real point is that there are ways to improve the way that cost estimation is done, and innovation could prove to be very helpful in improving the usefulness of cost-benefit analysis. There are good reasons to believe that the cost estimates that we see now are biased against regulation. We know that past cost-benefit analysis techniques have been inadequately evaluated and improved. By both looking back at past cost-benefit analysis to learn from past mistakes, and looking forward with a creative eye toward ways to improve estimations, we can help increase the accuracy of cost-benefit predictions and ultimately the wisdom of our regulatory choices.

The Sum of All the Fallacies

This Part has described eight fallacies of cost-benefit analysis. Each of these fallacies, individually, would bias the technique against regulation—together they amount to a virtual Berlin Wall blocking good regulations.

Tackling these fallacies may seem overwhelming, and the problems of cost-benefit analysis so great that it might seem that we would be better off dumping the technique rather than fixing it. But getting discouraged and giving up is not the answer. The bias within cost-benefit analysis is the result of proregulatory groups having been largely absent from the debate for nearly three decades. Once both sides join the discussion over how cost-benefit analysis ought to be conducted, and the public gets involved, real progress will have a strong chance.

With the agenda described in the last eight chapters, proregulatory groups and active citizens have the tools they need to take down the antiregulatory edifice in cost-benefit analysis. The suggestions outlined herein are concrete and can be readily implemented.

First, whenever countervailing risks are taken into account, ancillary benefits must be counted as well. It is both counterintuitive and clearly unfair to look for unexpected costs without looking for unforeseen benefits. The days of focusing on the negative consequences of regulations while ignoring positive side effects need to end.

Second, the wealth-health tradeoff must be recognized for what it is—a sham, devoid of meaningful content, designed to shut down regulations. The assumption underlying the health-wealth tradeoff, that higher income causes people to be healthier, is contradicted by the most recent research on the subject, which shows that education—associated with both higher wages and better health—is likely driving the correlation between health and wealth. If anything, the health-wealth tradeoff shows that improving health can improve economic productivity. Whenever an antiregulatory speaker claims that "wealth equals health," there should be someone else at the podium—or at least a heckler in the audience—to speak the truth.

Third, the life-years method—currently in vogue at the top levels of government—must be abandoned as theoretically incoherent and empirically ungrounded. Using life-years to measure regulatory benefits devalues the lives of older Americans, and is unrelated to people's actual risk preferences. The value of a statistical life, based on people's actual willingness to pay to avoid risk, is the gold standard for estimating the value of life-saving regulations.

Fourth, the quality adjusted life-years (QALY) method must never get off the ground. This method has all of the problems of life-years, plus it fails to take account of people's inherent ability to adapt to life-changing illnesses. Because of this failure, the lives of people with disabilities or chronic aliments will be systematically undervalued. The Americans with Disabilities Act may provide a legal hook to rein in the use of this technique, but matters should never get to that point; this method should not be used in cost-benefit analysis. Public opposition to its fundamental unfairness should be enough to stop its use before it starts.

Fifth, though discounting may be appropriate for regulations targeted at long-latency diseases, there must also be upward adjustments to account for dread over the latency period, as well as the involuntary nature of the risk and suffering associated with long-latency diseases. Applying a straight discount rate borrowed from the *Wall Street Journal* financial pages will systematically understate the benefits of avoiding long-latency diseases.

Sixth, discounting in the intergenerational context amounts to punting one of the most important moral questions of our time. Discounting the value of regulatory benefits that accrue to future generations is as arbitrary as discounting benefits affecting people west of the Mississippi River—unfair and unjustifiable. The current practice of discounting benefits to future generations radically understates our obligations to our children, grandchildren, and future progeny, and results in too little action on pressing issues like global climate change. We cannot punt on this issue, and must face up to the fundamentally moral question of what we owe future generations.

Seventh, existence value is an important part of cost-benefit analysis, and people's preferences to preserve endangered species and stretches of untouched wilderness—even when they do not plan to use those natural resources—should be respected. Technical problems with existence values admit of technical solutions. Simply valuing all existence values at zero because of the difficulty of deriving accurate estimates from stated-preference studies is not the best solution.

Finally, in our dynamic market-based economy, industry can adapt, and cost estimations need to take this fact into account. In its current form, cost-benefit analysis tends to assume that industry and the cost of complying with regulations are static. But the reality is that, given the chance, industry has shown great ingenuity in reducing the costs of regulatory compliance. Many examples from past experience show that environmental and public health goals can be achieved for cheaper than expected.

This is clearly a full agenda. Proregulatory groups and citizens that care about having sensible and strong regulations have some serious work in store for them, make no mistake. However, this mountain is not insurmountable, and the view from the top will be well worth the effort.

PART III | Instituting
Regulatory
Rationality

Regulatory Hurdles

Part II, "Eight Fallacies of Cost-Benefit Analysis," detailed fallacies of cost-benefit analysis that have become prominent, in part, because for the past three decades the conversation about how cost-benefit analysis should be conducted has been dominated by antiregulatory interest groups. These fallacies bias cost-benefit analysis against regulation. In order for cost-benefit analysis to serve as a neutral tool of policy analysis, and accurately identify wealth-maximizing regulations, these fallacies need to be eliminated. Proregulatory interest groups, as well as informed citizens, can use these chapters as the foundation of an agenda for reforming the methodology of cost-benefit analysis, in order to reclaim it for the benefit of the general public rather than for the narrow purposes of antiregulatory interests.

The biases of cost-benefit analysis, however, are not only in the methodology—how cost-benefit analysis is conducted—but also institutional—how cost-benefit analysis is used. In the current structure of review, regulations must clear two separate cost-benefit hurdles before they are approved—first the Office of Management and Budget (OMB), and then the courts. If an agency's cost-benefit analysis is deemed inadequate, or if the costs are deemed greater than the benefits, then the agency is sent back to the drawing board. Cost-benefit analysis tends to block regulation, without acting equally to spur regulation. This situation came about because the modern institutions of regulatory review were built on the false belief that agencies have a systematic tendency to overregulate. Otherwise, a one-way ratchet designed to make regulations less stringent would not make sense.

OMB AND COST-BENEFIT ANALYSIS

As discussed in earlier chapters, cost-benefit analysis has been closely associated with OMB review since President Reagan's executive order was adopted in 1981. That order established that OMB would conduct a centralized review of all new major regulations to ensure compliance with cost-benefit criteria. The Reagan order was motivated by a belief, shared by many of his supporters, that the administrative state had grown too strong, that its influence was too prevalent in the economy, and that many regulations were unjustifiable burdens on economic growth. The cure to the evils of the administrative state was twofold: cost-benefit analysis and the centralization of executive authority.

Reagan's centralized review process required the agencies to weigh regulatory costs against regulatory benefits. OMB acted as the final judge of whether regulations were cost-benefit justified. This centralized review process took substantial power away from agency heads that had previously operated on their own initiative. The power taken from the agencies was given to the newly formed Office of Information and Regulatory Affairs (OIRA). Although a version of this system has been in place for nearly three decades, and we have become accustomed to centralized regulatory review, it is difficult to overstate the significance of that power transfer.

As discussed earlier, President Clinton largely retained this structure. Clinton's executive order did make some important revisions by increasing the transparency of the process and making room for consideration of "qualitative measures," including "distributive impacts" and "equity."[428] President George W. Bush kept the Clinton order for six years, and then made a few changes to increase the importance of OIRA review. The same fundamental institutional arrangement, with OMB and OIRA at the center reviewing agency regulations against cost-benefit criteria, has now been in place for a quarter-century.

It is important to note that individual OIRA administrators can have an important impact on how regulatory review is conducted. In addition to the formalized mechanism of regulatory review—defined in the executive order— an administrator can use his or her position in the White House to help set and carry out the administration's regulatory agenda. Agency decisions can be influenced as much through the internal administration back-channel as through official action. This is true not only for the OIRA administrator, but other officials as well—the *Washington Post* has documented the extent to which Vice President Dick Cheney was a master at working the back-channel to effect his regulatory goals.[429] The internal back and forth between administration officials likely leads to both beneficial and unfortunate results, depending on the administration and the prevailing political winds. Although these behind-the-scenes machinations are no doubt important, little can be done ahead of time to structure them. Selecting highly qualified and honest civil servants and political appointees of high integrity is therefore extremely important.

Nonetheless, the institutions of regulatory review do matter. As currently structured, the role of OIRA is generally to determine whether the benefits of the regulation exceed its costs (its role in coordinating agency action currently takes a back seat). OIRA mostly seeks to ensure that the agency regulation is not too stringent, and does not impose higher economic costs than are justified. OIRA does not generally look into whether the regulation is too lax,[430] and whether cost-benefit analysis would call for a stronger regulatory response. OIRA, then, tends to act as a one-way ratchet turning regulation down but not up. Because there is no comparable formalized procedure geared to increasing regulatory stringency, regulations tend to be less stringent than would be economically efficient.[431]

A 2003 General Accounting Office (GAO) review of OIRA found that, out of the seventeen rules that had been "significantly changed" during review—fourteen of which came from the Environmental Protection Agency (EPA)—none had been made more stringent. Of the EPA rules, six had been changed to eliminate or delay specific provisions; four adopted lower-cost regulatory alternatives, and three were sent back for revisions in calculations.[432] In that report, the GAO noted that "attention to the cost side of the economic effects was most prevalent in OIRA's comments and suggestions."[433] Other studies have found that OIRA review "almost always suggested that agencies delay or weaken safety, health, and environmental protections in some way."[434]

WHAT DEREGULATION?

OIRA has a tendency to scrutinize new regulations more than decisions to deregulate. New regulations are delayed; old regulations are dispatched with haste. Yet deregulatory decisions can also benefit greatly from cost-benefit analysis. Deregulation can be just as costly, in terms of adverse impacts on social welfare, as inefficient regulation. Nixing an efficient regulation, or replacing an imperfect regulation with an even more imperfect nonregulated market, can be just as harmful as implementing an overly harsh regulation. To be neutral, cost-benefit analysis should be applied equally to regulatory and deregulatory decisions.

Under the Reagan executive order, the cost-benefit analysis of deregulatory decisions was not even considered. Getting rid of inefficient regulation was the objective of OMB and of cost-benefit analysis; deregulation was the goal to be achieved. Subjecting deregulation to cost-benefit analysis would have seemed nonsensical to those who believed that every deregulatory decision was, by definition, economically justified. In the 1980s and early 1990s, OIRA applied cost-benefit analysis to new regulations, but required "no cost analysis for [proposals] that relax[ed] existing standards."[435]

The Clinton executive order changed things, defining the "significant regulatory actions" that would be subject to cost-benefit analysis to include deregulatory decisions.[436] OIRA now says it reviews deregulatory decisions,[437] and agencies produce cost-benefit analyses of deregulatory decisions. On its face, it would seem that the Clinton order addressed this particular bias by subjecting deregulatory decisions to the same kind of scrutiny as proposed regulations.

However, under the George W. Bush administration, it appears that deregulatory decisions are not subject to such strict OIRA review. In 2002, the EPA promulgated a rule relaxing the New Source Review provision of the Clean Air Act, to allow old, dirtier, "grandfathered" power plants to undertake plant upgrades without becoming subject to stricter emissions controls. Though this rule clearly would have significant environmental and economic impacts, the EPA claimed that the economic consequences of the rule would be minor, making OIRA review unnecessary under the terms of the executive order. OIRA did not contest the EPA's determination, and after a weak attempt to get the EPA to conduct a cost-benefit analysis, eventually agreed that neither OIRA approval, nor even a formal cost-benefit analysis, was needed.

It is inconceivable that weakening the New Source Review provision was economically insignificant and would result in a net benefit for the environment. The National Association of Public Administration, the EPA's own Office of Inspector General, the American Lung Association, and a host of environmental groups have stated that the new rule will result in increased levels of air pollution. Given the well-documented effects of air pollution on health, the economic impact generated from increases in health risks alone likely justified a cost-benefit analysis and OIRA review. The argument that the new rule will have little economic impact is further undermined by the scope of the New Source Review provision, which covers all "stationary sources," meaning any facility "which emits or may emit any air pollutant"—a tremendous number of facilities including power plants, factories, and oil refineries. Even small changes in the New Source Review rules will, given its scope, deeply affect these important economic actors, with ripple effects throughout the economy. With the adverse environmental impacts and the important effects on industry, no reasonable person could believe that the weakening of the New Source Review rules will not result in a very significant overall economic effect.

OIRA's failure to require a cost-benefit analysis of the New Source Review rule shows the relative indifference OIRA currently shows toward deregulatory decisions. Though new regulations are subject to deep scrutiny and are often weakened as a result of OIRA intervention, deregulatory decisions have not always been examined with the same rigor.

One of the most powerful critiques of OIRA review and its use of cost-benefit analysis is that it merely responds to agency action and does not initiate regulation. Under the framework of the existing executive order, OIRA primarily serves an inhibitory role for the regulatory state. No similar formal mechanism exists to excite the agencies into action. There have been efforts on the part of individual OIRA administrators—both formal and informal—to spur agency action, but these efforts have been ad hoc and outside the context of official regulatory review.

The decision not to regulate can be as costly as the decision to regulate too much. Efficient regulations deliver large benefits, and counteract important failures of the unregulated market. Just as regulations impose some cost on the economy, the lack of regulation, if regulation is called for, also imposes costs in the form of reduced social welfare. The pollution of a valuable natural resource, like breathable clean air, for a low-value purpose—say, to allow cars to use leaded gasoline—can have enormous consequences. In the case of lead, increases in pollution levels are associated with a reduction in intelligence quotients (IQs) among children. This can lead to large losses of economic productivity, not to mention losses in welfare and human potential. A lack of regulation in that case imposes very large social costs. An agency's decision *not* to regulate, then, can easily be as costly as a decision to regulate too much.

Some steps have been taken to use OIRA to spur regulation. First, OIRA administrators are free to use their position to informally spur regulation. For example, Sally Katzen, the OIRA administrator under Clinton, has been credited with working behind the scenes to encourage regulatory efforts. She recalls holding meetings with agency heads in order to prod regulatory action.[438] These efforts are naturally difficult to track, but may play an important role, depending on the administration.

There have also been small steps to formalize the regulation-forcing role. In 2001, OIRA announced a new practice of issuing "prompt letters" designed to spur agencies into regulatory action.[439] Fourteen prompt letters have been issued on a number of matters. In some cases, OIRA has called on agencies to regulate in new areas—for example, by requesting OSHA to consider elevating promotion of automatic external defibrillators in the workplace.[440] The prompt letters have also been used to request more information from agencies in areas that they already regulate, such as a request to the EPA about its implementation of a beach-protection act.[441]

Yet even prompt letters have not been an unmitigated boon for those who favor regulation. Prompt letters were envisioned by their creator,

John Graham, to be useful both for spurring deregulation as well as regulation.[442] One of the most important prompt letters, which went out in 2003, asked the independent agencies to consider forty-nine regulatory reform proposals, most of which had been submitted to OIRA by industry groups.[443] These proposals included revoking consumer-protection rules like the three-day cooling-off period for purchases made from door-to-door salesmen, and the rule requiring mobile-phone providers to allow customers to maintain phone numbers when switching companies.

Another tool of the deregulatory agenda is its issuance of "hit lists" of expensive regulations.[444] Since the days of Ronald Reagan's Presidential Task Force on Regulatory Relief, central regulatory review has included efforts to find "bad" regulations and encourage agencies to deregulate. During the first year of the current Bush administration, OIRA requested suggestions for regulations that should be changed or eliminated to reduce burdens on industry.[445] It selected twenty-three of the suggestions for "high priority review."[446] OIRA has continued this practice, calling each year for new nominations to its hit list. There is no comparable effort to identify hit lists of regulatory inaction with significant, adverse social welfare consequences.[447]

Moreover, both the hit lists and the prompt letters are somewhat ad hoc mechanisms, not enshrined in the executive order establishing OMB review, and not firmly ingrained in the institutional practices of OIRA. The job of simply reviewing regulations that bubble up from agencies is nearly overwhelming—twenty-two OIRA staff are responsible for reviewing six hundred regulations a year—or twenty-seven per analyst per year, or about one every two weeks. Given the staggering complexity of some regulations, this is a Herculean (and perhaps impossible) task. With current levels of staffing and responsibility, the prompt letters and hit lists must take a backseat to OIRA's primary role—checking regulations against cost-benefit criteria, mainly to ensure that costs do not exceed benefits. The attempts by OIRA to undertake a formal proactive role are in some cases laudable, but also inadequate.

DELAY

One important criticism of OMB review in the past is that it delayed rulemaking. By requiring agencies to submit their rules to OIRA for approval, centralized review adds another significant step in the already long and contentious rulemaking process. In addition, delay can be used as a tactic to avoid regulation altogether—infinite stalling is an effective way to kill new regulation, and can avoid some of the political consequences of being more direct. Both the Reagan and George H. W. Bush administrations were heavily criticized for silently suffocating new regulations through long delays. When agencies sent disfavored regulations into the regulatory review process, they often feared that the regulations would never come out.

In his executive order, President Clinton implemented some measures to cut down on the delay associated with OMB review. Most importantly, he placed a ninety-day cap on OIRA's timeline, subject to a thirty-day extension. The cap has remained in place even under the Bush administration. Under John Graham, the number of regulations that have stalled in OIRA for longer than ninety days dropped considerably.[448]

However, the actual delay associated with OMB review is not reducible to the time it spends in the formal OIRA review process. OIRA now enters into consulting relationships with agencies well in advance of formal review. It is impossible to measure the impact of OIRA's earlier involvement on the speed of regulatory development. Tellingly, the number of return letters and "voluntary" rule withdrawals has also increased. It is quite possible that the delay associated with OIRA's involvement has merely shifted from the formal review process to the long informal negotiation between OIRA and the individual agencies. Overall, there has been, and may continue to be, significant delay associated with OIRA review.

JUDICIAL REVIEW AND COST-BENEFIT ANALYSIS

Courts play a very prominent role in the American administrative state. Under the Administrative Procedure Act (APA)—passed in the mid-1940s in reaction to the New Deal—the actions of federal agencies like OSHA and the EPA can generally be reviewed by courts. Judicial review of agency action serves a variety of purposes. It helps ensure that agencies act according to their governing statutes; follow proper procedures; remain accountable to political actors like Congress and the president;[449] act in accordance with the constitutional rights of individuals, organizations, or groups; and avoid actions that are "arbitrary, capricious, [or] an abuse of discretion."[450]

In addition to the general provisions of the APA, judicial review of agency actions is sometimes governed by more specific statutory requirements. Some statutes provide standards for judging agency rules that are stricter than those of the APA,[451] while others preclude judicial review of certain agency actions (although courts maintain the power to review agency decisions for constitutionality[452]).

Because of this important power of review, courts have played a significant role in shaping many environmental, health and safety regulations over the years. In some instances, courts have insisted on specific changes, or struck down rules that they believed did not pass muster. More generally, the threat of judicial veto exerts constant pressure on agencies—though many decisions are ultimately upheld, there is always a risk that a court will overturn an agency rule. Further, courts have also imposed a variety of analytic requirements on agencies by forcing them to provide strong justification for their actions. Some commentators believe that these requirements have significantly hampered the ability of agencies to carry out regulation.[453]

Cost-benefit analysis arises in two ways during the course of judicial review. Most straightforwardly, because courts review the basis of agency decisionmaking, they sometimes examine the cost-benefit analyses that are performed by agencies. Secondly, courts themselves sometimes use cost-benefit principles to evaluate the propriety of agency rules.[454]

Earlier chapters have described examples of when courts have found agency cost-benefit analysis wanting. In *Corrosion Proof Fittings v. EPA*,[455] Judge Jerry Edwin Smith of the Fifth Circuit was critical of the cost-benefit analysis prepared by the EPA in defense of a proposed asbestos ban. In that case, in response to an industry challenge, the court disagreed with the manner in which the EPA had conducted portions of its cost-benefit analysis.[456] As discussed earlier, Judge Smith held that the EPA had improperly failed to discount the health benefits of the ban over the course of the latency period, between exposure to asbestos and the manifestation of health impacts. Judge Smith further faulted the EPA for failing to compare the asbestos ban "to an improved workplace in which currently available control technology is utilized."[457] The court was also unhappy with what it referred to as a "double-counting of the costs of asbestos use"[458] and took issue with the use by the EPA of an unquantified benefits category, holding that "[w]hile the [Toxic Substances Control Act] contemplates a useful place for unquantified benefits beyond the EPA's calculation, unquantified benefits never were intended as a trump card allowing the EPA to justify any cost calculus, no matter how high."[459]

Because many agency decisions are justified by cost-benefit analysis, it should come as no surprise that courts have examined these cost-benefit analyses and have halted agency actions because they found flaws.[460] The judicial decisions also have important prospective consequences because practices that courts find objectionable cannot be used to justify future regulations. Courts thus shape not only the final rules, but also the methodology of cost-benefit analysis through this process.

Sometimes, courts also require agencies to conduct cost-benefit analysis. Some statutes are quite explicit about the need for agencies to balance costs against benefits, but many statutes are vague or are silent on the matter. In some of these cases, such as the Toxic Substances Control Act, which is discussed above, courts have nonetheless found in the statute a requirement that agencies engage in cost-benefit analysis. In fact, Cass Sunstein has suggested a presumption that agencies must utilize cost-benefit principles when exercising their discretion in areas in which congressional statutes are unclear.[461]

Cost-benefit analysis, then, is an important part of the judicial review of agency decisions. Unfortunately, like the use of cost-benefit analysis in OMB review-of-agency decisions, the institutional context of the judicial treatment of cost-benefit analysis creates an antiregulatory bias.

AGENCY INACTION

Although agency action is generally subject to review, it is often much harder for plaintiffs to get courts to take a look at agency inaction. This imbalance means that cost-benefit analysis more often arises in the context of a plaintiff asking a court to overturn an agency action. In this institutional context, cost-benefit analysis is used to impede regulation. It is not similarly used in a proactive sense, to induce regulation that would increase social welfare. Deference to agency inaction therefore creates an important bias in how cost-benefit analysis is used.

There are several reasons why agency inaction is less subject to review than agency action.[462] Even when courts hear cases about agency inaction, they grant agencies significant latitude on these matters.[463] If Congress has not established clear timelines for particular action, courts generally commit the decision over whether to act to agency discretion. As one commentator put it, "[W]hile an agency's refusal to initiate or complete a rulemaking procedure is usually reviewable, such 'action-forcing' suits are typically more difficult to win than suits challenging enacted rules."[464] However, the important recent Supreme Court decision of *Massachusetts v. EPA* (discussed later) may indicate a renewed interest on the part of the courts to spur agencies forward in certain kinds of agency-inaction cases.

REMEDIES

Another source of antiregulatory bias arises from the remedies available to plaintiffs if courts find that agency action has been improper. Most commonly, the agency action is set aside, which can be troubling for any proregulatory interest seeking review. Even if an agency action is allowed to stand, any victory by a proregulatory interest may be illusory, as agencies tend not to worry too much about adverse court decisions if the court fails to overturn the agency rule. The result is that proregulatory groups are in a bind when they seek to increase the stringency of an agency action.

In cases in which an agency acts, two types of challenges are typical. On the one side, industry representatives will challenge a rule, arguing either that there should be no rule, or that the stringency of the rule should be decreased. On the other side, the proregulatory interest—such as a labor union or an environmental group—might challenge the regulation, arguing that it is not stringent enough. The potential payoffs for the two sides, however, are markedly different.

If the industry side is successful, and the court agrees that there is inadequate justification for the stringency of the new rule, then the court can vacate the regulation while the agency reconsiders the matter. The agency can then either reduce the stringency of the regulation or provide better justification for the original rule. Industry benefits either way, reaping both short-term and potential long-term benefits. In the short term, the state of affairs prior to agency action—often, no regulation or underregulation—is restored. The industry costs associated with the new regulation are, at the very least, delayed. If the agency comes back with a weaker regulation, that is worse for industry than no regulation but still better than the earlier regulation. In either case, bringing the suit is a win-win proposition for the industry side.

The situation is different for the proregulatory interests, which challenge rules that they feel are insufficiently stringent. They are faced with a difficult dilemma. If they are successful, and the court agrees that the agency has failed to justify its low level of stringency, then the rule may be set aside awaiting further agency consideration. At least in the short term, that outcome is worse than if the weak rule had just gone through unchallenged. Furthermore, there is a significant possibility that the agency will simply find additional justification for the original decision—the proregulatory interest, then, sees no benefit whatsoever from the "successful" challenge, while suffering an important cost during the delay period.

In the D.C. Circuit, which is the court that hears many cases seeking review of agency decisions, some attempt has been made to mitigate this problem through the use of the remand without vacatur remedy. In these cases, the court finds for the plaintiff, but allows the agency regulation to stand, pending reconsideration of the rule by the agency. Thus, the plaintiff has the advantage of the weak (but still better than nothing) regulation in place while the agency considers whether to propose a stricter rule, or find additional justification for the weak rule.

The remand with vacatur remedy is not a panacea. First, and perhaps most importantly, the possibility of a regular remand with vacatur is significant, so that proregulatory plaintiffs must balance the probability of this remedy against the possible benefits of challenging the regulation. If the remand without vacatur remedy were used exclusively, this would not be a problem. Further, critics of the remand without vacatur remedy have found that agencies tend to ignore these rulings—because their proposed rule is allowed to stand, they have little incentive to prioritize any action to address the court's order.[465] So, the benefit to the proregulatory interest becomes speculative if the agency can simply sit on a ruling for a long time rather than promptly examining a more strict regulatory option.

Because of these remedy problems, it makes sense for the antiregulatory interest to challenge agency rule-makings, and argue that cost-benefit analyses have been inadequately performed, or that an agency's rationale does not conform to cost-benefit principles. In contrast, there is less incentive for a proregulatory group to make the opposite argument—that an agency failed to account sufficiently for a regulatory benefit, and thus regulated less stringently than it should have.

CONCLUSION

Because of its place within the structure of regulatory review, cost-benefit analysis generally serves an antiregulatory purpose. In both OMB and the courts, cost-benefit analysis is a hurdle that regulations must clear, but it is rarely used to spur agencies to action. This institutional arrangement means that we have less regulation and less stringent regulations than we should— meaning less environmental protection, and more cases of preventable death, sickness, and injury than we can afford.

Shaky Foundation

If agencies are by nature overzealous, failing to adequately account for costs and generally overregulating and overburdening the economy, then it makes sense for central reviewers and judges to put in place a scheme designed primarily to apply the brakes, so long as the central reviewers can be counted on to be more neutral than agencies. This has been the operating theory of the system of regulatory review since President Reagan's 1981 executive order. Both prongs of this argument, however, are faulty. First, there is no reason to believe that agencies systematically overregulate. Second, it is naïve to expect that the Office of Information and Regulatory Affairs (OIRA) will be systematically better at maximizing social welfare than regulatory agencies.

DEBUNKING THE BUREAUCRATIC BOOGEYMAN

Several theories of agency behavior posit that agencies tend to overregulate. These theories of the "overzealous agency" have not withstood the test of time. The first theory maintains that regulating agencies will be captured by special-interest groups, which encourage the agencies to pursue regulatory agendas that benefit the special interest at the expense of the general good. This argument is a spin on classic collective action theory, which states that large diffuse groups will be less able to organize than small groups with concentrated interests. Proregulatory groups, according to the story, gain access to agencies, and impose costs willy-nilly on American businesses and consumers, in the pursuit of their narrow agendas.

This story, however, runs afoul of both collective-action theory and the legislative process as it actually works. Proponents of this theory must argue that special interest groups—such as environmental organizations and consumer protection groups—will have greater power in the administrative process than industry groups. But collective-action theory predicts just the opposite: Environmental and consumer groups will have the most difficulty organizing themselves into effective lobbying blocks. Industry, with fewer players and more at stake for each firm, will have the advantage. That prediction is vindicated in our actual process in which environmental and consumer groups are dwarfed by industry trade associations, individual corporate lobbying, and the general probusiness and antitax lobbies.

A second theory posits that the heads of unchecked agencies will engage in empire-building, seeking to increase their own prestige and power by enlarging their agency's budget and mandate. The result of this effect is "agencies gone wild," overregulating and projecting their power into every corner of American life in an egomaniacal rush. As discussed earlier, this theory, propounded by William Niskanen, a member of President Reagan's Council of Economic Advisers, held significant sway for many years, in both public-policy circles as well as the academy.

This view also has grave problems. The strongest refutation of the empire-building theory has come from Daryl Levinson,[466] who argued that agency heads do not necessarily face incentives to increase their agencies' budgets or mandates. There is a wide variety of other goods that agency heads could pursue—such as prestige, nicer offices, intellectually stimulating work, leisure time, and future employment prospects, that may or may not dovetail with increasing agency budgets and mandates. It may make more sense for an agency to "go along to get along" and treat industry with a light hand in order to accrue favors that will be useful in the job market. In any case, an argument for why increasing budgets and mandates is the best course of action for the opportunistic bureaucrat has not been convincingly put forward.

Even if agency heads did pursue an empire-building agenda, it would probably make more sense to regulate in more areas, but less stringently. Less strict regulation will be less controversial, leading the agency to be able to pursue regulation in more areas. However, the cost-benefit test and Office of Management and Budget (OMB) review are ill suited to protect against this kind of empire building. Furthermore, both Congress and the president exercise influence over the agencies. In many cases agency heads have no choice but to respond to the demand of their political masters.

Some agencies are widely believed to have a proregulatory tilt. For example, Sally Katzen, OIRA director under Clinton, thinks that the Environmental Protection Agency (EPA) tends to have a more proregulatory focus than other agencies. Katzen has written, "[I]n my experience senior political appointees at EPA clearly stand out from their colleagues at other agencies for both the intensity of their enthusiasm for their agency's mission and their faith in regulatory solutions."[467] She notes that "EPA has a singular history of attracting highly motivated and intelligent political and career staff dedicated to its institutional mission."[468] She also notes that in recent presidential administrations, "there were a significant number of senior officials … who had previously been environmental activists or state or local environmental officials and who had forcefully advocated the importance of protecting—indeed, improving—the environment."[469]

But if some agencies are perceived as proregulatory, others agencies have traditionally been perceived as antiregulatory. The Army Corps of Engineers and the Department of Energy do not draw on the pool of former activists for their political and civil servant staffs. In many agencies, working for the regulated industry both prior to and after a stint in government is not uncommon. Further, the particular biases of the political staff will shift according to the administration currently in office. Few would accuse the administration of George W. Bush of filling agencies with former environmental activists.

Moreover, because of the overlapping mandates of federal agencies and the widespread collaboration needed to carry out sophisticated regulatory programs, the overregulating tendencies of some agencies will be in tension with the underregulating tendencies of others. When, either on their own initiative or at the request of OIRA, the EPA sits down with the Department of Energy, a number of competing interests are represented, and it is not clear that systematic overregulation will be the result.

In the end, there is no persuasive reason to believe that agencies pervasively tend to overregulate, rather than underregulate. This is not to say that agencies are perfect—no doubt, they have all the flaws associated with any institution. These include a lack of perfect information, personal desires that conflict with the public good, and simple laziness. However, the sum total of these failings does not point to across-the-board overregulation. If anything, given the human tendency to avoid confrontation, protect the status quo, and avoid change, we might think that agencies tend towards inertia and inaction. Rather than just a check, they might sometimes need an occasional prod.[470] The result of the widely held but incorrect view of the overzealous regulator is a formal system of regulatory review that is needlessly skewed against regulation and does not best promote economic efficiency.

THE QUESTION OF OIRA'S NEUTRALITY

Because of OIRA's special place as the centralized reviewer of major regulations, it is sometimes thought to be a neutral arbiter, one that cannot become captured by any particular special interest or become overly enamored with a particular narrow regulatory outlook. Courts—which also oversee agency actions—have several structural features, established by the Constitution, to ensure their independence, including the life tenure of federal judges. This is not the case with OIRA, which, in fact, operates with less transparency and oversight than traditional regulatory agencies, and is far more subject to political accountability than the courts.

OIRA is not governed by the normal procedural requirements, including notice of rulemaking, opportunity for public comment, and judicial review, that tend to increase the ability of the general public to add its input to the regulatory process and decrease the influence of special interests. With normal agencies, the goings-on are very much in public view—many of the steps that agencies take must be explained to the public under the Administrative Procedure Act, and agencies—as a matter of both law and habit—are continually holding public meetings and accepting public comment. Further, the judiciary, exercising judicial review of agency decisions, has traditionally been a source of oversight. Because OIRA decisions are not subject to judicial review, that oversight is absent.

Further, OIRA is not as transparent as regular agencies. Although there have been reforms in this area, and the Reagan days of OIRA acting in a near-total shroud of darkness are over, it remains difficult for outsiders to fully observe the ins and outs of OIRA review.[471] As late as 2003, the Government Accounting Office (GAO) has found that OIRA reviews are "not always transparent to the public." The GAO complained about OIRA's failure to disclose why rules were withdrawn from review, the poor quality of its disclosure about contacts with outside parties, and the transparency problems associated with informal OIRA review of regulations.[472] The transparency problems involved with informal review have become more pronounced as agencies have begun reaching out to OIRA in advance of formal review in order to avoid being shut down by OIRA at the end of a long process. Often, it is during the informal back and forth between OIRA and an agency that the most important changes are made.[473] This lack of transparency provides more opportunity to shun the public interest in favor of the needs of politically connected special interests. If Justice Brandeis was correct, and "sunshine is the best disinfectant," then the OIRA process raises very serious contamination threats.

This lack of the traditional structures of agency control has been defended on the grounds that OIRA is closer to the president than other agencies. The argument is that because the president is responsible to a national constituency, he (or she) will be less sensitive to the kinds of special-interest pressure that might dominate the agencies.[474] It is relatively cheap to capture an agency compared to capturing the president, because the president is responsible to a wide array of stakeholders. As the number of competing interests that a policymaker must take account of increases, it becomes less likely that any particular group can control that individual.

This argument resonates with the one put forward by James Madison in the *Federalist Papers*, in which he argued that a large republic, by incorporating many diverse interests, can help defeat the influence of "factions."[475] In Madison's view, extending the territory and populace within a single nation would make it less likely that any particular group would be able to form a majority, and thus impose its will on the minority. The backers of OIRA appropriate the spirit of this argument to claim that the president, who governs on the whole range of issues, is less likely to become beholden to a particular interest group than a specialized agency.

Experience and theory, however, show that this hope is not well founded. First, as an elected official, the president will be attentive to those groups that can provide him with the resources, support, and votes to win elections for himself and his party.[476] Experience with direct presidential-level review of agency decisionmaking—which took place under the Council of Competitiveness during the administration of George H. W. Bush—has been atrocious. The sad story of former Vice President Dan Quayle, traveling the country to hold closed-door sessions with big Republican donors, before silently killing regulations while leaving "no fingerprints,"[477] should dispel any myth we have about presidential neutrality. Vice President Dick Cheney's efforts to protect the content of meetings held with industry lobbyists when formulating energy policy in the early days of the George W. Bush administration casts further doubt on the interest of the White House to stay above the fray. The image of a president who can avoid the taint of special interest politics is naïve.

Even if it turned out that the president was able to put aside special interest politics for the good of the nation, OIRA is not the president. It is nearly as difficult for the president to personally keep track of the goings-on at OIRA as it would be to keep track of the internal workings of a regulatory agency. Just because OIRA is located in the executive office of the president does not mean that the president will realistically exercise a significant level of control. It would be strange to argue, for example, that interest groups are less able to influence the Office of the U.S. Trade Representative, simply because it is located within the executive office of the President. It is difficult to imagine that groups would be significantly benefited in their lobbying efforts if the U.S. Trade Representative headed a separate cabinet department.

The strongest argument in favor of OIRA neutrality is that there is no specific interest group to which OIRA is responsible. The EPA works with the same environmental groups and the same regulated industries over and over again. It is called before the same congressional committees repeatedly. The Occupational Safety and Health Administration (OSHA) is responsible to labor, and the lobbying groups representing business. OIRA, because it covers the entire regulatory field, does not have a clear constituency.

The lack of a constituency can be both a strength and a weakness—OIRA may be less subject to pressure than a typical agency, but the lack of a constituency could translate into less political power in intramural administration debates. The question of OIRA's constituency will differ from administration to administration. Under Presidents Reagan and George H. W. Bush, there was a strong contingent of antiregulatory activists, both regulated industry as well as individuals committed to a particular worldview. In those years, it is easy to imagine that antiregulatory interests acted as OIRA's constituency in both a positive and negative sense—influencing OIRA's agenda but also giving it greater influence in internal deliberations. An OIRA administrator who is not responsive to these antiregulatory interests is forced to "go it alone," gaining independence but trading a source of political support. This situation creates as strong an incentive to be responsive to narrow special interests—if somewhat different—as that faced by any administrative agency.

CONCLUSION

It is not correct to assume that all agencies systematically overregulate. The theoretical arguments that pro-regulatory interest groups have captured regulatory agencies, or that bureaucrats will systematically pursue strategies leading to overly stringent regulation are unpersuasive. Even if some agencies will tend to overregulate, there will be other agencies that will have offsetting antiregulatory biases. Thus, a central regulator should not be charged merely with checking overzealous agencies.

Even if such a central regulatory check was needed, OIRA cannot reasonably be expected to fulfill that task. Even if OIRA was a perfect representative of the president, there is no reason to believe that a president will not be responsive to the needs of narrow special interests. And even if the president exactly represented the will of the nation, OIRA's place in the executive office of the president does not mean that it perfectly represents the president's views. Further, OIRA does not have the same kind of constituency as traditional regulatory agencies, because it covers the entire field of regulation. That situation is both a potential source of independence, but also a weakness. Without cultivating relationships with interest groups, the OIRA administrator is forced to "go it alone" in internal administration disputes, relying on the strength of his or her arguments—and personal relationships and esteem—rather than political power. For certain administrators that may be enough, but the situation is fraught with potential special-interest pressure, just as it is in the case of traditional agencies.

In summary, because the underlying logic of the current structure of regulatory review is faulty, the set of hurdles that now confront agencies predictably leads to underregulation. The next chapter discusses how the system can be reformed, building on its strengths and counteracting its weaknesses, to increase the rationality of our system of regulatory review.

Rethinking OIRA

The current institutions of regulatory review were constructed based on a flawed theory of the systematically overregulating agency. A new system, which reflects the reality that agencies will both over- and underregulate, is needed. To start, the idea of central review of regulations need not be scrapped. Although the current system is biased against regulation, there are ways to reform it so that it can lead to a more rational system of regulation, without unfairly and unwisely hindering agencies.

First, a new executive order to define a new role for the Office of Information and Regulatory Affairs (OIRA) is needed. This executive order would set out new guidelines for how OIRA is to approach cost-benefit analysis by changing the focus away from checking agencies and toward agenda-setting and the calibration of regulatory stringency. Further, the executive order will prioritize the non-cost-benefit analysis function of OIRA, including interagency coordination and harmonization, and distributional analysis.

OIRA OVERSIGHT

The first order of business for a new executive order is to further increase the transparency of OIRA and public participation in its decisions. Important steps took place during the Clinton and George W. Bush administrations, but further steps need to be taken. Although full APA review, with judicial oversight, may be unrealistic for many of OIRA's decisions, the general openness of how agencies conduct their business should be the gold standard.

As an initial matter, it is important to recognize that OIRA is different from traditional agencies in relevant ways. When agencies conduct rulemaking, they set out binding rules with the force of law—in effect, they act like specialized legislatures, specifying and filling-in congressional statutes. The rulemaking process is where much of the Administrative

Procedure Act (APA) process is focused, with rules about public participation and transparency designed to ensure that the public is not shut out of the rulemaking process. Much of OIRA's work is not rulemaking, but rather the analysis and negotiation of proposed rules. That process is not easily subject to APA review. However, OIRA does undertake some rulemaking-like activity. For example, OIRA publishes a set of guidelines—called the Office of Management and Budget (OMB) *Circular A-4*—which describes how agencies should conduct cost-benefit analysis.[478] Later on, we will encourage it to do more, for example, by harmonizing scientific standards across agencies.

At the very least, when OIRA sets out general guidelines concerning the regulatory apparatus as a whole, such as the *Circular A-4*, those rules should be the subject of traditional notice and comment rulemaking. These procedures have been created to ensure that agencies adequately consider the various interests that are affected by its actions, and engage in reasoned analysis to support their decisions. It is not difficult to see a role for judicial review in these rulemaking processes. Independent oversight of executive agencies has been a hallmark of our system of administrative law for many decades. Because of the vast power given to agencies, and their relatively insulated position, which removes them from direct electoral accountability, supplemental accountability measures have been developed. Courts have served a useful role in ensuring that underrepresented viewpoints are adequately considered by agencies, and procedures to inform the public of agency action, and require agencies to solicit and respond to comments from the public, ensure that agency action does not take place entirely under the radar. When OIRA makes general rules, it should be subject to the same—or a similar—regime.

Further, OIRA should be subject to the same rules regarding transparency, such as the rules concerning public meetings, that govern agencies. Not every meeting that OIRA conducts needs to be made public, but the same kinds of meetings that, when conducted by agencies, would be subject to open meetings requirements, should also be public when conducted by OIRA. It is not uncommon for agencies to conduct a meeting of stakeholders that includes a general invitation to the public—that kind of practice can be imported to OIRA as well.

Finally, it is important that the reforms of the Clinton and George W. Bush administrations be preserved and strengthened. For example, John Graham instituted rules concerning the release of information to the public about meetings held at OIRA. These rules should be formalized and made a permanent part of OIRA's marching orders.

Centralized review of regulation has always been justified, in part, as a checking function. President Reagan's executive orders note that one purpose of review is "to reduce the burdens of existing and future regulations."[479] Even the Clinton order states that "[t]he American people deserve a regulatory system ... that protects and improves their heath, safety, [and] environment ... without imposing unacceptable or unreasonable costs on society." As discussed, this checking function has come to dominate OIRA review of regulation, as the antiregulatory stance of the originators of executive office review became institutionalized in the description of OIRA's mission.

For cost-benefit analysis to become a neutral tool of policy analysis, so that it serves neither anti- nor proregulatory interests, this checking function has to be supplemented. Reformed cost-benefit analysis has an important role to play in centralized review, but not exclusively to check agencies. It must also spur them to action when needed. Such analysis can help prioritize agency action, place governmental resources and regulations where they are most needed, and address the most pressing problems first. Agenda-setting and prioritization should be core functions of a reformed cost-benefit analysis.

Agencies already undertake a substantial amount of effort to set their regulatory agendas, but there is a place for centralized review to help facilitate and rationalize this process. Data about how well agency programs are performing can be collected and analyzed according to cost-benefit criteria, though such efforts to date, including OMB's Program Assesment Rating Tool (PART), have been problematic.[480] Likewise, research into new regulatory areas can be compiled at the central level, so that the prospective returns to regulatory action can be analyzed. There are distinct advantages to involving a central body in this process. A central prioritizing body can facilitate the sharing of information across agencies that is useful for prioritization. It can also avoid the parochialism that sometimes characterizes agencies, and can rise above intra-agency conflicts and assess which programs and prospective programs should be given priority. Finally, only a central body can set priorities across agencies, and mediate in areas in which agency responsibilities overlap. For these reasons, at least, there is an important role for a central body—using cost-benefit analysis as one input—to participate in agenda-setting and prioritization.

OIRA can also help invigorate petitions for rulemaking as a way of identifying areas in which new rules are needed. Under the current regulatory system, it is not uncommon for groups to petition agencies for new regulation. If agencies deny petitions for rulemaking—as they often do—the judicial review of those denials is quite deferential. There is no formal way to include cost-benefit analysis in this petition process. A newly enhanced agenda-setting role for OIRA should include the review of denials of petitions for rulemaking that involve agency inaction. If those petitions are supported by credible cost-benefit analyses, but are denied by the agency, petitioners should have the right to appeal to OIRA before seeking judicial review. OIRA could then examine the cost-benefit analysis, and if there is a strong enough case for regulation, either mediate between the agency and the groups, or issue a finding of fact that a regulation is justified. That finding could then be taken to the courts, where the agency's determination that regulation was not needed would be given substantially less deference. At the very least, the agency would have to develop a reasoned response to OIRA's findings. The process would create a mechanism for cost-benefit analysis to be used directly to spur agencies to action.

By allowing citizens and groups to use cost-benefit analysis to justify new regulatory actions, this petition process would give proregulatory interests the opportunity to use cost-benefit analysis to forward their cause, and would also increase participation in the setting of agencies' agendas. Although it will remain important for individual agencies, as well as the central regulatory review office, to maintain a large degree of control over the specifics of agenda-setting, there is also an important role for affected interests. Because of the structure of regulatory review, there is currently ample opportunity for affected interests to bog down the regulatory process; it is time to create a countervailing opportunity to get the process started.

CALIBRATION RATHER THAN CHECKING

In addition to this prioritization function, cost-benefit analysis can calibrate the stringency of agency regulation. Rather than be a check on regulation, the most appropriate and natural role for cost-benefit analysis is to help find the regulatory sweet spot, the optimal point that is between not enough and too much.

Once we identify a pressing social problem, we must still answer the question of how (and how much) to address it. That is where cost-benefit analysis can again be helpful. We cannot hope to eliminate every risk in society. We can hope, however, to mitigate and reduce some risks through intelligent governmental policy. Cost-benefit analysis helps us achieve efficient levels of regulation by identifying how much of a given risk we should eliminate, so that we spend social resources according to people's actual preferences about risk.

Calibrating stringency does not always mean reducing stringency, a view that sometimes seems to have been implemented by OIRA. Because regulatory calibration is the role most closely related to the checking function currently performed by OIRA, it is important that calibration be understood as having the potential to increase as well as decrease regulatory stringency. In the current system, agencies and OIRA sometimes act as advocates on opposite sides of a negotiation on regulatory stringency, with the agency advocating for greater stringency, and OIRA advocating for less stringency. This adversarial process might be desirable if OIRA were not ultimately the effective judge in this contest. With the antiregulatory advocate also acting as the decisionmaker, however, the result is miscalibrated, overly lax regulation.

It would be wasteful to add a third level of bureaucracy to adjudicate the competing claims of the agency and OIRA. Therefore, both the agencies and OIRA must step back from their past advocate roles and take new roles as collaborators seeking the correct and efficient level of regulation. OIRA must take the first step, by clarifying in words and deed its intent to look for ways to increase net benefits—both by decreasing costs and increasing benefits. Once agencies are taken out of the role of defending regulatory stringency, and instead have to justify their choices against claims that they are both too weak and too strong, a more balanced inquiry and relationship will have been created.

COORDINATION AND HARMONIZATION

From its genesis during the Reagan presidency, centralized review of agency regulation was justified on the grounds that it would coordinate and harmonize the activities of the disparate federal agencies. The original Reagan executive order listed several purposes of regulatory review, among them to "minimize duplication and conflict of regulations" and to promote political accountability.[481] The second Reagan executive order, which set out the annual regulatory planning process, also created a "coordinated process," to "increase the accountability of agency heads" and to "enhance public and Congressional understanding of the administration's regulatory objectives."[482] Likewise, harmonization and coordination were important justifications for centralized review under the Clinton executive order, which seeks "to enhance planning and coordination" of new and existing regulation. Coordination is mentioned throughout the order as a goal of centralized review and planning.[483]

The coordination process under the Reagan administration took place largely under the second executive order, issued in 1985. Under this order, agencies were required to submit "an overview of the agency's regulatory policies, goals, and objectives for the program year,"[484] which was reviewed, compiled, and published by OIRA after being circulated for comment to the other agencies. Whenever an agency wished to deviate from the plan, it needed to "immediately advise" OIRA and submit the new action for review. Except in emergencies, the agency was not allowed to move forward with the proposed action until OIRA had completed its review. Under the Clinton executive order, a similar planning process was put in place. Early in each year, the heads of the federal agencies were to meet to "seek a common understanding of priorities and to coordinate regulatory efforts," and from that "common understanding" to create a regulatory plan "of the most significant regulatory actions that the agency reasonably expects to issue ... in that fiscal year." A working group of agency heads was also created and given the job of "identifying and analyzing important regulatory issues."[485]

Informal coordination no doubt occurred as well during all administrations. Because OIRA sees all of the most important regulations and becomes familiar with the territory, roles, and interests of many agencies, OIRA can play an important alarm-sounding role when regulations may conflict, by, for example, sending out draft rules to agencies that may be impacted. This kind of informal coordination is clearly of benefit to the regulatory system, and could be the basis for a more formal process.

Although these coordination efforts—both formal and informal—are praiseworthy, they often took a secondary role to the checking function of OIRA. OIRA resources have traditionally been stretched thin just in reviewing the cost-benefit analyses prepared by agencies for important rules. In addition, the Reagan regulatory planning requirements largely left the task of identifying potential areas of cooperation and conflict to the agencies themselves, with no centralized review of the overall regulatory effort taking place. The meetings, working groups, and idea exchanges that took place under the Clinton order likewise relied upon agency heads and staff to perform the coordinating role, assuming that once all of the agencies were in the same room, potential synergies would become apparent. But without a sustained independent effort from the center, it was unlikely that actors would be able to coordinate on their own.

The main lesson from the efforts of past administrations is that a central body, given the task of identifying potential areas of overlap, conflict, and potential cooperation is needed to usefully coordinate the disparate federal agencies. This coordination effort must be specifically funded and staffed with appropriate experts. Without these resources, there is a high probability that agencies would continue working at cross purposes, or at least spending too much to achieve their regulatory goals.

Without a centralized body to ensure coordination, it is up to individual federal agencies, and sometimes private parties, to ensure that necessary cooperation takes place. In West Virginia, mountaintop mining—the practice of blasting away the entire tops of mountains in order to get at coal deposits—poses a significant environmental threat. There are several federal agencies, as well as state authorities, responsible for permitting and monitoring this activity. In order to ensure proper coordination of the various federal and state bodies, environmental groups were forced to file a lawsuit in federal court,[486] eventually winning an order from the court enjoining new mining permits and staying old ones. As part of the settlement agreement between the defendants and the environmentalists, a Memorandum of Understanding was finally signed between four different federal authorities—the Environmental Protection Agency (EPA), the Office of Surfacing Mining, the Army Corps of Engineers, and the Fish and Wildlife Service—and the state environmental agency, setting out detailed procedures to "improv[e] coordination among" the agencies.[487] These kind of ad hoc coordination measures, which sometimes come about only after court intervention, are inadequate. Clearly, this is an area in which a centralized body can make an important contribution.

Harmonization is also an important task that can be performed by a centralized reviewing office. As it currently stands, the various federal agencies have little in the way of uniform policies on a wide range of subjects, from how risks are assessed, to the science used as the basis for agency decisions. Harmonization can bring various agencies more in line with one another by creating more uniform standards and policies applied across the regulatory agencies.

Some efforts have been made to increase OIRA's harmonization function. In 2001, Congress passed the Information Quality Act (IQA). OIRA released guidelines in January 2002 and 2004 under the IQA establishing some standards of "objectivity" as well as for the peer review of "scientific information" that the agency intends to disseminate.[488] Though agencies retain some discretion to choose the mechanism for peer review, in some cases, for "highly influential information," OIRA sets certain requirements on the expertise of peer reviewers and other matters.

Placed as a rider on a large appropriations bill, the bill passed without debate. (Many members of Congress were probably unaware of its existence.) As discussed earlier, Jim Tozzi, a former OIRA staffer during the Reagan administration, was a major player in moving the IQA. The IQA has come under heavy scrutiny because of fears that it acts as a mechanism for industry groups unhappy with regulators to put another monkey wrench in the regulatory works.

The specifics of the IQA, and certainly the process of its adoption, leave much to be desired, but the increased role of OIRA in harmonizing scientific procedures is generally a positive development. Only a central review office can develop generally applicable guidelines on the use of scientific studies and expertise. Although agencies should be allowed to engage in some level of experimentation, having a central regulator to collect and disseminate best practices while ensuring that agencies meet minimal requirements can improve the quality of agency decisionmaking.

The "science policy" judgments relating to the assessment of cancer risks illustrate that further harmonization would be useful. Because we do not conduct human experiments to determine whether chemicals pose a cancer risk, scientists both within and outside the agency must make do with animal experiments, in vitro tests, and epidemiological studies. Data from these studies must then be used to estimate the risks posed by a carcinogen to the general public. Several science-policy judgments must be made, however, when extrapolating from these data sources to estimate human risks, including, for instance, assumptions about how to translate high-dose responses in rats to low-dose responses in humans. Because there are no clear answers to how to best make these assumptions, different federal agencies have come to different conclusions, leading to large disparities in how cancer risks are estimated. Thus, the same chemical in the same concentration could be deemed not a threat by one agency, but labeled a real risk by another—leading to uneven levels of regulation across agencies and regulatory incoherence.

In 1983, a major call for standardization of science-policy judgments came from a National Research Council publication referred to as the Red Book.[489] The Red Book identified fifty important science-policy decisions that could have an impact on regulatory standards.[490] The science-policy decisions included whether "positive results outweigh negative results"[491] in comparable epidemiological studies, whether "a positive result from a single animal study [is] sufficient,"[492] and whether "dose-response relations [should] be extrapolated according to best estimates or according to upper confidence limits."[493] The Red Book called not only for agency guidelines, but also for a comprehensive interagency policy with respect to science-policy judgments on cancer risk assessment.[494] The Red Book gave a long set of reasons justifying harmonization, including diminution of biases, the efficient internalization of the latest scientific research, and the promotion of uniformity across agency decisions.[495]

Despite this—and many other—calls for harmonization, no uniform guidelines exist for how federal agencies should deal with these science-policy judgments. Some agencies, such as the Food and Drug Administration (FDA), do not even have agency-wide guidelines.[496] Though there are many areas of agreement—such as a general no-threshold assumption for carcinogens[497]—there are also important areas in which the agencies have different policies. A 2001 General Accounting Office (GAO) report on the EPA, the FDA, and the Occupational Safety and Healthy Administration (OSHA) found "some notable differences in the agencies' specific approaches, methods, and assumptions."[498] As just one example, OSHA and the EPA and the FDA use different assumptions when scaling between dosages administered to a laboratory rat and equivalent dosages in humans. OSHA uses a linear scale based on body weight,[499] while the FDA and the EPA generally use a default of body mass to the three-quarters power—although the common FDA and EPA "policy" is only formalized by a draft agreement that the agencies are not required to follow.[500] Given the large number of similar science-policy judgments that are required to estimate human carcinogenicity from animal experiments and epidemiological studies, the cumulative effect can be significant.

Along similar lines, Justice Breyer, in his book on risk regulation, argues for the need for a centralized coordinating body, noting that interagency coordination efforts "typically suffer from their ad hoc status ... [and] rarely exist long enough, or have sufficient authority, to see that their recommendations are implemented."[501] It is unlikely that interagency dialogue and agreements will be able to resolve these differences. The authority of a centralized body will be needed to ensure uniform approaches across the various federal agencies. This mission is fundamentally important. Cancer guidelines that are followed across the agencies will reduce arbitrariness and increase transparency; generate political accountability for these essentially values-based decisions; save time and resources by allowing the decisions to be made once, instead of during every study; and facilitate the incorporation of the newest scientific research. The importance of the harmonization function must be recognized, and it should not continue to take a back seat to the "checking" function of centralized regulatory review.

There are important limits to how much we want federal agencies to be coordinated and harmonized. Though it makes sense for agencies not to step on each other's toes, it also makes sense for agencies to have the freedom to experiment and develop new approaches to regulatory problems. Over-coordination and over-harmonization could stifle innovation and lead to more drone-like administration of the nation's laws—hardly desirable outcomes. It makes sense to avoid too much coordination early in the development of a policy to allow experimentation and dialogue among agencies. Later on, however, the benefits of coordination grow, and the costs of reduced innovation are lessened. At this point, it makes sense for a central body to ensure that agencies have a coherent overall strategy to tackle a social problem. Achieving an appropriate balance may not be easy, but we have clearly erred on the side of under-coordination and under-harmonization, with agencies sometimes conflicting with one another and working at cross purposes, and with mismatched assumptions leading to incoherent regulatory results. There is, then, an important role for central regulatory review that extends beyond cost-benefit analysis.

DISTRIBUTIONAL ANALYSIS

Because cost-benefit analysis selects regulations that maximize net benefits across the entire population, subpopulations could be saddled with regulatory costs while other groups might enjoy the bulk of the benefits. Over the course of many regulations, some of these effects might cancel out, as the beneficiaries of one regulation could be duly burdened by another regulation. But if the regulatory system as a whole is burdening some groups significantly more than others—or unfairly benefiting certain subpopulations—then there is a clear concern about the equity and fairness of the administrative state.

There are many ways that the distribution of regulatory costs and benefits may be unfair. For example, a particular subpopulation may be shut out from receiving the same regulatory benefits that many others enjoy. In Louisiana, local residents and environmental groups have dubbed the area along the Mississippi River industrial corridor as "Cancer Alley" to reflect fears that elevated pollution levels have resulted in increased instances of rare cancers and unexplained "cancer clusters."[502] If a particular group is repeatedly denied regulatory benefits that accrue to other populations, then clearly the distribution is unfair.

Likewise, the distribution of regulatory costs could fall disproportionately on a subpopulation. A measure that added a small increment of increased safety to a large population but resulted in massive economic losses for a small population—such as the loss of use of some otherwise productive asset—would raise distributional issues as well. Although the regulation may nevertheless be justified, some measure to ease the consequences for this specific population may also be warranted.

Finally, a regulation may effectuate an undesirable transfer of wealth from poorer to richer. It can be the case, for example, that if historic landmarks are preserved, relatively wealthy local landowners benefit from increased property values, but less affluent members of society are harmed when future development is hindered, leading to fewer new housing or job creation opportunities.

President Reagan's executive order was not concerned with distributional matters. The administration was resolutely focused on reducing the total amount of regulation by stopping new regulation and deregulating whenever politically possible. It was unsurprising that ensuring equitable and fair distribution of the effects of regulation fell by the wayside. President Clinton's order did mention distributional concerns, and required agencies to consider "distributive impacts" with "equity" as potential "costs" of regulations in cost-benefit analysis.[503] It does not make sense, however, to think of the distributional effects of a regulation as a cost of a regulation. A particular regulatory regime may have distributional effects that are generally favored or disfavored, but they are not properly understood as either costs or benefits of a particular regulation. Rather, distributional effects must be judged by reference to some framework of distributional justice.

In general, economic analysis tends to disregard distributional impacts, favoring wealth-maximizing regulation regardless of how that wealth is distributed. Consistently with this view, in its *Circular A-4*, OIRA instructs agencies to consider the distribution of regulatory effects separately from cost-benefit analysis. Economists generally do not favor tinkering with the distributional impacts of particular regulations.[504] Rather, the thinking goes, it is better for agencies to maximize the net benefits of regulation, and then for some central mechanism—such as a tax and transfer system—to achieve a socially desirable distribution of resources. That way, we have efficient regulations that maximize net wealth, and we can then distribute that wealth as we see fit. Or, as they say, first, we should make the pie as big as possible; then, we can start dividing it.

For this centralized redistributive mechanism to work properly, there must be an understanding of the net distributive consequences of the regulatory system, that is, how the cumulative costs and benefits of regulations are borne by the American public and its many subpopulations. Absent information about how the large set of federal regulations affects the distribution of wealth in society, it is impossible for a central redistributional mechanism like the tax-and-transfer system to adequately achieve distributional goals. Simply attending to straightforward measures of inequality[505]—such as income and wealth disparities—will fail to take into account the large number of ways that the regulatory system can create inequalities in the well-being and quality of life enjoyed by different subpopulations within the United States. For example, measures of wealth and income do not capture important variables such as life expectancy. Without specific information on how the regulatory state affects the distribution of wealth and welfare across the population, it is impossible for a redistributional program to make up for systematic regulatory bias, leading to serious questions about the fair distribution of social goods.

Unfortunately, very little of this kind of analysis has been done. OIRA, which is in the position to require agencies to conduct distributional analysis, has not focused on this question, devoting its resources to the checking function of centralized review. For example, in the *Circular A-4*, which gives detailed instruction on many aspects of cost-benefit analysis for agencies, a scant two paragraphs are devoted to measuring the distributional effects of regulations. Similarly, the annual report issued by OIRA, which gives the costs and benefits of regulations across the many agencies of the federal government, does not include an analysis of the distribution of those costs and benefits, nor an analysis of the overall distributional effects of the regulatory system.

There may be, indeed, a systematic bias in the process of promulgating regulations in the American administrative state. Throughout the process of setting an administrative agenda; and proposing, adopting, and enforcing regulations, there are many openings where special interests can influence decisionmakers. This would not be a problem if all interests were equally represented, but we know that they are not. Those interests that are smaller, better organized, and better funded will tend to win out in the regulatory "lottery," making it not much of a lottery at all. In addition, there may be reasons why deeply held biases, personal and institutional, can affect which regulations are proposed and adopted, and which are not. The environmental justice movement—which argues, among other things, that environmental goods have been historically distributed on the basis of race—has spent considerable effort trying to fight such pervasive, but sometimes subtle, sources of bias.

Distributional analysis is not an easy undertaking, but it is a necessary corollary to cost-benefit analysis. Cost-benefit analysis, on its own terms, excludes concern for the distribution of the benefits and burdens of regulations. This omission is acceptable only if a separate effort is undertaken to account for these effects. Increasing aggregate wealth is a perfectly legitimate goal of regulation, but ignoring the distributional impacts of governmental action, and risking the perpetuation and exacerbation of socio-economic inequality is not tolerable. Critics of cost-benefit analysis are indeed correct that without efforts to distribute the burdens and benefits of regulations fairly, cost-benefit analysis loses much of its normative allure.

OIRA can make several changes to facilitate distributional analysis. For example, it can establish guidelines for how agencies should conduct distributional analysis, and then require agencies to follow those guidelines, with the same rigor that it uses to enforce its cost-benefit analysis mandate. OIRA has been largely successful in convincing the agencies that they must conduct cost-benefit analyses if they hope to get their regulations through the central review process. It is now up to OIRA to do a similar job with distributional analysis. Once the agencies have incorporated distributional effects into their regulatory impact analyses, OIRA will have the job of tallying these effects, to gather a picture of how the efforts of the regulating agencies are affecting different populations. Once this cumulative picture has been created, decisionmakers in Congress and the presidential administration will have the information they need to counteract systematic regulatory bias. Perhaps most importantly, the public will have the information it needs to hold political actors accountable for their actions—or failure to act—to fairly distribute regulatory benefits and burdens.

One might question why it would be wise to expand OIRA's powers given concerns that OIRA itself will be afflicted by various public choice pathologies. Because such pathologies are omnipresent across the government, however, if the harmonization and coordination of important government functions is to be undertaken, it will have to be undertaken by an imperfect agency. Given its original mission and current authority, OIRA seems best placed to achieve these goals.

Balancing the Scales

Courts must also take steps to take the antiregulatory bias out of judicial review. Hopefully, a recent decision in the Supreme Court presages greater openness to review of regulatory inaction, but many other steps are necessary to balance the scales of judicial review.

MASSACHUSETTS V. EPA

In the fall of 1999, a number of environmental groups filed a petition asking the Environmental Protection Agency (EPA) to regulate the emission of greenhouse gases from motor vehicles under the authority given by the Clean Air Act. The EPA received voluminous public comments, and reviewed a National Research Council report, commissioned by the White House. Entitled *Climate Change: An Analysis of Some Key Questions*, the report found that human activities were increasing the level of greenhouse gases in the atmosphere, resulting in increased temperatures. Nonetheless, the EPA denied the petition.

The EPA gave two reasons for why it would not regulate greenhouse gas emissions from cars. First, the EPA argued that the Clean Air Act does not give it the authority to promulgate regulations to combat climate change, because greenhouse gases are not "pollution" under the definitions of the act. Second, the EPA argued that even if the act did give it this authority, it had made a discretionary decision not to regulate. It maintained that because the link between human influences and global warming could not be "unequivocally established," it was unwise to issue mandatory regulations.[506] The EPA, under President Bush's vision, was more interested in a comprehensive system—that included the participation of developing countries—than a "piecemeal approach" to climate change.

Groups seeking the regulation of greenhouse gases, including a number of states, sought review in the D.C. Circuit. They argued that the EPA had failed in its duty to issue mandatory regulation when air pollutants threatened the public health.

In late 2005, the D.C. Circuit ruled two to one in favor of the EPA. Each of the three judges wrote separate, and largely disparate, opinions. The "majority" opinion, written by Judge A. Raymond Randolph, found that the Clean Air Act "gives the Administrator considerable discretion."[507] Further, the EPA administrator need not "exercise his discretion solely on the basis of his assessment of scientific evidence," but instead, "policy judgments also may be taken into account."[508] Citing the "scientific uncertainty about the causal effects of greenhouse gases on the future climate of the earth," as well as a number of "policy considerations," such as the fact that motor vehicles were not solely responsible for climate change, and concerns that "unilateral regulation of U.S. motor vehicle emissions could weaken efforts to persuade developing countries" to reduce greenhouse gas emissions, Judge Randolph concluded that "the EPA Administrator properly exercised his discretion under [the Clean Air Act] in denying the petition for rulemaking."[509] Writing separately, Judge David B. Sentelle took a different approach, arguing that because of constitutional standing requirements, the plaintiffs could not pursue their case.[510] Judge Sentelle joined Judge Randolph in finding for the defendants.

Judge David S. Tatel, the final judge on the panel, dissented.[511] Judge Tatel argued that the EPA's decision did not fall within an area in which the agency enjoyed statutory discretion. Although noting that courts are "particularly deferential in reviewing an agency refusal to institute rulemaking,"[512] Judge Tatel stated that the Clean Air Act "plainly limits the Administrator's discretion ... to determining whether the statutory standard for endangerment has been met. The Administrator has no discretion either to base that judgment on reasons unrelated to this standard or to withhold judgment for such reasons."[513] Judge Tatel found that, "[i]n effect, the EPA has transformed the limited discretion given to the Administrator under [the Clean Air Act]—the discretion to determine whether or not an air pollutant ... may reasonably be anticipated to endanger public health or welfare—into the discretion to withhold regulation because it thinks such regulation bad policy."[514]

After having lost in the D.C. Circuit, the plaintiffs petitioned the Supreme Court for review. The Supreme Court heard and decided the case, finding in favor of the petitioners and dealing a significant blow to the Bush administration. The Supreme Court's decision in *Massachusetts v. EPA*[515] issued on April 2, 2007, was closely contested, dividing five to four with the court's more conservative members joining two spirited dissents.

The Court held that the EPA had not offered sufficient justification for its failure to initiate regulatory proceedings.[516] It began by noting that agencies enjoy broad discretion to carry out their statutory duties, and that review of agency inaction is especially deferential. Citing *Heckler v. Chaney*, an important 1985 case, the Court found that agency discretion "is at its height when the agency decides not to bring an enforcement action"[517] and that those decisions are "not ordinarily subject to judicial review."[518] The Court, however, also made reference to the long-standing doctrine that, "[t]here are key differences between a denial of a petition for rulemaking and an agency's decision not to initiate an enforcement action"[519] such that agency refusal to regulate decisions are subject to judicial review; however "such review is extremely limited and highly deferential."[520]

In looking at the EPA's decision not to regulate, the Court found that this decision rested "on reasoning divorced from the statutory text."[521] Although acknowledging that the Clean Air Act does invest the EPA with discretion to decide whether an air pollutant endangers public health, the Court found that this discretion was "not a roving license to ignore the statutory text."[522] To the contrary, EPA's "reasons for action or inaction must conform to the authorizing statute." Under the Clean Air Act, this meant that "EPA can avoid taking further action only if it determines that greenhouse gases do not contribute to climate change or if it provides some reasonable explanation as to why it cannot or will not exercise its discretion to determine whether they do."[523] The Court found the EPA's "laundry list of reasons not to regulate"[524] an inadequate substitute for a reasoned judgment based on the statutory standard of whether a pollutant endangered public health or welfare.

There were two dissents in this case, one authored by Chief Justice John Roberts and the other by Justice Antonin Scalia. Justice Scalia disagreed with the majority's determination on how the EPA exercised its discretion, finding the reasons given by the EPA for deciding not to regulate to be "perfectly valid."[525] Further, even if the discretion of the agency to not act was limited to areas in which the EPA found there to be too much scientific uncertainty—the gloss that the Scalia dissent gives to the majority opinion—Justice Scalia would have found that the EPA had met that burden. Chief Justice Roberts essentially agreed with Judge Sentelle that the plaintiffs did not have standing to pursue the case, and stated that Massachusetts' claim that, in the twenty-first century, it stands to lose coastal land from the rising sea level induced by climate change was "pure conjecture."[526]

Massachusetts v. EPA was significant because it required agencies to defend, according to a statutory standard, their decisions not to initiate rulemaking proceedings, rather than allowing such agencies simply to wave their hands in the direction of abstract "policy concerns." It is possible that *Massachusetts v. EPA* is a one-of-a-kind decision, involving special factors like state plaintiffs and a major environmental threat. Still, it provides an example of how review of inaction can be structured, and indicates a potential for a new direction for the judicial review of agencies.

FIXING COST-BENEFIT ANALYSIS IN THE COURTS

By subjecting certain kinds of agency inaction to judicial review according to relatively strict statutory guidelines, the *Massachusetts v. EPA* decision helps balance out the current institutional bias in how cost-benefit analysis is used. So, for example, a court might set aside an agency decision not to regulate, on the grounds that such regulation could increase social welfare. Even after this decision, however, significant biases remain. For cost-benefit analysis to play a truly neutral role in regulatory decisionmaking, the courts must continue to reform how they approach review of agency decisions.

Judicial review of agency inaction—while perhaps somewhat strengthened by *Massachusetts v. EPA*—remains weak. Even in finding that the particular agency inaction was unjustified, the Court reiterated that review of agency inaction decisions is "extremely limited and highly deferential." Although the Court found that the EPA had given reasons that were insufficient, because they did not relate to the statutory standard, it seems that the EPA will have broad discretion within the statutorily proscribed zone. The EPA and other agencies are likely to learn quickly—justifying their inaction according to statutory standards rather than broad-ranging policy concerns. Thus, although *Massachusetts v. EPA* is an important development that will help trim agency discretion to refuse to act, agencies will nonetheless continue to enjoy broad latitude.

The courts have a long way to go before the institutional context of cost-benefit analysis within judicial review is free of antiregulatory bias. *Massachusetts v. EPA* is an important step because it establishes a roadmap that judges can use in the future to guide more robust review of agency-inaction decisions in the area of rulemaking. But courts can go significantly further to establish that they will look closely at the decisions of agencies not to pursue regulations that are welfare-maximizing. In this context, the petition process discussed above can be helpful. It gives proregulatory interests the opportunity to build a record showing that regulations are justified. Most importantly, it creates a context in which courts can review inaction decisions.

Massachusetts v. EPA also does not address the problem of remedies. That the Court did set aside the agency's decision does not mean that a regulation is automatically put in place. Rather, the status quo—nonregulation—is preserved while the agency considers whether to regulate, or offer an alternative justification for failing to regulate. Thus, despite a proregulatory victory, delay—the outcome favored by antiregulatory groups—is maintained, potentially for a long time. Again, this asymmetry reduces the incentive for proregulatory groups to pursue these kinds of cases.

Steps need to be taken to augment the remedies that are currently given to proregulatory groups. First, the remand without vacatur remedy is very appropriate if the victorious plaintiff is a proregulatory interest, and that interest would prefer the proposed regulation rather than the preregulatory state of affairs. Moreover, the tendency of agencies to ignore the non-vacatur remedy can be counteracted. A fairly straightforward approach would be for courts to place relatively strict timetables on agencies under remand without vacatur orders, so that the agency has no choice but to appear back before the court within a fixed period of time to give an account of itself.

By changing how courts review agency inaction and how they treat agencies when they have failed to justify the level of regulatory stringency that they have chosen, cost-benefit analysis could play a more even-handed role in the judicial setting. Both of these reforms will make courts a place where cost-benefit analysis can be used for proregulatory ends, properly balancing the scales between proregulatory and antiregulatory interests.

CONCLUSION

The association between cost-benefit analysis and the institutions of regulatory review has significantly tainted the practice of cost-benefit analysis in the eyes of many proregulatory interests such as consumer groups, organized labor, and environmentalists. This is mostly because of their negative feelings—often fully justified—about Office of Management and Budget (OMB) review. These feelings were especially justified in the early days of OMB review, under Presidents Ronald Reagan and George H. W. Bush, when OIRA was the place good regulations went to die.

The close association of the institutions of regulatory review and cost-benefit analysis has also deeply affected how we view cost-benefit analysis. Most commentators and policymakers view cost-benefit analysis as a way of checking agency behavior, to ensure that regulatory costs do not exceed regulatory benefits.

But there is nothing in the nature of cost-benefit analysis that so limits its role. Theoretically, cost-benefit analysis can be used to increase stringency—by checking to ensure that tighter controls do not deliver higher net benefits than weaker controls. Cost-benefit analysis can also be used as part of agenda-setting, to ensure that we address the most pressing problems first. It can be used to spur agencies to action. All of these functions can be realized if and only if both OIRA and the courts change how they use cost-benefit analysis and review regulations.

The link between regulatory review and cost-benefit analysis has also needlessly limited the role of centralized review of agency action. There are other important tasks that can and should be carried out by a central reviewer—coordination and harmonization are clear examples. Furthermore, a central office is in the best position from which to look at the aggregate distributional impacts of the regulatory system. Distributional analysis lies outside the purview of cost-benefit analysis, but is fundamentally necessary if our regulatory system is to be just, as well as efficient.

Perhaps most importantly, we must recognize that cost-benefit analysis is not a panacea. Cost-benefit analysis does have an important place in policymaking. By quantifying the costs and benefits of regulation in economic terms, it is an extremely useful contribution to a democratic, participatory, and deliberative decisionmaking process, in which politicians, experts, interest groups, and ordinary citizens collectively make decisions about governmental actions. But the rightful place of cost-benefit analysis is not at the center of decisionmaking—rather it should be a tool that serves a broad democratic debate.

Cost-benefit analysis is not the answer to all of our problems; it is an inexact science at best. It must also be augmented with discussions of our values, political debate, and analysis of non-cost-benefit factors like who bears the benefits and burdens of regulation.

EPILOGUE: SELF-FULFILLING PROPHECIES

Overall, this book presents an optimistic view of the future of cost-benefit analysis and central regulatory review. Through reform, systematic antiregulatory biases can be removed, and centralized regulatory review can use cost-benefit analysis to prioritize and calibrate regulatory action. Further, cost-benefit analysis can be augmented with distributional analyses of the cumulative effects of regulation. The result of these reforms would be an administrative state that is more efficient and fair, and delivers more environmental, health and safety protection for less cost. Proregulatory interests, clearly, have much to gain if this vision of cost-benefit analysis is realized.

This vision, however, is sharply at odds with the past experience of proregulatory interests with cost-benefit analysis. They were introduced to cost-benefit analysis as it gained prominence as part of the large-scale effort on the part of the Reagan campaign and administration to vilify the administrative state and scale back the gains made by proregulatory interests. They became justifiably skeptical as Office of Information and Regulatory Affairs (OIRA) during the Reagan presidency gained a reputation as a "black hole" where good regulations were sent to die. These proregulatory interests became deeply pessimistic about cost-benefit analysis, and have alternatively fought hard against its use and ignored it as a legitimate tool of policy analysis.

That deep pessimism has continued to this day. Environmental groups and other proregulatory interests have largely ceded the development of methodologies for cost-benefit to antiregulatory interests and scholars. The result has been that these methodologies have become skewed, undercounting benefits and overestimating costs. Further, in the system of executive and judicial review of agency decisions, cost-benefit analysis has been commonly used to strike down or weaken regulations, but rarely to spur regulation or increase regulatory stringency.

Because proregulatory interests have not engaged in the debate about how to conduct cost-benefit analysis, their pessimism towards the technique has largely become self-fulfilling. Although there have been times in the last twenty-five years when administrations and congressional leaders have ignored proregulatory interests, there have been other times when these interests have had the ears of important leaders in the executive and legislative branches. Unfortunately, proregulatory groups failed to take advantage of these opportunities and the cause of their pessimism—the antiregulatory bias within cost-benefit analysis—became more deeply entrenched.

It is not clear that the American public shares the skepticism of proregulatory groups toward cost-benefit analysis. Although it may be possible to gain some rhetorical advantage by couching opposition to cost-benefit analysis in moral terms—arguing that it is impermissible to "put a value on human life"—the American public is aware that environmental, health and safety regulations are costly. They are willing to bear the costs of these regulations, up to a point. The impression that proregulatory groups refuse to "place a value" on regulation allows antiregulatory interests to portray environmentalists, labor unions, and consumer groups as zealots, seeking "big government" at all costs. Clearly, that is not the desire of the American public. A balanced approach, which recognizes the need for regulation but also recognizes the need for economic growth and prosperity, is more likely to be palatable to the average voter.

This optimistic view of cost-benefit analysis can become a new self-fulfilling prophecy. If proregulatory groups take up the cause of reforming cost-benefit analysis and augmenting centralized review through distributional analysis, and increased coordination and harmonization within the federal agencies, we will see changes in how cost-benefit analysis is conducted. Cost-benefit analysis has been stunted by the bad environment in which it has grown for the past quarter century. Having both sides participate in the discussions holds the promise of leading to real improvements in how cost-benefit analysis is conducted and used.

This book's optimistic tone flows in large part from its reconstructed vision of cost-benefit analysis. But it also rests on two fundamental beliefs. First, that proregulatory interests are capable of moving beyond their resistance to cost-benefit analysis. Second, that these groups can effectively advocate for their new position in our democratic system.

Proregulatory groups have moved beyond old positions in the past, when they have found them limiting or incorrect. There have been several prominent examples in recent years in which environmental groups have embraced regulatory techniques that a few years earlier were widely viewed with skepticism. Most striking is the embrace of economic incentives as a means of achieving environmental goals, as opposed to the command-and-control system that historically has driven much environmental regulation. In the 1990 amendments to the Clean Air Act, environmental groups supported the Acid Rain Program, which is based on a system of tradeable permits for emission of the pollution that causes acid rain. Despite initial, very serious doubts about this approach, the program has proved to be a very large success, cutting down on pollution and achieving regulatory goals at fairly low costs. The experience has led many environmental groups to embrace economic-incentive approaches in the context of climate change. The leading groups currently support a cap-and-trade mechanism for cutting down on greenhouse gas emissions, and a carbon tax has also been acknowledged by environmentalists as a desirable means of fighting climate change. Cost-benefit analysis and marketable permits are conceptually very different, but these examples show that environmental groups are capable of learning and discovering the benefit of regulatory approaches that were initially foreign to them. Likewise, environmentalists and other proregulatory interests have the capacity to see the usefulness of cost-benefit analysis and enter the debate on how it should be done and used.

Finally, it is also possible to be cautiously optimistic about the ability of our democratic process to allow proregulatory groups the opportunity to effectively present their views of how cost-benefit analysis should be performed. There are many reasons to despair about the state of democracy in America—from the influence of special interests, the use of incumbent protection mechanisms like gerrymandered districts, the failure of campaign finance reform, the politicization of the media, and the general quality of political discussion. But there are reasons for hope as well—our political system remains a democracy, with the people ultimately holding the reins of power. That hope is always at a zenith during a presidential election cycle, especially if no incumbent is running. It is during these times that many things seem possible, and the transformative power of democratic politics is at its maximum.

Cost-benefit analysis need not be simply a tool for antiregulatory administrations to stall new regulation and cut back on old regulation. It has the potential to play a much more useful role in the American regulatory state—increasing rationality, transparency, and leading to more effective and efficient regulations. Proregulatory groups and the American public have much to gain by reforming cost-benefit analysis and its place in regulatory review. The question now is whether proregulatory groups will take up this cause, and whether they can make their case effectively to political leaders and to the voters upon which everything ultimately depends. We very much hope that they will.

ACKNOWLEDGMENTS

RETAKING RATIONALITY DEVELOPED out of a series of conversations between Dean Richard L. Revesz and Michael A. Livermore during 2006 and 2007 when Livermore was a postdoctoral fellow at the Center for Environmental and Land Use Law at New York University School of Law. The book builds on research and scholarly work that Dean Revesz has conducted with several coauthors over the last decade. In particular, "Part II, Eight Fallacies of Cost-Benefit Analysis," draws from Samuel Rascoff and Richard L. Revesz, "The Biases of Risk Tradeoff Analysis: Toward Parity in Regulatory Policy," 69 *University of Chicago Law Review* 1763 (2002); Laura Lowenstein and Richard L. Revesz, "Anti-Regulation Under the Guise of Rational Regulation: The Bush Administration's Approaches to Valuing Human Lives in Environmental Cost-Benefit Analyses," 34 *Environmental Law Reporter* 10,954 (2004); Richard L. Revesz, "Environmental Regulation, Cost-Benefit Analysis, and the Discounting of Human Lives, 99 *Columbia Law Review* 941 (1999); and "Part I, Decisions Are Made by Those Who Show Up," and "Part III, Instituting Regulatory Rationality," draw from Nicholas Bagley and Richard L. Revesz, "Centralized Oversight of the Regulatory State," 106 *Columbia Law Review* 1260 (2006). Special thanks are due to the coauthors of these pieces. The Filomen D'Agostino and Max E. Greenberg Research Fund at the New York University School of Law and the Hewlett Foundation provided financial support. Stephanie J. Tatham was an outstanding research assistant.

We greatly appreciate the detailed comments of Nicholas Bagley, Michael Caplan, E. Donald Elliott, Jay Furman, Roderick M. Hills Jr., Sally Katzen, Judge Robert Katzmann, Jerome Kern, Jennifer A. Kozlowski,

Michael E. Levine, Jerry L. Mashaw, Lia Norton, Rick Pildes, Euston Quah, Elizabeth Rohlfing, Andrew Schwartz, Richard Stewart, Kenji Yoshino, and several anonymous referees. We are especially grateful to Kenji Yoshino for his counsel in bringing this book to fruition as well as for his inspired editorial insights.

NOTES

Prologue

1 Elaine Scarry, *Speech Acts in Criminal Cases, in* LAW'S STORIES: NARRATIVE AND RHETORIC IN THE LAW 166 (Peter Brooks & Paul Gewirtz eds. 1996).

2 *Id.*

3 A fascinating study conducted of people with brain damage to a specific region of the brain showed that these individuals were more likely to make strictly utilitarian moral choices that typical people find very troubling—such as choosing to throw a switch to avoid a train accident that would have killed ten people, but in the process diverting the train in such a way that the death of two different individuals results. *See* Benedict Carey, *Brain Injury Said to Affect Moral Choices*, N.Y. TIMES, Mar. 22, 2007, at A19.

Part I

4 This line comes to us from the television show, *The West Wing*, Season 1, Episode 22 (NBC television broadcast May 17, 2000). The episode was written by Aaron Sorkin, and the character who spoke the line was President Jed Bartlet, played by Martin Sheen. *See* TV.com, The West Wing, http://www.tv.com/the-west-wing/what-kind-of-day-has-it-been/episode/809/summary.html (last visited Nov. 15, 2007). Sorkin apparently attributes the line to Woody Allen. *See* The West Wing Episode Guide, What Kind of Day Has It Been, http://www.westwingepguide.com/S1/Episodes/22_WKODHIB.html (last visited Nov. 15, 2007) (comment originally posted at TheWestWing@egroups.com by "Jenn" from notes taken at a Harvard Law School Forum with Aaron Sorkin). It seems to be, then, a revision of

a saying widely attributed to Allen, "Eighty percent of life is just showing up." *See* Danny Heitman, *Showing Up Gets Prize in Little League*, THE ADVOCATE (Boca Raton, La.). June 29, 2007 at E1 (discussing Allen quote and 2001 column by William Safire, confirming the Allen quote and discussing whether original line was that ninety percent of life was showing up).

5 OFFICE OF MANAGEMENT AND BUDGET (OMB), DRAFT 2007 REPORT ON THE COSTS AND BENEFITS OF FEDERAL REGULATION, (Mar. 8, 2007) http://www.whitehouse.gov/omb/inforeg/2007_cb/2007_draft_cb_report.pdf. Economist Mark Crain has estimated that the total costs of regulation in 2005 was $1.127 trillion dollars. *See* Cesar Conda, *A Detour Past Congress: What Bush Can Do for the Economy*, WKLY. STANDARD (Wash. D.C.) Jan. 22, 2007.

6 For a recent sustained critique, arguing that cost-benefit analysis is fundamentally flawed, see FRANK ACKERMAN & LISA HEINZERLING, PRICELESS: ON KNOWING THE PRICE OF EVERYTHING AND THE VALUE OF NOTHING (2004).

7 Richard L. Revesz was a member of the Science Advisory Board Committee on Environmental Economics between 1997–2000. During his time there, when the guidelines were being overhauled, environmental groups were noticeably absent from the Committee's meetings. In off-the-record conversations with environmentalists at the time, a high-ranking officer at a prominent national environmental group explained the absence by stating that cost-benefit analysis was a no-man's land that groups were unwilling to endorse, even tacitly.

8 *See, e.g.*, Safe Drinking Water Act, 42 USC §§ 300f –300j-26 (2000).

9 *See, e.g.*, STEPHEN BREYER, BREAKING THE VICIOUS CIRCLE: TOWARD EFFECTIVE RISK REGULATION (1993); RICHARD POSNER, CATASTROPHE: RISK AND RESPONSE (2004).

10 *See, e.g.*, Corrosion Proof Fittings v. EPA, 947 F.2d 1201 (5th Cir. 1991).

11 *See, e.g.*, STEPHEN HOLMES & CASS R. SUNSTEIN, THE COST OF RIGHTS: WHY LIBERTY DEPENDS ON TAXES (2000).

12 In addition to the criticism discussed above, there are several other more formal criticisms of cost-benefit analysis. *See, e.g.*, MATTHEW D. ADLER & ERIC A. POSNER, NEW FOUNDATIONS OF COST-BENEFIT ANALYSIS (2006) (discussing, *inter alia*, cycles created by shifting preferences); Duncan Kennedy, *Cost-Benefit Analysis of Entitlement Problems: A Critique*, 33 STAN. L. REV. 387 (1981) (arguing that indeterminacy threatens coherence of cost-benefit analysis); Amy Sinden, *In Defense of Absolutes: Combating the Politics of Power in Environmental Law*, 90 IOWA L. REV. 1405 (2005) (same); Cass R. Sunstein, *Willingness to Pay Versus Welfare*, (AEI-Brookings Working Paper No. 06-38, Dec. 2006) *available at* http://www.aei.brookings.org/admin/authorpdfs/page.php?id=1347&PHP

SessID=ec973f15b18bad53b82e02f0ee13a053 (arguing that net economic benefit maximization itself is not morally significant). These kinds of formal problems are interesting in a theoretical sense, but they are not sufficient, on their own, to argue that cost-benefit analysis cannot be useful. However, all of these points are complex, and are not addressed fully here.

13 *See* ACKERMAN & HEINZERLING, *supra* note 6; Steven Kelman, *Cost-Benefit Analysis: An Ethical Critique*, 5 J. GOV'T & SOC. REG. 33 (1981).

14 *Cf.* commodity fetishism in Marxist theory. KARL MARX, CAPITAL VOL. I: A CRITIQUE OF POLITICAL ECONOMY 163–177 (Pelican Books 1976) (1867).

15 In the words of Michael Oppenheimer, former Chief Scientist for Environmental Defense Fund (EDF), "It seems like you're balancing huge uncertainties, so how can you take it seriously." Interview with Michael Oppenheimer, Prof. of Geosciences and Int'l Aff., Princeton U., in New York, N.Y. (March 5, 2007).

16 Steven Shavell, *A Note on Efficiency vs. Distributional Equity in Legal Rulemaking*, 71 AM. ECON. REV. (PAPERS AND PROC.) 414 (1981); David A. Weisbach, *Should Legal Rules Be Used to Redistribute Income?* 70 U. CHI. L. REV. 439 (2003).

17 This argument tracks the one made in JOHN HART ELY, DEMOCRACY AND DISTRUST (1980).

18 Wede Graham, *Dark Side of the New Economy*, ONEARTH, Spring 2007, *available at:* http://www.nrdc.org/onearth/07spr/ports1.asp.

19 TVA v. Hill, 437 U.S. 153 (1978).

20 *See,* ROBERT PERCIVAL ET AL., ENVIRONMENTAL REGULATION: LAW, SCIENCE, AND POLICY 875 (2006).

21 *Cf.* ROBERT A. KATZMANN, REGULATORY BUREAUCRACY: THE FEDERAL TRADE COMMISSION AND ANTITRUST POLICY (1981) (discussing differing perspectives of lawyers and economists).

22 Washington University in St. Louis, Faculty Experts at Washington University School of Law: Murray Weidenbaum, http://new-info.wustl. edu/sb/page/normal/521.html (last visited Nov. 15, 2007).

23 Murray L. Weidenbaum and R. DeFina, *The Cost of Federal Regulation of Economic Activity*, Wash. D.C.: American Enterprise Institute (1978); *see also* Judith Miller, *Report by a Nader Group Measures Dollar Benefits of U.S. Regulations; Professor Defends Study*, Oct. 10, 1979, at A24. For a similar exercise, a bit earlier, *see* Murray L. Weidenbaum, *The High Cost of Government Regulation*, 18:4 BUS HORIZONS (Aug. 1975).

24 *Reagan's Choice*, TIME, Feb. 2, 1981, at 59.

25 *See, e.g.,* Murray L. Weidenbaum, *The High Cost of Governmental Regulation*, CHALLENGE, Nov.-Dec. 1979, at 32–39.

26 *Id.*

27 *Id.*

28 AMERICAN ENTERPRISE INSTITUTE, BENEFIT-COST ANALYSES OF SOCIAL REGULATION: CASE STUDIES FROM THE COUNCIL ON WAGE AND PRICE STABILITY (James C. Miller III & Bruce Yandle, eds., 1979); James C. Miller, *Environmental Protection: The Need to Consider Costs and Benefits*, HIGHWAY USERS Q. (1976).

29 AMERICAN ENTERPRISE INSTITUTE, REFORMING REGULATION (Timothy B. Clark, James C. Miller, & Marvin H. Kosters eds., 1980).

30 Christopher DeMuth, *Defending Consumers Against Regulation*, AM. SPECTATOR, Jan. 1978, at 1 *available at* http://www.chrisdemuth.com/id47.html.

31 *Id.*

32 Christopher DeMuth, *Domestic Regulation and International Competitiveness*, (paper presented at Harvard University, May 1980).

33 *See, e.g.*, Christopher DeMuth, *Constraining Regulatory Costs: The White House Review Programs*, REGULATION Jan.-Feb. 1980, at 13 Christopher DeMuth, *Constraining Regulatory Costs: The Regulatory Budget*, REGULATION, Mar.-Apr. 1980, at 29.

34 Curtis W. Copeland, *The Role of the Office of Information and Regulatory Affairs in Federal Rulemaking*, 33 FORDHAM URB. L.J. 1257, 1264 (2006).

35 *Id.*

36 *Id.*

37 *See supra* note 24.

38 Commission on Presidential Debates, Debate Transcript, October 28, 1980, *available at* http://www.debates.org/pages/trans80b.html.

39 Edward Cowan, *Choice of 2d Economic Aid Reported*, N.Y. TIMES Mar. 17, 1981, at D1.

40 Exec. Order No. 12,291, 46 Fed. Reg. 13,193 (Feb. 17, 1981).

41 Clyde H. Farnsworth, *Move to Cut Regulatory Costs Near*, N.Y. TIMES, Feb. 14, 1981, at 2.

42 John D. Graham, Administrator, OIRA, *Smarter Regulation—Progress and Unfinished Business*, Prepared for Harvard University Kennedy School of Government Seminar on New Directions in Regulation (2003) *available at* http://www.whitehouse.gov/omb/inforeg/speeches/030925 graham.html.

43 Ed Magnuson, *Three Steps Forward, Two Back*, TIME Aug. 29, 1983.

44 *Id.*

45 Chris Mooney, *Paralysis by Analysis, Jim Tozzi's Regulation to End All Regulation*, 36 WASH. MONTHLY 23 (May 2004).

46 Dan Davidson, *Jim Tozzi, Center for Regulatory Effectiveness, Nixon's 'Nerd' Turned Regulations Watchdog*, FederalTimes.com, Nov. 11, 2002.

47 Mooney, *supra* note 45.

48 Davidson, *supra* note 46.

49 *See* Miller, *supra* note 23 (describing report of the Corporate Accountability Research Group).

50 Farnsworth, *supra* note 41.

51 E. Donald Elliott, *TQM-ing OMB: Or Why Regulatory Review Under Executive Order 12,291 Works Poorly and What President Clinton Should Do About It,* 57 L. & CONTEMP. PROBS. 167, 169 (1994).

52 Richard H. Pildes & Cass R. Sunstein, *Reinventing the Regulatory State,* 62 U. CHI. L. REV. 1, 5 (2005).

53 Erik D. Olson, *The Quiet Shift of Power: Office of Management & Budget Supervision of Environmental Protection Agency Rulemaking Under Executive Order 12,291,* 4 VA. J. NAT. RESOURCES L. 1, 31–35 (1984).

54 Alan B. Morrison, *OMB Interference With Agency Rulemaking: The Wrong Way to Write a Regulation,* 99 HARV. L. REV. 1059 (1986).

55 *Id.* at 1064.

56 *Id.*

57 *Id.*

58 *Id.* at 1066.

59 133 Cong. Rec. E3449-01 (Sep. 9, 1987) (Extension of remarks by Hon. Harry A. Waxman).

60 EPA: *Investigation of Superfund and Agency Abuses (Part 3); Hearing Before the H. Subcomm. on Oversight and Investigations of the H. Comm. on Energy and Commerce,* 98th Cong. (1983).

61 *Id.*

62 The fates of intellectual architects of the Executive Order in the Reagan administration diverged considerably. Weidenbaum was seen as playing a more background role in the early days of the administration, having been appointed several months after the administration took office. Edward Cowan, *Amid Stormy Debates, A Low-Key Style,* N.Y. TIMES, Nov. 8, 1981, §3, at 6. At the time, there were several other important players giving economic advice to President Reagan, including David A. Stockman, the budget director appointed by President Reagan who spearheaded Reagan's campaign to cut the federal budget (and who was recently indicted for bank fraud and conspiracy to obstruct justice). *See* Jeremy W. Peters, *Reagan Budget Chief Is Charged With Fraud,* NYTIMES. COM, Mar. 27, 2007, http://www.nytimes.com/2007/03/27/business/ 27stockman.web.html; Landon Thomas Jr., *Stung By A Fraud Indictment, A Power Broker Punches Back,* N.Y. TIMES, Apr. 15, 2007, §1, at 1.

Weidenbaum failed to establish a "close relationship" with the President. Jonathan Fuerbringer, *Economic Council's Time of Change,* N.Y. TIMES, Nov. 17, 1982. Reagan was said to be "underwhelmed" by Weidenbaum. Hobart Rowen, *The CEA Gets a Reprieve,* WASH. POST, Mar. 3, 1985 at F1. After a dispute over military spending in which Weidenbaum—consistent with his views about limiting government— wanted to see cuts in the defense budget, Weidenbaum ultimately quit in protest. *See* Ronald Reagan, Letter Accepting Murray L. Weidenbaum's

Resignation (July 23, 1982) *available at* http://www.reagan.utexas.edu/ archives/speeches/1982/72382c.htm. Shortly after his resignation, Weidenbaum said "On balance, we really haven't cut the budget. When you add that [defense spending] to the big tax cuts, you get such horrendous deficits." George J. Church, *Hope and Worry for Reaganomics*, TIME, Sept. 6, 1982, at 44.

William Niskanen lasted a bit longer, but during his tenure, Reagan developed a more adversarial relationship with the Council of Economic Advisors. Reagan even "seriously considered dismantling the Council." Peter T. Kilborn, *Man in the News: An Economic Adviser With a Different View: Beryl Wayne Sprinkel*, N.Y. TIMES, Feb. 22, 1985, at D1. Eventually Reagan appointed Beryl W. Sprinkel, a "company man," *id.* (quoting Weidenbaum), to the position of Chairman. With that appointment, Niskanen resigned. *Id.*

Miller left OIRA after just one year, moving on to another position within the Reagan Administration, as chairman of the Federal Trade Commission (FTC). He then went on to serve as the director of the Office of Management and Budget from 1985–1988. *Regulatory Accounting: Costs and Benefits of Federal Regulations: Hearing Before the H. Comm. On Gov't Reform*, 107th Cong. (Mar. 12, 2002) (statement of James C. Miller III, Counselor, Citizens for a Sound Economy) *available at:* http://www. freedomworks.org/informed/issues_template.php?issue_id=908.

After Miller's departure from OIRA, the job of defending cost-benefit analysis fell to Miller's replacement, Christopher DeMuth. DeMuth was not always an unmitigated fan of cost-benefit analysis as the best mechanism to keep regulatory costs under control—arguing in 1980 that a "regulatory budget," which set an absolute cap on regulatory costs was preferable in some ways. Nevertheless, in defending cost-benefit analysis against charges from consumer advocates that it was "institutionally biased against health-safety regulation" DeMuth asked, "What's the alternative? Consulting a Ouija board?" Robert Pear, *Fiscal Plan Bears the Tell-Tale Signs of Cost-Benefit Analysis*, N.Y. TIMES, Feb. 14, 1982, §4, at 2 (quoting Mark Green, former head of Ralph Nader's Congress Watch). He also touted its usefulness in forwarding antiregulatory goals, stating that because of the review process, the Reagan administration had not issued new major regulation 20 months after taking office, the first such regulatory drought in over a decade. Caroline E. Mayer, *Regulatory Campaign Falters; Setbacks Take Toll, 'Last Ball Hasn't Been Hit'*, WASH. POST Aug. 22, 1982, at H1. DeMuth also argued that, of all Reagan's antiregulatory efforts, the effectiveness of regulatory review at stopping new regulation was "the major accomplishment of the administration." *Id.*

In addition to his role as the chief in charge of centralized review and cost-benefit analysis of new regulations, DeMuth replaced Miller as the

Executive Director of the President's Task Force on Regulatory Reform. As head of OIRA and the Task Force, DeMuth was referred to as the Reagan Administration's "deregulatory chief." Caroline Shifrin, *Deregulation Falling Short, DeMuth Told*, WASH. POST, Nov. 18, 1982, at D1. He also spearheaded Administration efforts to take regulatory reform from the "regulatory level" to the "statutory level." Edward Cowan, *What's New in Deregulation? The Push Is On for Legislation*, N.Y. TIMES, Oct. 10, 1982, §3, at 27.

Many of these same players who participated in creating the cost-benefit analysis structure have continued to play important roles in the ongoing debate. After his time in the Reagan administration, James Miller III continued to pursue his antiregulatory agenda. Miller has a position at Citizens for a Sound Economy Foundation, another conservative think tank with an antiregulatory stand. Citizens for a Sound Economy, for example, was a member of the Cooler Heads Coalition, which, until its closure in 2006, was a prominent climate change "skeptic" that opposed measures to limit greenhouse gas emissions. Cooler Heads Coalition, *GlobalWarming.org*, Feb. 3, 2004, http://www. globalwarming.org/node/538.

After his career in the Reagan Administration, William Niskanen continued his advocacy against regulation as the chairman of the Cato Institute, an influential libertarian think tank. Cato supports a broad range of antiregulatory work; as a minor example, on Friday March 9, 2007—the day that the EU announced broad new measures to combat climate change—Cato played host to Václav Klaus, the President of the Czech Republic in a forum entitled "Facing a Challenge of the Current Era: Environmentalism." In a web promotion for the talk, Cato noted that "Klaus recently took issue with global warming alarmists, asserting 'Global warming is a false myth and every serious person and scientist says so.'" Cato Institute, Czech President Challenges Global Warming Alarmism (Mar. 7, 2007) http:// www.cato.org/homepage_item.php?id=497.

However, Niskanen has also become frustrated with the inability of cost-benefit analysis to provide an effective check against regulation. Writing in 2003, Niskanen criticized a proposal by fellow conservative commentators to increase the importance of cost-benefit analysis, arguing that the production of "more lonely numbers" will not help curb overzealous regulators. William Niskanen, *More Lonely Numbers*, 26 REGULATION 22 (2003). Nevertheless, Niskanen's antiregulatory views, and his ideas about the overreaching nature of bureaucracies, have become ingrained into the regulatory review apparatus that was constructed during his time in the Reagan administration.

In 1986, Jim Tozzi, along with Thorne Auchter—OSHA chief under Reagan—founded Federal Focus, an industry funded group that fought government efforts to collect data on deaths from secondhand smoke. After founding a lobbying firm dedicated to representing businesses in their regulatory affairs, Tozzi founded the for-profit Center for Regulatory Effectiveness, a conservative think tank largely funded by industry. Mooney, *supra* note 45. Tozzi and the Center were instrumental in passage of the Data Quality Act. The Act, which was attached as a rider to a huge appropriations bill in 2000, requires OMB to develop guidelines to ensure the "quality, objectivity, utility, and integrity of information ... dissemenated by federal agencies...." Treasury and General Government Appropriations Act for Fiscal Year 2001, Pub.L. 106-554 §515 (2001). Groups displeased with government information can make challenges under the Act, a provision that has been much more heavily used by industry groups than consumer or environmental organizations. Rick Weiss, *Data Quality Act Is Nemesis of Regulation*, WASH. POST, Aug. 16, 2004, at A1. The Act has been credited with stopping important regulations including control of the herbicide atrazine—which has been found to cause sexual deformeties in frogs and the European Union has banned as over fears that it interferes with natural hormones—after Tozzi's group, with financial backing from the manufacturer of atrazine, filed a complaint under the Act. *Id.*

After his time at OIRA and the Task Force, Christopher DeMuth continued to take an active role forwarding an antiregulatory agenda. In 1986, he was chosen to head the American Enterprise Institute (AEI), the conservative think tank that has funded the work of many antiregulatory scholars. In that role, he has joined others at AEI at promoting an antiregulatory agenda, with cost-benefit analysis as the tool of choice to trim back regulation. *See, e.g.*, CHRISTOPHER DEMUTH ET AL., AN AGENDA FOR FEDERAL REGULATORY REFORM (1997).

63 Peter M. Shane, *Political Accountability in a System of Checks and Balances: The Case of Presidential Review of Rulemaking*, 48 ARK. L. REV. 161, 168 (1995).

64 Bob Woodward & David S. Broder, *Quayle's Quest: Curb Rules, Leave 'No Fingerprints'*, WASH. POST Jan. 9, 1992, at A1.

65 *See* Susan Reed, *Enemies of the Earth*, PEOPLE, Apr. 1992 (reporting that environmental groups saw the Council "a backdoor through which industry has entered to water down regulations it finds too costly"); Caroline De Witt, Comment, *The President's Council on Competitiveness*, 6 ADMIN. L.J. AM. U. 759 (1993).

66 Thomas O. Sargentich, *Normative Tensions in the Theory of Presidential Oversight of Agency Rulemaking*, 7 ADMIN. L.J. AM. U. 325 (1993) (citing OMB Watch report).

67 Woodward & Broder, *supra* note 64.

68 Elena Kagan, *Presidential Administration*, 114 HARV. L. REV. 2245, 2281 (2001).

69 Woodward & Broder, *supra* note 64.

70 *Id.*

71 *Id.*

72 Pildes & Sunstein, *supra* note 52, at 5–6.

73 Exec. Order No. 12,866 § 2(f), 58 Fed. Reg. 51,735 (1993) ("'significant regulatory action' means any regulatory action that is likely to result in a rule that [*inter alia*] may … [h]ave an annual effect on the economy of $100 million or more…").

74 *Id.* § 6(b)(4).

75 *Id.* § 1(a).

76 *Id.* § 6(b)(2).

77 This view was later bolstered by a piece written after the end of the Clinton Administration by Elena Kagan, the former Deputy Assistant to the President for Domestic Policy and Deputy Director of the Domestic Policy Council, in the Harvard Law Review, *supra* note 68, which detailed how Clinton harnessed the administrative state to achieve his own progressive political ends. On this view, centralized cost-benefit review is part of the tool kit available to Presidents—progressive and conservative alike—to put their stamp on the bureaucratic apparatus.

78 Interview with Sally Katzen, former Dep. Dir. for Mgmt., OMB in Wash. D.C. (Feb. 20, 2007).

79 *Id.*

80 *Id.*

81 *Id.*

82 The final Guidelines for Preparing Economic Analyses were released in 2000. EPA, GUIDELINES FOR PREPARING ECONOMIC ANALYSES (2000) *available at* http://yosemite.epa.gov/ee/epa/eed.nsf/webpages/Guidelines. html. At the time this book went to press, the EPA is again updating the Guidelines.

83 *See supra* note 7.

84 The Center for Responsive Politics, on its website, opensecrets.org, categorizes lobbying expenditures according to industry. In the "environmental" industry—which includes the major environmental organizations—there was $8.7 million spent on lobbying during 2005. The biggest single spender was the Natural Resources Defense Council, at $820,000. By contrast, the "electric utility" industry accounted for $86.9 million in lobbying expenditures in the same period. The biggest spender was Southern Co, with $12.9 million in expenditures; and there are several with over $1 million. Naturally, not all of that lobbying related directly to environmental issues; but, some of it certainly was—for example, Southern Co. has two issues listed under its lobbying profiled "Environment/Superfund" and "Utilities." In any case, these number provide a rough sense of the scope of the disparity in lobbying firepower

between industry and environmental interests. Center for Responsive Politics, Lobbying Database, Top Industries 2005, http://opensecrets. org/lobbyists/overview.asp?showyear=2005&txtindextype=i (last visited Nov. 15, 2007).

85 Interview with Wesley Warren, Dir. of Programs, NRDC, in Wash. D.C. (Nov. 30, 2006).

86 *Id.*

87 Telephone interview with Eric Haxthausen, Snr. Pol. Advisor, The Nature Conservancy (Dec. 9, 2006).

88 *Supra* note 85.

89 *Id.*

90 *Id.*

91 CASS R. SUNSTEIN, THE COST-BENEFIT STATE: THE FUTURE OF REGULATORY PROTECTION (2002). Sunstein has written very extensively on the subject of cost-benefit analysis and risk regulation. *See e.g.* CASS R. SUNSTEIN, LAWS OF FEAR: BEYOND THE PRECAUTIONARY PRINCIPLE (2005); CASS R. SUNSTEIN, RISK & REASON: SAFETY, LAWS, AND THE ENVIRONMENT (2004); CASS R. SUNSTEIN, AFTER THE RIGHTS REVOLUTION: RECONCEIVING THE REGULATORY STATE (1990).

92 Early legislative initiatives focused on the EPA. *See* Environmental Technologies Act of 1994, H.R. 3870, 103d Cong. 2d Sess (Feb. 22, 1993); Risk Assessment Improvement Act of 1994, H.R. 4306, 103d Cong. 2d Sess. (Apr. 28, 1993).

93 *See* Risk Assessment and Cost-Benefit Act of 1995, H.R. 1022, 104th Cong. 1st Sess. (Feb. 23, 1995).

94 *See e.g.* Comprehensive Regulatory Act of 1995, S. 343, 104th Cong. 1st Sess. (Feb. 2, 1995); Regulatory Improvement Act of 1998, S. 981, 105th Cong. 2d Sess. (June 27, 1997); Regulatory Improvement Act of 1999, S.746, 106th Cong. 1st Sess. (March 25, 1999); Regulatory Improvement Act of 2000, H.R. 3311 106th Cong, 1st Sess. (Nov. 10, 1999).

95 As just one of myriad examples, ex-Congressman Richard Pombo, a rancher and member of the "property rights movement" made a name for himself, and earned the ire of environmental groups, for his efforts to weaken the Endangered Species Act. *See All Things Considered: Pombo Seeks to Weaken Endangered Species Act* (NPR radio broadcast July 22, 2005) *available at* http://www.npr.org/templates/story/story.php?story Id=4766959.

96 One of the first uses of this term was by Richard W. Parker, *Grading the Government*, 70 U. CHI. L. REV. 1345 (2003).

97 *See, e.g., id.*

98 Parker cites to some of the press coverage given to these regulatory scorecards, as well as the reactions of several prominent policymakers and commentators. *Id.*

99 John F. Morrall III, *A Review of the Record*, REGULATION 25, 30 tbl. 4 (Nov.-Dec. 1986).

100 For criticism of the Morrall study, see Parker *supra* note 96; *supra* note 6.

101 Tammy O. Tengs et al., *Five-Hundred Life-Saving Interventions and Their Cost-Effectiveness*, 15 RISK ANALYSIS 369 (1995).

102 *See* Tammy O. Tengs & John D. Graham, *The Opportunity Costs of Haphazard Social Investments in Life-Saving Programs*, *in* RISKS COSTS AND LIVES SAVED: GETTING BETTER RESULTS FROM REGULATION (Robert Hahn ed., 1996).

103 *Risk Assessment and Cost-Benefit Analysis: Hearing Before the H. Committee on Science,* 104th Cong., 1st Sess. 79 (Jan. 31, 1995) (testimony of John D. Graham).

104 Another important figure during this time was Cass Sunstein, who while generally progressive, has embraced cost-benefit analysis and many of the methodological suggestions that have come from antiregulatory commentators.

105 *Reforming Regulation to Keep America's Small Businesses Competitive: Hearing Before the H. Subcom. on Reg. Reform and Oversight of the H. Comm. On Small Bus.,* 108th Cong., Sess. 2 (May 20, 2004) (statement of Susan E. Dudley, Director of the Regulatory Studies Program, Mercatus Center).

106 *How to Improve Regulatory Accounting: Costs, Benefits, and Impacts of Federal Regulations, Part II: Hearing Before the H. Subcomm. on Energy Pol., Nat'l Resources, and Reg. Affairs of the H. Comm. On Gov't Reform,* 108th Cong., Sess. 2 (February 25, 2004) (statement of Susan E. Dudley, Director of the Regulatory Studies Program, Mercatus Center).

107 147 Cong. Rec. S7921–22 (July 19, 2001).

108 News Release, NRDC, NRDC Urges Senate to Reject OMB Regulatory Chief Nominee John D. Graham (March 8, 2001) *available at* http://www.nrdc.org/media/pressReleases/010308.asp.

109 *Id.*

110 PUBLIC CITIZEN, SAFEGUARDS AT RISK: JOHN GRAHAM AND CORPORATE AMERICA'S BACK DOOR TO THE BUSH WHITE HOUSE 3 (2001).

111 147 Cong. Rec. S7922–23 (July 19, 2001).

112 147 Cong. Rec. S7908 (July 19, 2001).

113 *Id.*

114 PUBLIC CITIZEN, *supra* note 110.

115 147 Cong. Rec. S7925 (July 19, 2001).

116 147 Cong. Rec. S7926 (July 19, 2001).

117 *See supra* note 85.

118 Cindy Skrycki, *Under Fire, EPA Drops the 'Senior Death Discount'*, WASH. POST, May 13, 2003.

119 Conversation with E. Donald Elliot, Partner, Willkie Farr & Gallagher LLP, in Wash., D.C. (Oct. 3, 2007). *See also* John D. Graham,

The Evolving Regulatory Role of the U.S. Office of Management and Budget, 1 REV. ENV'T & ECON. POL'Y 171 (2007).

120 News Release, OMB Watch, Bush Recess Appointment Threatens Public Protections (Apr. 4, 2007) (Quoting Rick Melberth, representative of OMB Watch, as saying of appointment, "At a time when the American people are growing more frustrated with back-room, special interest dealings at the White House, Bush has bypassed the transparency afforded by the Senate confirmation process.").

121 Robert Pear, *Bush Directive Increases Sway on Regulation*, N.Y. TIMES, Jan. 30, 2007, at A1 (citing primer produced by Mercatus Center and authored by Dudley).

122 *See, e.g.*, Osha Gray Davidson, *Reviews: Priceless*, ONEARTH, Spring 2004.; JOAN CLAYBROOK, PUBLIC CITIZEN, COMMENTS TO THE 2005 DRAFT REPORT TO CONGRESS ON THE COSTS AND BENEFITS OF FEDERAL REGULATIONS (July 29, 2005); OMB Watch, Pricing the Priceless (Mar. 20, 2002), http://www.ombwatch.org/article/articleview/616/1/134/.

123 *See, e.g.*, W. Kip Viscusi, *Monetizing the Benefits of Risk and Environmental Regulation*, 33 FORDHAM URB. L.J. 1003 (2006).

124 *See* Edmund L. Andrews, *Liberty and Security: New Scale for Toting Up Lost Freedom vs. Security Would Measure in Dollars*, N.Y. TIMES Mar. 11, 2003, at A13.

125 *Id.*

126 *Id* (quoting Charles Pena of the Cato Institute).

127 James K. Hammitt, Security at a Price, Letter to the Editor, N.Y. TIMES, March 14, 2003, at A28.

128 For an interesting example of this logic, see David Leonhardt, *What $1.2 Trillion Can Buy*, N.Y. TIMES Jan. 17, 2007, at C1.

129 See *supra* note 6, at 216–19.

130 The irony of Nader, for example, supporting cost-benefit analysis has not been lost. *See* Andrews, *supra* note 124. However, it should be noted that earlier, before Reagan placed cost-benefit analysis in the conservative corner, Nader used cost-benefit analysis arguments in support of progressive causes; in fact, he even worked with W. Kip Viscusi on a report studying the adverse environmental effects of dams in the west. RICHARD L. BERKMAN & W. KIP VISCUSI, DAMMING THE WEST: RALPH NADER'S STUDY GROUP REPORT ON THE BUREAU OF RECLAMATION 75 (1973) (cited in *supra* note 123).

131 Robert A. Simons & Kimberly Winson-Geideman, *Determining Market Perceptions on Contamination of Residential Property Buyers Using Contingent Valuation Surveys*, 27:2 J. REAL ESTATE RESEARCH 193 (2005).

132 See Magnus Johannesson, Per-Olov Johansson & Richard M. O'Connor, *The Value of Private Safety Versus the Value of Public Safety*, 13 J. RISK & UNCERTAINTY 263 (1996) (comparing willingness to pay for safety features in automobiles versus roads).

133 This has been true even during Democratic administrations. *See* Sally Katzen, *A Reality Check on An Empirical Study: Comments on "Inside the Administrative State,"* 105 MICH. L. REV. 1497 (2007).

134 *See* Daniel A. Farber & Paul A. Hemmersbaugh, *The Shadow of the Future: Discount Rates, Later Generations, and the Environment,* 46 VAND. L. REV. 267, 268 n.3 (1993) (noting OIRA's use of a $1 million per life saved value in evaluating the asbestos ban).

135 John Morrall III, PhD, OIRA, OMB Revised Comments (Feb. 25, 2000) (testimony before the EPA Science Advisory Board (SAB) Committee on Environmental Economics) (on file with the authors).

Part II

136 RISK VERSUS RISK: TRADEOFFS IN PROTECTING HEALTH AND THE ENVIRONMENT (John D. Graham & Jonathan Baert Wiener eds. 1995) [hereinafter RISK VERSUS RISK]. The Graham and Wiener book was not the first work on countervailing risks; Graham himself produced earlier work, including a much cited study on auto fuel efficiency. *See* Rober W. Crandall and John D. Graham, *The Effect of Fuel Economy Standards on Automobile Safety,* 21 J. L. & ECON. 97, 101–15 (1989).

137 *See, e.g.,* W. Kip Viscusi, *Regulating the Regulators,* 63 U. CHI. L. REV. 1423, 1437–55 (1996).

138 *See, e.g.,* Cass R. Sunstein, *Health-Health Tradeoffs,* 63 U. CHI. L. REV. 1533 (1996).

139 *See* AEI-Brookings, Council of Academic Advisors, http://www.aei.brookings.org/about/advisory.php?menuid=1 (last visited Nov. 15, 2007), and AEI-Brookings, Scholars, http://www.aei.brookings.org/about/scholars.php?menuid=1 (last visited Nov. 15, 2007).

140 *See* H.R. 3311, § 621(7)(C)(ii), 106th Cong., 1st Sess. (Nov. 10, 1999); S. 746, § 621(11), 106th Cong., 1st Sess. (Mar. 25, 1999); S. 981, § 624(h), 105th Cong. 2d Sess. (June 27, 1997); S. 343, § 636(2), 104th Cong., 1st Sess. (Feb. 2, 1995); H.R. 1022, § 105(4), 104th Cong., 1st Sess. (Feb. 23, 1995).

141 42 USC § 7412(f)(1)(C) (1994).

142 42 USC § 300g-1(b)(3)(C)(i)(VI) (1994).

143 OMB, INFORMING REGULATORY DECISIONS: 2003 REPORT TO CONGRESS ON THE COSTS AND BENEFITS OF FEDERAL REGULATIONS AND UNFUNDED MANDATES ON STATE, LOCAL, AND TRIAL ENTITIES 62 (2003).

144 *Id.*

145 Competitive Enterprise Institute (CEI), About CEI, http://www.cei.org/pages/about.cfm (last accessed Nov. 15, 2007).

146 Competitive Enterprise Institute v. Nat'l Highway Traffic Safety Admin. *("CEI II"),* 956 F.2d. 321 (D.C. Cir. 1992).

147 *Id.* at 326.

148 The NHTSA has proposed increased fuel efficiency for light trucks. *See* NHTSA, Final Rule, Average Fuel Economy Standard for Light Trucks, 49 C.F.R. 523, 533, 537 (NHTSA 2006). This proposal is controversial, and environmental groups have weighed in, arguing that the new standard is inadequate. *See id.*

149 In 2003, Americans consumed an average of 432 gallons of gasoline per year, the highest per capita rate of consumption. The average for all countries was 46 gallons per year, a shade over 10% of the U.S. rate of consumption. *See* World Resources Institute, EarthTrends, Transportation: Motor Gasoline Consumption Per Capita *available at* http://earthtrends. wri.org/searchable_db/index.php?theme=6&variable_ID=292&action= select_countries (last visited Nov. 22, 2007).

150 Whitman v. Am. Trucking Ass'ns Inc., 531 U.S. 457 (2001).

151 *Id.* at 495.

152 *See* Wiener and Graham, *Resolving Risk Tradeoffs* in RISK VERSUS RISK *supra* note 136, at 250.

153 *Id.* at 251.

154 *See id.* at 254–55.

155 *See id.* at 258.

156 *See id.* at 262–63.

157 Sunstein, *supra* note 138, at 1567.

158 Cass R. Sunstein, *Congress, Constitutional Moments, and the Cost-Benefit State*, 48 STAN. L. REV. 247, 296 (1996).

159 Sunstein, *supra* note 138, at 1562.

160 American Heart Association, *Aspirin in Heart Attack and Stroke Prevention*, http://www.americanheart.org/presenter.jhtml?identifier=4456 (last visited Nov. 15, 2007)

161 Sunstein, *supra* note 138, at 1541–42 (1996).

162 *See* Chris Whipple, *Redistributing Risk*, 9 REGULATION 37, 38 (May-June 1985).

163 *See* John D. Graham & Jonathan Baert Wiener, *Confronting Risk Tradeoffs*, in RISK VERSUS RISK *supra* note 136 (citing Christopher Anderson, *Cholera Epidemic Traced to Risk Miscalculation*, 354 NATURE 255 (1991)).

164 *See* LESTER B. LAVE, THE STRATEGY OF SOCIAL REGULATION: DECISION FRAMEWORKS FOR POLICY 15 (1981).

165 *See* EPA, OFFICE OF WATER, CONSTRUCTED WETLANDS FOR WASTEWATER TREATMENT AND WILDLIFE HABITAT, (1993), EPA832-R-93-005 *available at* http://www.epa.gov/owow/wetlands/construc/.

166 *See* Steven Piper & Jonathan Platt, *Benefits from Including Wetland Component in Water Supply Projects*, 124 J. WATER RESOURCES PLANNING & MGMT. 230 (1998).

167 *See* Jocelyn Kaiser, *Soaking Up Carbon in Forests and Fields*, 290 SCIENCE 922 (2000).

168 M. Shelef, *Unanticipated Benefits of Automotive Emission Control: Reduction in Fatalities by Motor Vehicle Exhaust Gas*, 146/147 SCI. TOTAL ENVTL. 93 (1994).

169 *Id.*

170 *See* Graham & Wiener, *supra* note 163, at 14.

171 *See e.g.* Dallas Burtraw et al., *Ancillary Benefits of Reduced Air Pollution in the United States from Moderate Greenhouse Gas Mitigation Policies in the Electricity Sector* (Resources for the Future Discussion Paper No. 01-61, 2001).

172 Dallas Burtraw & Michael Toman, *The Benefits of Reduced Air Pollutants in the U.S. from Greenhouse Gas Mitigation Policies* (Resources for the Future Discussion Paper No. 98-01, 1998) (estimates ranging from $2.88 to $78.85 per ton of carbon reduction).

173 *See* Burtraw et al., *supra* note 171.

174 W. KIP VISCUSI, FATAL TRADEOFFS: PUBLIC AND PRIVATE RESPONSIBILITIES FOR RISK 225 (1992).

175 It could be argued that the attentiveness effect that we describe actually changes people's preferences. We need not separate out that distinction here; it is enough to show that the lulling effect may be counteracted or complemented by an effect in the other direction. The impact of regulation on preferences is a complex topic for cost-benefit analysis, because it is not clear whether *ex-ante* or *ex post* preferences should be used to judge regulations. This is the heart of the willingness-to-pay/willingness-to-accept distinction. While these problems are theoretically interesting, and may in fact pose practical problems in some cases, they are beyond the scope of this work.

176 W. Kip Viscusi, *The Lulling Effect: The Impact of Child-Resistant Packaging on Aspirin and Analgesic Ingestions,* 74 AM. ECON. REV. (PAPERS & PROC.) 324 (1984).

177 *Id.* at 327.

178 In another body of his scholarly output, Viscusi has discussed the ancillary environmental benefits that accrue from various CO_2 pricing schemes. *See* Roy Boyd, Kerry Krutilla, and W. Kip Viscusi, *Energy Taxation as a Policy Instrument to Reduce CO_2 Emissions: A Net Benefit Analysis,* 29 J ENVTL. ECON. & MGMT. 1, 8–10 (1995); W. Kip Viscusi et al., *Environmentally Responsible Energy Pricing*, 15:2 ENERGY J. 23, 31–41 (1994). Nevertheless, he does not consider those types of ancillary benefits in his discussions of risk tradeoffs.

179 Sunstein, *supra* note 138, at 1535. In Sunstein's presentation of the problem—and the methodology—ancillary benefits are absent.

180 In *American Trucking*, for instance, Judge Williams writes: "Legally, then, EPA must consider positive identifiable effects of a pollutant's presence in the ambient air in formulating air quality criteria under

§ 108 (of the Clean Air Act) and NAAQS under § 109." Whitman v. Am. Trucking Assn's, Inc., 175 F.3d 1027, 1052 (D.C. Cir. 1999). Judge Williams says nothing about the legal requirement to consider ancillary benefits, which presumably is no less compelling.

181 It is worth noting that Justice Breyer's formulation of risk-risk analysis in *American Trucking* was that under Section 109 of the Clean Air Act, the EPA Administrator "may consider whether a proposed rule promotes safety overall." Am. Trucking, 531 U.S. at 495. This does seem to leave the door open for consideration of ancillary benefits. However, Justice Breyer's concurrence focuses on ancillary risks, to the exclusion of ancillary benefits.

182 *See supra* note 140.

183 Mark Heil, EPA, *Evolving Considerations of Co-benefits in U.S. Analyses of Environmental Regulation*, U.S.-Japan Workshop on Climate Actions and Developmental Co-benefits, 10–14 (Mar. 5, 2007) *available at* http://www.epa.gov/ies/pdf/workshops/IES_Japan2007/presentations/Heil.pdf.

184 In 2002, an article on ancillary risks was published by Richard L. Revesz—one of the co-authors of this book—and Samuel Rascoff, calling attention to ancillary benefits. Samuel J. Rascoff & Richard L. Revesz, *The Biases of Risk Tradeoff Analysis: Towards Parity in Environmental and Health-and-Safety Regulation*, 69 U. Chi. L. Rev. 1763 (2002). After publication of this article, there was some additional recognition of the importance of ancillary benefits. Most prominently, in its 2003 guidelines on cost-benefit analysis, OIRA recommends that agencies account for both countervailing risks and ancillary benefits. This is generally a positive development, and helps alleviate some of the lengthy concerns that ancillary benefits are given short shrift. However, the section on countervailing risks and ancillary benefits takes up but half a page of the guidelines, and in order to counteract the long institutional bias in favor of looking for countervailing risks while ignoring ancillary benefits, OIRA will have to focus greater attention on changing how analysts approach non-targets risks and benefits. OMB, Circular A-4, *Regulatory Analysis: Memorandum to the Heads of Executive Agencies and Establishments* (Sep. 9, 2003).

185 *See* Wiener and Graham, *Resolving Risk Trade-offs, supra* note 152, at 230–33.

186 While recognizing that there are multiple groups involved in the legislative process, Graham and Wiener reason that legislators will "tend to hear only part of the story." *Id.* at 230.

187 *See,* generally, Gary S. Becker, *A Theory of Competition among Pressure Groups for Political Influence,* 98 Q. J. Econ. 371 (1983).

188 This is the case when existing sources are "grandfathered" in the regime, so that they do not face the same stringent regulation that new sources face. Such a regime exists in the Clean Air Act, for example.

189 Bruce Ackerman & William Hassler, Clean Coal/Dirty Air (1981).

190 *See* Wiener and Graham, *Resolving Risk Trade-offs*, *supra* note 152, at 232–33.

191 IPCC, Working Group I, Climate Change 2007: The Physical Science Basis; Summary for Policymakers (4th Assessment Rep. 2007).

192 IPCC, Working Group II, Climate Change 2007: Impacts, Adaptation, and Vulnerability; Summary for Policymakers (4th Assessment Rep. 2007).

193 *Id.*

194 According to the EPA, "CO_2 from fossil fuel combustion has accounted for approximately 77 percent of [global warming potential]-weighted emissions since 1990, growing slowly from 76 percent of total [global warming potential]-weighted emissions in 1990 to 79 percent in 2005." *See* EPA, *Inventory of U.S. Greenhouse Gas Emissions and Sinks: 1990–2005* ES-7, EPA430-R-07-002 (2007) *available at* http://www.epa.gov/climatechange/emissions/downloads06/07ES.pdf.

   "Electricity generators consumed 36 percent of U.S. energy from fossil fuels and emitted 41 percent of the CO_2 from fossil fuel combustion in 2005. The type of fuel combusted by electricity generators has a significant effect on their emissions. For example, some electricity is generated with low CO_2 emitting energy technologies, particularly non-fossil options such as nuclear, hydroelectric, or geothermal energy. However, electricity generators rely on coal for over half of their total energy requirements and accounted for 93 percent of all coal consumed for energy in the United States in 2005." *See id.* at ES-8.

195 42 USC §§ 7651–51o (2000).

196 *See* Dallas Burtraw et al., *The Costs and Benefits of Reducing Acid Rain*, (Resources for the Future, Discussion Paper No. 97-31, 1997).

197 Ctr. for Biological Diversity v. NHTSA, No. 06-71891, 14,871 (9th Cir. Nov. 15, 2007).

198 *See Regulatory Review Process*, 138 Cong. Rec. S3806–09 (Mar. 18, 1992) (Letter by James McRae read into the Congressional Record).

199 *OMB Interference in OSHA's Efforts to Protect Worker Health and Safety*, 138 Cong. Rec. S3858–59 (Mar. 18, 1992).

200 138 Cong. Rec. S3806–08 (Mar. 18, 1992).

201 *See OMB Risk/Risk Analysis*, 138 Cong. Rec. S10957–58 (July 30, 1992).

202 *Id.*

203 *See id.* ("Within a few days of the hearing, OMB backed down and allowed the OSHA rulemaking to go forward.").

204 *See, e.g.*, Aaron Wildavsky, *Searching for Safety* 59–66 (Social Philosophy and Policy Center 1988).

205 *See* Frank B. Cross, *When Environmental Regulations Kill: The Role of Health-Health Analysis*, 22 Ecol. L.Q. 729 (1995).

206 *See supra* note 137, at 1452.

207 Ralph L. Keeney, *Mortality Risks Induced by Economic Expenditures*, 10 Risk Anal. 147 (1990). Keeney uses some other data for redundancy, see *id.*, but the 7.25 number comes from the Kitagaw and Hauser Study.

208 *Id.*

209 To perform the conversion to 2006 dollars, the U.S. Department of Labor Bureau of Labor Statistics inflation calculator *available at* http://www.bls.gov/cpi/ was used.

210 Randall Lutter, John Morrall, & W. Kip Viscusi, *The Cost-Per-Life-Saved Cutoff for Safety-Enhancing Regulations*, 37 Econ. Inq. 599 (1999).

211 *Id.* at 605.

212 *See* Sunstein, *supra* note 138.

213 *See supra* note 207.

214 The phrase even has its own Wikipedia entry, see Wikipedia, *Statistical Murder*, http://en.wikipedia.org/wiki/Statistical_murder (last visited Nov. 15, 2007).

215 John Stossel, ABC's 20/20, Speech Given at Hillsdale College: The Real Cost of Regulation (May 2001) *available at* http://www.hillsdale.edu/hctools/imprimis_archive/2001/05/.

216 Int'l Union, UAW v. OSHA (*"Lockout/Tagout I"*), 938 F.2d 1310 (D.C. Cir. 1991).

217 *Id.* at 1312.

218 *Id.* at 1326 (Williams, J., concurring).

219 *See* Int'l Union, UAW v. Johnson Controls, Inc., 886 F.2d 871, 918 (7th Cir. 1989) (en banc) (Easterbrook dissenting).

220 *See* Am. Dental Ass'n. v. Martin, 984 F.2d 823, 826 (7th Cir. 1993) (Posner).

221 Am. Trucking, 531 U.S. at 496 (2001).

222 141 Cong. Rec. H2234, 2255 (Feb. 27, 1995).

223 Keeney, *supra* note 207, at 149.

224 *Id.*

225 A summary of recent findings can be found in, Gina Kolata, *A Surprising Secret to a Long Life: Stay in School*, N.Y. Times, Jan. 3, 2007, at A1 (noting that researchers have found that education "obliterates any effects of income" on life expectancy).

226 James P. Smith, Rand Corp., Unraveling the SES-Health Connection (2005) *available at* http://www.rand.org/pubs/reprints/2005/RAND_RP1170.pdf.

227 No statistically significant correlation for income, a weak correlation between wealth and some health indicators on some measurements, but not on others. In general, the health-wealth connection pales compared to the health-education connection. See *id.*

228 *Id.* at 119.

229 The Keeney study uses 1980, so his number was $27,801. This figure was converted to 2006 dollars using the U.S. Department of Labor Bureau of Labor Statistics inflation calculator. U.S. Department of Labor, Inflation Calculator, *available at* http://www.bls.gov/cpi/ (last visited Nov. 15, 2007).

230 OCCUPATIONAL SAFETY AND HEALTH ADMINISTRATION, PROTECTING WORKERS IN CONFINED SPACES: SUMMARY OF THE FINAL REGULATORY IMPACT ANALYSIS (1993).

231 *See* Michael J. Moore & W. Kip Viscusi, *The Quantity-Adjusted Value of Life,* 26 ECON. INQUIRY 269 (1988).

232 *Id.* at 370

233 *Id.*

234 *Id.*

235 EPA, REVIEW OF NATIONAL AMBIENT AIR QUALITY STANDARDS FOR OZONE: POLICY ASSESSMENT OF SCIENTIFIC AND TECHNICAL INFORMATION, OAQPS STAFF PAPER 6-8 (2007) *available at* http://www.epa.gov/ttn/naaqs/standards/ozone/data/2007_01_ozone_staff_paper.pdf.

236 EPA has created a graphic representation of these competing trends. *Cars Are Getting Cleaner, But People Are Driving More.* U.S. EPA, Office of Mobile Sources, *Automobiles and Ozone,* EPA400-F-92-006, (Fact Sheet OMS-4, Jan. 1993) *available at* http://www.epa.gov/otaq/consumer/04-ozone.pdf.

237 *See* EPA, *supra* note 235.

238 EPA's own estimates of compliance with its 1997 ozone air quality standard was $48 billion per annum. Randall Lutter, *Is EPA's Ozone Standard Feasible?* (AEI-Brookings Joint Center Regulatory Analysis 99-6, 1999). Others estimates are significantly higher. For example, Randall Lutter, of the AEI-Brookings Joint Center, estimated that attainment of the 1997 ozone standard by 2010 is infeasible in one city, which would have attainment costs of over $1 trillion per year, and potentially prohibitively expensive in seven other major cities, for which attainment by 2010 would cost approximately $70 billion per year. *Id.* at 11.

239 Tammy O. Tengs et al., *Five-Hundred Life-Saving Interventions and Their Cost-Effectiveness,* 15 RISK ANALYSIS 369 (1995).

240 *See, e.g.*, EPA, TECHNICAL ADDENDUM: METHODOLOGIES FOR THE BENEFIT ANALYSIS OF THE CLEAR SKIES ACT OF 2003 (2003); EPA, CONTROL OF EMISSIONS FROM NONROAD LARGE SPARK-IGNITION ENGINES, AND RECREATIONAL ENGINES (MARINE AND LAND-BASED), 67 FED. REG. 68,242–301 (NOV. 8, 2002).

241 Letter from David Certner, Director of Federal Affairs, AARP, to Lorraine Hunt, OIRA (May 5, 2003) *available at* http://www.whitehouse.gov/omb/inforeg/2003report/346.pdf.

242 Memorandum from John Graham, Administrator, OIRA, to the President's Management Council (May 30, 2003) *available at* http://www.whitehouse.gov/omb/inforeg/pmc_benefit_cost_memo.pdf.

243 Michael A. Livermore attended a meeting on September 14, 2006 when life-years was discussed. *See* EPA, Minutes of the EPA EEAC Public Meeting Sept. 14–15, 2006 *available at* http://www.epa.gov/sab/06minutes/eeac_09_14-15_06_minutes.pdf. Some of the panelists opposed the life-years method as economically unsound, but other members of the panel disagreed, and stressed the importance to them of use of the life-years method. *See also* EPA, Chris Dockins, Kelly Maguire & Nathalie Simon, *Willingness to Pay for Environmental Health Risk Reduction When There Are Varying Degrees of Life Expectancy: A White Paper* (Aug. 22, 2006) [hereinafter EPA *Life-Years White Paper*] *available at* http://yosemite.epa.gov/ee/epa/eermfile.nsf/vwAN/EE-0495-01.pdf/$File/EE-0495-01.pdf (providing background on the life-years method for the Sept. 14 SAB EEAC meeting).

244 *See* B.S. FIELD & M. FIELD, ENVIRONMENTAL ECONOMICS: AN INTRODUCTION 44 (1997) ("The fundamental idea of value is tied to willingness to pay; the value of a good to somebody is what that person is willing to pay for it.").

245 One possible solution to this would be to increase the valuation of life-years as the number of expected years in a person's life decreases. A version of this solution has been proposed by John Graham. *See supra* note 242.

246 EPA *Life-Years White Paper*, *supra* note 243.

247 *Id.* at 7–8 (citing Pratt and Zeckhauser study).

248 *Id.* at 8–9 (citing Eeckhoudt and Hammitt study). This is only the case when people have a bequest motive—the desire to leave an inheritance when they die. *Id.*

249 *Id.* at 9–10.

250 Ann Alberini et al., *Does the Value of a Statistical Life Vary with Age and Health Status? Evidence from the United States and Canada*, (Resources for the Future Working Paper No. 01-19, 2001).

251 The study did find a 30% reduction for Canadians after age 70. *Id.* It is unclear what to make of this fact.

252 Joseph Aldy & W. Kip Viscusi, *Adjusting the Value of a Statistical Life for Age and Cohort Effects*, (Resources for the Future Discussion Paper No. 06-10, 2006); W. Kip Viscusi & Joseph Aldy, *Labor Market Estimates of the Senior Discount for the Value of Statistical Life*, (Resources for the Future Discussion Paper No. 06-12, 2006).

253 Thomas Kniesner et al., *Life-Cycle Consumption and the Age-Adjusted Value of Life*, 5 CONTRIBUTIONS ECON. ANAL. & POL'Y 1524 (2006).

254 EPA *Life-Years White Paper*, *supra* note 243 (citing two studies by Aldy and Viscusi).

255 *See, generally,* John K. Horowitz & Kenneth E. McConnell, *Willingness to Accept, Willingness to Pay, and the Income Effect*, 51 J. ECON. BEHAVIOR & ORG. 537 (2003).

256 *See, e.g.,* Todd H. Wagner et al., *Does Willingness to Pay Vary By Race/Ethnicity? An Analysis Using Mammography Among Low-Income Women*, 58 HEALTH POL'Y 275 (2001).

257 *See supra* note 16.

258 Jonathan Oberlander et al., *Rationing Medical Care: Rhetoric and Reality in the Oregon Health Plan*, 164 CAN. MED. ASS'N J. 1583 (2001).

259 *Id.*

260 *Id.*

261 Michael J. Astrue, *Pseudoscience and the Law: The Case of the Oregon Medicaid Rationing Experiment*, 9 ISSUES L. & MED. 375 (1994) (citing OREGON HEALTH SERV. COMM, PRIORITIZATION OF HEALTH SERVICES: A REPORT TO THE GOVERNOR AND LEGISLATURE app. C-13 (1991)).

262 *Id.*

263 *See* Matthew D. Adler, *Welfare Polls: A Synthesis*, 81 N.Y.U. L. REV. 1875, 1885 (2006).

264 *See id.* at 1885–86. This "time trade off" method is widely used in QALY surveys, although it is not always clear that people understand the tradeoffs that they are making. *See* Trude M. Arnesen & Mari Trommald, *Roughly Right or Precisely Wrong? Systematic Review of Quality-of-Life Weights Elicited with the Time Trade-Off Method*, 9 J. HEALTH SERV. RES. & POL'Y (2004); Trude M. Arnesen & O.F. Norheim, *Quantifying Quality of Life for Economic Analysis: Time Out for Time Trade Off*, 29 MED. HUMAN. 81 (2003).

265 Tammy O. Tengs et al., *Oregon's Medical Ranking and Cost-Effectiveness: Is There Any Relationship?*, 18 MED. DECISION MAKING 99, 101 (1996).

266 *Id.*

267 *See* Pildes & Sunstein, *supra* note 52.

268 Cass R. Sunstein, *Lives, Life-Years, and Willingness to Pay*, 104 COLUM. L. REV. 205, 246 (2004) *available at* http://www.mercatus.org/publications/pubid.1393/pub_detail.asp.

269 Susan E. Dudley et al., *Public Interest Comments on the Office of Management and Budget's 2002 Draft Report to Congress on the Costs and Benefits of Federal Regulation* 12 (2002).

270 Am. Trucking, 175 F.3d. 1027 at 1039–40.

271 *Id.* at n.5.

272 OMB, MAKING SENSE OF REGULATION: 2001 REPORT TO CONGRESS ON THE COSTS AND BENEFITS OF REGULATIONS AND UNFUNDED MANDATES ON STATE LOCAL AND TRIBAL ENTITIES 50 (2001).

273 *Id.*

274 *Id.*

275 *See* Cass R. Sunstein, *Illusory Losses,* (AEI-Brookings Working Paper 07-07, 2007) *available at* http://www.aei-brookings.org/admin/authorpdfs/page.php?id=1380&PHPSESSID=6636fb0327858687a109818771f608d1.

276 *See e.g.,* ADAPTATION TO CHANGING HEALTH: RESPONSE SHIFT IN QUALITY-OF-LIFE RESEARCH (Carolyn E. Schwartz & Mirjam A.G. Sprangers eds., 2000).

277 J. Heyink. *Adaptation and Well-being,* 73 PSYCHOLOGICAL REPORTS 1331 (1993).

278 *See* Astrue, *supra* note 261.

279 The results of several studies are summarized in James K. Hammitt, *Methodological Review of WTP and QALY Frameworks for Valuing Environmental Health Risks to Children* (Paper presented at OECD VERHI-Children Advisory Group Meeting, Sept. 2006).

280 Kenshi Itaoka et al., *Age, Health, and the Willingness to Pay for Mortality Risk Reductions: A Contingent Valuation Survey in Japan* (Resources for the Future Working Paper, 2006) *available at* http://www.rff.org/Documents/RFF-DP-05-34.pdf.

281 Kevin Haninger & James K, Hammitt, *Willingness to Pay for Quality-Adjusted Life Years: Empirical Inconsistency Between Cost-Effectiveness Analysis and Economic Welfare Theory* (Harv. Ctr. for Risk Anal. Working Paper, 2006) *available at* http://www.oecd.org/dataoecd/ 1/27/37585720.pdf.

282 *Id.* at 4.

283 *See id.* at 2 (citing several studies).

284 Cass R. Sunstein & Arden Rowell, *On Discounting Regulatory Benefits: Risk, Money, and Intergenerational Equity* (AEI-Brookings Joint Ctr. for Reg. Stud. Working Paper No. 05-08, 2005) *available at* http://ssrn.com/abstract=756832. It is worth noting that Sunstein augments his views on discounting with a notion of inter-generational responsibility that helps alleviate some of its negative effects.

285 W. Kip Viscusi, *Equivalent Frames of Reference for Judging Risk Regulation Policies,* 3 N.Y.U. ENVTL. L.J. 431, 436 (1995).

286 *See, e.g.,* Susan W. Putnam & John D. Graham, *Chemicals Versus Microbials in Drinking Water: A Decision Sciences Perspective,* 85 J. AM. WATER WORKS ASS'N 57 (1993).

287 OMB, *supra* note 184, at 33. The 7% discount rate is the OMB's "default position." *Id.* Where regulations primarily affect consumption, OMB recommends a lower discount rate—specifically 3 percent. *Id.* OMB also allows for the possibility of even lower discount rates to be used for

"sensitivity analysis," alongside the 3 and 7 percent recommended rates, in the context of regulations that benefit future generations. *Id.* at 36.

288 EPA, *supra* note 82, at 52 (2000).

289 AL GORE, EARTH IN THE BALANCE: ECOLOGY AND THE HUMAN SPIRIT 190–91 (1992).

290 Lisa Heinzerling, *Regulatory Costs of Mythic Proportions*, 107 YALE L.J. 1981 (1998).

291 GEOFFREY TWEEDALE, MAGIC MINERAL TO KILLER DUST, TURNER & NEWALL AND THE ASBESTOS HAZARD 21 (2001) (citing Chief Inspector of Factories and Workshops, Annual Report of the Chief Inspector of Factories and Workshops for the Year 1898 (1899)).

292 MARK R. POWELL, SCIENCE AT EPA: INFORMATION IN THE REGULATORY PROCESS 290 tbl. E1 (1999).

293 *Id.*

294 51 Fed. Reg. 3738, 3748 (1986); 54 Fed. Reg. 29,460, 29,487 (1989).

295 *See* Letter from Robert P. Bedell, Deputy Admr., Office of Information and Regulatory Affairs to A. James Barnes, Acting Deputy Admr., EPA (Mar. 27, 1985), *reprinted in* PETER S. MENELL & RICHARD B. STEWART, ENVIRONMENTAL LAW AND POLICY 104 (1994).

296 *Id.*

297 Corrosion Proof Fittings v. EPA, 947 F.2d 1201 (5th Cir. 1991).

298 *Id.* at 1211.

299 *Id.* at 1218.

300 *Id.*

301 *See e.g.,* Maureen L. Cropper & Frances G. Sussman, *Valuing Future Risks to Life*, 19 J. ENVTL. ECON. & MAGMT. 160 (1990).

302 Cognitive biases and heuristics present a general problem to both revealed preference and stated preference studies. Because people do not process information perfectly, their preferences as expressed in market transactions (or stated preference studies) may not be an accurate reflection of their "true" preferences—those preferences that would be expressed given perfect information and decisionmaking powers. The nature of people's "true" preferences—as distinct from their actual choices—is complex and controversial. We do not address this general problem. We raise the issue of cognitive biases here because it is likely to be particularly grave in the context of long-latency diseases, though we recognize that they are potentially problematic in all stated preference studies and market transactions.

303 Anna Alberini et al., *Willingness to Pay for Mortality Risk Reductions: Does Latency Matter?* (Resources for the Future Working Paper 04-13, 2004) *available at* http://www.rff.org/Documents/RFF-DP-04-13.pdf.

304 *Id.*

305 *See* Michael J. Moore & W. Kip Viscusi, *Discounting Environmental Health Risks: New Evidence and Policy Implications*, 19 J. ENVTL. ECON. & MGMT.

S-51 (1990) (summarizing past work and conducting new study). This particular Moore & Viscusi piece is flawed because it relies on a life-years model to estimate the implied discount rate—problems with the life year model render its conclusions highly suspect.

306 *See, e.g.*, Christine Jolls et al., *A Behavioral Approach to Law and Economics*, 50 STAN. L. REV. 1471, 1538–41 (1998).

307 BRUCE ACKERMAN & ANNE ALSTOTT, THE STAKEHOLDER SOCIETY 141 (1999).

308 Gregory S. Berns et al., *Neurobiological Substrates of Dread*, 312 SCIENCE 754 (May 5, 2005).

309 *Id.* at 754.

310 *Id.*

311 *Id.* at 756

312 *See, e.g.*, Paul Slovic, *Perceptions of Risk*, 236 SCIENCE 280 (1987).

313 Whether workplace risk is voluntary or not is actually contestable, as the circumstances of some job-seekers may restrict their choices beyond the point where "voluntary" would seem to apply. Cass Sunstein has recommended we think of job risk as falling on a continuum, based on a set of factors relevant to voluntariness. *See* Cass R. Sunstein, *Bad Deaths*, 14 J. RISK & UNCERTAINTY 259, 272 (1997).

314 News Release, Nat'l Ski Areas Ass'n, Facts about Skiing/Snowboarding Safety (Mar. 2006) *available at* March 2006, http://www. nsaa.org/nsaa/press/0506/facts-about-skiing-and-snowboarding.asp.

315 *See* Sunstein, *supra* note 313.

316 *Cf.* Cass R. Sunstein, *A Note on "Involuntary" vs. "Voluntary" Risks*, 8 DUKE ENVTL. L. & POL'Y F. 173 (arguing that whether risks are perceived as voluntary or involuntary "often depend[s] on confusion and selective attention" and should therefore not overly concern rational regulators).

317 Maureen L. Cropper & Uma Subramania, *Public Choice Between Lifesaving Programs: The Tradeoff Between Qualitative Factors and Lives Saved*, 21 J. RISK & UNCERTAINTY 117 (2000). In that study, avoidability—which can be understood as voluntariness—was one of several "qualitative" factors studied. The authors found that the more avoidable a risk, the less respondents were willing to pay for regulators to eliminate it. In the same study, the authors also looked at "blame," which they associated with voluntariness. They found that blame was not a statistically significant indicator of people's program preferences.

318 *Id.*

319 George Tolley et al., *State-of-the-Art Health Values*, *in* GEORGE TOLLEY ET AL., VALUING HEALTH FOR POLICY: AN ECONOMIC APPROACH 339–44 (1994).

320 *Id.*

321 The chapter deals primarily with environmental risks because health and safety risk reductions are generally enjoyed by the current generation, while environmental protection measures can take many decades to bear fruit. However, in the instances where risk reduction benefits in the health and safety context are enjoyed by future generations, the arguments are the same.

322 In advance of the 2007 G8 meeting in Germany, President Bush announced a plan to convene a meeting of top greenhouse gas emitting nations to develop country specific goals. Congressman Edward Markey offered the following comment: "The president's goals are not aspirational, they're procrastinational." Deborah Zabarenko, *Pelosi Says Bush "In Denial" on Warming*, REUTERS, June 1, 2007, *available at* http://www.reuters.com/article/latestCrisis/idUSN01327213. The G8 meeting itself produced an agreement on the part of involved nations to consider meeting tough emission standards to combat climate change, but no concrete commitments.

323 *See e.g.,* Johanna Neuman & Richard Simon, *Waxman: White House Misled Public on Global Warming*, L.A. TIMES, Jan. 30, 2007 (discussing study conducted by Union of Concerned Scientists that found government scientists had felt pressure to downplay threat of climate change). *Cf.* Andrew C. Revkin, *U.S. Agency Admits to Link Between Human Activity and Global Warming*, INT'L HERALD TRIBUNE, Wed. Jan. 10, 2007 *available* at http://www.iht.com/articles/2007/01/10/news/climate.php.

324 POSNER, *supra* note 9.

325 NICHOLAS STERN, CABINET OFFICE, HER MAJESTY'S TREASURY, THE ECONOMICS OF CLIMATE CHANGE: THE STERN REVIEW (2006).

326 *Id.*

327 *See* ROBERT C. LIND, DISCOUNTING FOR TIME AND RISK IN ENERGY POLICY 5–6 (1982).

328 IPCC, WORKING GROUP III; CLIMATE CHANGE 2007: MITIGATION OF CLIMATE CHANGE; SUMMARY FOR POLICYMAKERS (4TH ASSESSMENT REP. 2007).

329 *Supra* note 287, at 35.

330 Likewise, in THE STERN REVIEW, *supra* note 325—a cost-benefit analysis of climate change action undertaken by the treasury of the U.K.—the ethical considerations of discounting in the intergenerational context are given significant attention, but a form of discounting is eventually embraced. The authors of the Stern Review offer growth in consumption rates, and the potential of civilization destroying catastrophes, to justify discounting—both arguments addressed later in this chapter. While the Stern Review does take the distinction between latency and the intergenerational context seriously, it ultimately comes to incorrect conclusions about the wisdom of discounting.

331 Cass. R. Sunstein & Arden Rowell, *On Discounting Regulatory Benefits: Risk, Money, and Intergenerational Equity* (Univ. of Chi. Law Sch. John M. Olin Law and Econ. Working Paper Series, No. 252, 2005).

332 *Id.*

333 *Supra* notes 191 & 192.

334 *Id.*

335 United Nations Statistics Division, *Social Indicators, Indicators on Income and Economic Activity*, http://unstats.un.org/UNSD/demographic/products/socind/inc-eco.htm (last visited May 11, 2007). These numbers are for nominal GNP. Using a purchasing power measure, which takes into account the local cost of living, the per capita GNP of the United States and Bangladesh in 2004 were $43,500 and $2,200, respectively, as estimated by the CIA. *See CIA, CIA World Factbook, Rank Order GDP Per Capita*, https://www.cia.gov/cia/publications/factbook/rankorder/2004rank.html (last visited May 11, 2007).

336 STERN REVIEW *supra* note 325.

337 Nick Bostrom, *Existential Risks*, 9 J. EVOLUTION AND TECH. 1 (2002) *available at* http://www.jetpress.org/volume9/risks.html.

338 Susan W. Putnam & John D. Graham, *Chemicals Versus Microbials in Drinking Water: A Decision Sciences Perspective*, 85 J. AM. WATER WORKS ASS'N 57, 60 (1993).

339 *See* K. J. Arrow et al., *Intertemporal Equity, Discounting, and Economic Efficiency, in* CLIMATE CHANGE 1995: ECONOMIC AND SOCIAL DIMENSIONS OF CLIMATE CHANGE 125, 132 (James P. Bruce et al. eds., 1996) ("[S]ociety cannot set aside investments over the next three centuries, earmarking the proceeds for the eventual compensation of those adversely affected by global warming."); Daniel A. Farber & Paul A. Hemmersbaugh, *The Shadow of the Future: Discount Rates, Later Generations, and the Environment*, 46 VAND. L. REV. 267, 297 (1993); Robert C. Lind, *Intergenerational Equity, Discounting, and the Role of Cost-Benefit Analysis in Evaluating Global Climate Policy*, 23 ENERGY POL'Y 379, 381–82 (questioning society's ability to make transfers across several generations).

340 Tyler Cowen & Derek Parfit, *Against the Social Discount Rate, in* JUSTICE BETWEEN AGE GROUPS AND GENERATIONS 144, 148 (Peter Laslett & James S. Fishkin eds., 1992); Farber & Hemmersbaugh, *supra* note 339, at 291; James C. Wood, *Intergenerational Equity and Climate Change*, 8 GEO. INT'L ENVTL. L. REV. 293, 321 (1996).

341 David W. Pearce & R. Kerry Turner, ECONOMICS OF NATURAL RESOURCES AND THE ENVIRONMENT 223–24 (1990); *see* Morrall, *supra* note 99, at 28 (without discounting "all rules yielding continuous benefits are worth any amount of immediate costs").

342 *See* Robert Solow, *An Almost Practical Step Toward Sustainability*, 19 RESOURCES POL'Y 162, 168 (1993).

343 *See, e.g.*, Garry D. Meyers & Simone C. Muller, *The Ethical Implications, Political Ramifications and Practical Limitations of Adopting Sustainable Development as National and International Policy* 4 BUFF. ENVTL. L.J. 1 (1996).

344 1987 report of the World Commission on Environment and Development (often referred to as the Brundtland Report, after its chair, the then Prime Minister of Norway). WORLD COMMISSION ON ENVIRONMENT AND DEVELOPMENT, OUR COMMON FUTURE (1987).

345 Two influential accounts, one based in international law, the other in economics, have been given by Edith Brown Weiss and Robert Solow, respectively. Brown Weiss gives an interpretation of sustainable development rooted in the tradition of international law, in which three basic principles make up the core of sustainable development. Edith Brown Weiss, *Intergenerational Equity: A Legal Framework for Global Environmental Change, in* ENVIRONMENTAL CHANGE AND INTERNATIONAL LAW: NEW CHALLENGES AND DIMENSIONS 385 (Edith Brown Weiss ed. 1991). First, the principle of conservation of options requires each generation to preserve the natural and cultural resource bases so that the options available to future generations are not unduly restricted. Second, the principle of conservation of quality requires each generation to prevent a worsening of the planet's environmental quality. Third, the principle of conservation of access requires each generation to provide its members with equitable rights of access to the legacy of past generations, and to conserve this access for the benefit of future generations. *See generally* EDITH BROWN WEISS, IN FAIRNESS TO FUTURE GENERATIONS: INTERNATIONAL LAW, COMMON PATRIMONY, AND INTERGENERATIONAL EQUITY (1988).

   In contrast, according to economist Robert Solow, sustainability requires that each future generation have the means to be as well off as its predecessors. Solow, *supra* note 342. Solow argues that each generation must use its nonrenewable and environmental resources in a way that does not detract from the ability of future generations to have a similar standard of living. He admits that certain unique and irreplaceable resources, like certain national parks, should be preserved for their own sake, but maintains that the consumption of non-unique natural and environmental resources ought to be permissible as long as they are replaced by other resources such as equipment or technological knowledge.

346 Compare Weiss, *Intergenerational Equity*, *supra* note 345, at 404 with Solow, *supra* note 342, at 167.

347 Compare Weiss, *Intergenerational Equity*, *supra* note 345, at 404, with Solow, *supra* note 342, at 168.

348 Compare Weiss, *Intergenerational Equity*, *supra* note 345, at 403, with Solow, *supra* note 342, at 168.

349 Alaskan Wilderness Sailing and Kayaking Society, *Prince William Sound Natural History,* http://www.alaska.net/~awss/pws.html#anchor600856 (last visited Nov. 20, 2007).

350 Valdez Convention & Visitors Bureau, *A Short History of Valdez,* http:// www.valdezalaska.org/history/shortHistoryValdez.html (last visited Nov. 20, 2007).

351 U.S.G.S., *Largest Earthquakes in the World Since 1900,* June 27, 2006, http://earthquake.usgs.gov/regional/world/10_largest_world.php.

352 City of Valdez, *Port of Valdez Home,* http://www.ci.valdez.ak.us/port/ index.html (last visited Nov. 20, 2007).

353 The exact amount is disputed.

354 EPA, Oil Program: Exxon-Valdez, http://www.epa.gov/oilspill/exxon.htm (last visited Nov. 20, 2007).

355 Richard T. Carson et al., *Contingent Valuation and Lost Passive Use: Damages from the Exxon Valdez Oil Spill,* 25 ENVTL. & RESOURCE ECON. 257, 278 (2003).

356 News Release, U.S. Dep. of Justice, *Exxon to Pay Record One Billion Dollars in Criminal Fines and Civil Damages in Connection with Alaskan Oil Spill* (Mar. 13, 1991) *available at* http://www.epa.gov/history/topics/ valdez/02.htm.

357 Robert Barnes, *Justices to Examine Punitive Damages in Exxon Oil Spill,* Wash. Post, Oct. 30, 2007, at A3. An updated timeline of the case is kept by the law firm, Keller Rohrback. Keller Rohrback, Exxon Valdez, http://www.krclassaction.com/Default.aspx?tabid=1444 (last visited Nov. 20, 2007).

358 *See* Alex Fryer, *Bush's Gatekeeper Weighs Costs, Benefits of New Regulation,* SEATTLE TIMES, Sept. 29, 2004, at A1 *available at* http://seattletimes. nwsource.com/html/nationworld/2002049154_graham29m.html; OFFICE OF MANAGEMENT AND BUDGET, OFFICE OF INFORMATION AND REGULATORY AFFAIRS, STIMULATING SMARTER REGULATION: 2001 REPORT TO CONGRESS ON THE COSTS AND BENEFITS OF REGULATIONS AND UNFUNDED MANDATES ON STATE, LOCAL, AND TRIBAL ENTITIES 48–50, tbl. 9 (2002). Note that the OMB report does recognize the "unquantified" benefits of the roadless rule.

359 *See* Frank B. Cross, *Natural Resource Damage Valuation,* 42 VAND. L. REV. 269 (1989).

360 *See* THE NATURE CONSERVANCY, CONSOLIDATED FINANCIAL STATEMENTS (2006) *available at* http://www.nature.org/aboutus/annu-alreport/files/arfinancials2006.pdf.

361 *See* Carson *supra* note 355.

362 Also some groups had different valuations, *id.*

363 Susan Dudley and Daniel Simmons, Mercatus Center, *Public Interest Comment on The Environmental Protection Agency's Proposed Information Collection on Willingness to Pay Survey: Phase III Cooling Water Intake Structures* (2005) *available at* http://www.mercatus.org/repository/ docLib/MC_RSP_PIC2005- 01EPACVPhaseIIINon-use_050131.pdf.

364 *Id.*

365 David Throsby, *Determining the Value of Cultural Goods: How Much (Or How Little) Does Contingent Valuation Tell Us?*, 27 J. CULTURAL ECON. 275 (2003).

366 Peter A. Diamond & Jerry A. Hausmann, *Contingent Valuation: Is Some Number Better than No Number?*, 8:4 J. ECON. PERSPECTIVES 45, 47 (1994).

367 Susan Dudley, Mercatus Center, *Public Interest Comment on the Office of Management and Budget's Draft 2003 Report to Congress on the Costs and Benefits of Federal Regulation,* 12 (2003) *available at* http://www.mercatus.org/repository/docLib/MC_RSP_PIC2003-11OMBBC Report_030429.pdf.

368 Diamond & Hausmann, *supra* note 366.

369 Dudley, *supra* note 367.

370 Kenneth Arrow's impossibility theorem shows that the aggregation of preferences may not follow basic rationality constraints. Kenneth J. Arrow, *A Difficulty in the Concept of Social Welfare*, 58 J. POL. ECON. 328 (1950).

371 This technique is difficult to implement in the regulatory process. First, it is somewhat tautological; past decisions are used as the justification for future decisions, when those past decisions themselves need justification. Furthermore, in our flawed democratic system, there is no guarantee that the actions of the people's representatives are true representations of the people's aggregate willingness to pay to protect those natural resources. Because of imperfections in the political process, a legislature or agency might over or under protect, and yet remain in office in the future. Nevertheless, there is a theoretical technique for measuring existence value—through a perfect democratic political process.

372 There are other challenges that we do not discuss here. For example, some have argued that even if existence value is real, it cannot bear on a person's welfare, and therefore, preferences for existence value should be excluded from the cost-benefit calculation. One version of this argument is put forward by Matthew D. Adler and Eric A. Posner in their recent book *New Foundations of Cost-Benefit Analysis* in which they support a non-economic justification for cost-benefit analysis as a relatively cheap procedure to identify welfare increasing governmental projects. They argue that in order for a preference to be relevant, it must concern a state of the world that affects the preference holder. Because Adler and Posner reject the economic justification of cost-benefit analysis their arguments are not directly addressed here.

373 For just one example of an industry group using problems with contingent valuation studies to attack the use of existence value, see Letter from National Roofing Contractors Association to Lorraine Hunt, OIRA, (May 5, 2003) (on file with authors) (arguing that contingent valuation "is so fundamentally flawed as to warrant exclusion altogether").

374 W.H. Desvousges et al., *Measuring Natural Resource Damages with Contingent Valuation: Tests of Validity and Reliability, in* CONTINGENT VALUATION: A CRITICAL ASSESSMENT (Jerry A. Hausman ed., 1993).

375 Ohio v. Dept. of Interior, 880 F.2d 432 (D.C. Cir. 1989).

376 *See, e.g.*, CONTINGENT VALUATION *supra* note 374 (collection of paper and comments from an industry funded conference held in Washington D.C. in April of 1992).

377 Report of the NOAA Panel on Contingent Valuation, 58 Fed. Reg. 4601, 1, app. 1, app. 5 (Jan. 15, 1993).

378 *Id.*

379 *Id.*

380 *See, e.g.*, EPA, CONTROL OF EMISSIONS FROM NONROAD LARGE SPARK-IGNITION ENGINES AND RECREATIONAL ENGINES (MARINE AND LAND-BASED), 67 Fed. Reg. 68,242–301 (Nov. 8, 2002); U.S. EPA, FINAL REGULATORY SUPPORT DOCUMENT (RSD): CONTROL OF EMISSIONS FROM UNREGULATED NONROAD ENGINES (2002), http://www.epa.gov/otaq/regs/nonroad/2002/r02022.pdf; EPA, TECHNICAL ADDENDUM: METHODOLOGIES FOR THE BENEFIT ANALYSIS OF THE CLEAR SKIES ACT OF 2003 (2003), http://www.epa.gov/air/clearskies/tech_adden.pdf.

381 Much has been written about the ozone layer and the Montreal Protocol. *See e.g.* RICHARD A. BENEDICT, OZONE DIPLOMACY: NEW DIRECTIONS IN SAFEGUARDING THE PLANET (1991); K. MADHAVA SARMA, STEPHEN O. ANDERSEN & LANI SINCLAIR, PROTECTING THE OZONE LAYER: THE UNITED NATIONS HISTORY (2002).

382 F. Sherwood Rowland Autobiography, http://nobelprize.org/nobel_prizes/chemistry/laureates/1995/rowland-autobio.html (last visited Nov. 20 2007).

383 Mario J. Molina, & F. Sherwood Rowland, *Stratospheric Ozone Sink for Chlorofluoromethanes: Chlorine Atom Catalyzed Destruction of Ozone*, 249 NATURE 810 (1974).

384 Walter Sullivan, *Tests Show Aerosol Gases May Pose Threat to Earth*, N.Y. TIMES Sept. 26, 1974, at A1.

385 NATIONAL ACADEMY OF SCIENCES, HALOCARBONS: EFFECTS ON STRATOSPHERIC OZONE (1976); NATIONAL ACADEMY OF SCIENCES, PROTECTION AGAINST DEPLETION OF STRATOSPHERIC OZONE BY CHLOROFLUOROCARBONS (1979); NATIONAL ACADEMY OF SCIENCES, CAUSES AND EFFECTS OF STRATOSPHERIC OZONE DEPLETION: AN UPDATE (1982); NATIONAL ACADEMY OF SCIENCES, CAUSES AND EFFECTS OF STRATOSPHERIC OZONE DEPLETION: UPDATE 1983 (1984).

386 EPA, Fully Halogenated Chlorofluoroalkanes: Final Rules, 43 Fed. Reg. 11,318 (Mar. 17, 1978); FDA, Certain Fluorocarbons (Chlorofluorocarbons) in Food, Food Additives, Drug, Animal Food,

Animal Drug, Cosmetic and Medical Device Products as Propellants in Self Pressurized Containers—Prohibition on Use, 43 Fed. Reg. 11,301 (Mar. 17, 1978).

387 Edward Stevens Atkinson Jr., *Chlorofluorocarbons and Stratospheric Ozone: Regulatory Background,* 36:3 THE AM. STATISTICIAN (Part 2: Proceedings of the Sixth Symposium on Statistics and the Env.) 301 (1982).

388 One interesting fact is that, for a time, the science on the connection between CFC emissions and the ozone layer began pointing in the wrong direction—toward less of a link. This science was eventually overruled by later findings, but points to a particular kind of pathology in the scientific development of knowledge, especially problematic in the area of environmental policymaking, that Professor Oppenheimer has dubbed "negative learning." *See* Michael Oppenheimer, *Negative Learning* in CLIMATE CHANGE [forthcoming].

389 Frank Camm et al., Social Cost of Technical Control Options to Reduce Emissions of Potential Ozone Depleters in the UNITED STATES, RAND N-2440-EPA (1986).

390 James K. Hammitt, *Are the Costs of Proposed Environmental Regulations Overestimated? Evidence from the CFC Phaseout,* 16 ENVTL. & RESOURCE ECON. 281 (2000).

391 *Id.*

392 Sally Katzen, *Cost-Benefit Analysis: Where Should We Go from Here?,* 33 FORDHAM URB. L.J. 1313 (2006).

393 *Id.* at 1315.

394 Hart Hodges, *Falling Prices: Cost of Complying with Environmental Regulations Almost Always Less Than Advertised* (Econ. Policy Institute Briefing Paper 1997) (citing Keith Mason, *The Economic Impact,* EPA J. (Jan/Feb. 1991)).

395 ROBERT V. PERCIVAL ET AL., ENVIRONMENTAL REGULATION 561 fig.4.8 (2d ed. 1996).

396 *Mandates Information Act: Hearing Before the S. Gov't Affairs Comm.,* 105th Cong. (1998) (statement of Sharon Buccino, Legislative Counsel, Natural Resources Defense Council (citing statement by L.A. Iacocca, Executive Vice President, Ford Motor Company, Sept. 9, 1970)).

397 John Anderson & Todd Sherwood, EPA, Comparison of EPA and Other Estimates of Mobile Source Rule Costs to Actual Price Changes (Presentation at the SAE Government Industry Meeting, D.C. (May 14, 2002).

398 Stockholm Environment Institute, *Costs and Strategies Presented by Industry During Negotiations of Environmental Regulations* (1999) *available at* http://www.york.ac.uk/inst/sei/pubs/ministry.pdf.

399 *See* National Institute of Environmental Health Sciences, Alphabetical Index of Health Topics, Dry Cleaners—Perchloroethylene, http://www.

niehs.nih.gov/external/faq/dryclean.htm (last visited July 3, 2007) (on file with author).

400 Lauraine G. Chestnut & David M. Mills, *A Fresh Look at the Benefits and Costs of the U.S. Acid Rain Program*, 77 J. ENVTL. MGMT. 252, 252–55 (2005).

401 EPA, ACID RAIN PROGRAM 2005 PROGRESS REPORT 10 (2006) *available at* http://www.epa.gov/airmarkets/progress/docs/2005report.pdf.

402 *Id.*

403 Chestnut & Mills, *supra* note 400, at 255.

404 Michael Grubb et al., *Economics of Changing Course: Implications of Adaptability and Inertia for Optimal Climate Policy*, 23 ENERGY POLICY 417 (1995) (discussing dynamic adaptation of firms to environmental rules).

405 Some find the idea that regulation can cut down on operating costs, improve products, or lead to more efficient internal processes to be implausible. They argue instead that the resources dedicated to environmental compliance cannot be used by a firm to increase productivity. In this view, business managers know best how to increase productivity, and it is unlikely that taking decisions about how firm resources will be spent out of their hands will lead to productivity gains. *See* Adam Jaffe & Karen L. Palmer, *Environmental Regulation and Innovation: A Panel Data Study*, 79 REV. ECON. & STATISTICS 610 (1997); Adam Jaffee et al., *Environmental Regulation and the Competitiveness of U.S. Manufacturing: What Does the Evidence Tell Us?* 33 J. ECON. LITERATURE 132 (1995). In a perfect marketplace, regulation could not lead to lower costs or higher profits, because all firms would be operating at maximum efficiency. In the imperfect real world marketplace, Porter notes that regulation can have several effects which spur innovation, including "signal[ing] companies about likely resource inefficiencies," "raising corporate awareness," "reducing uncertainty," "overcome[ing] organizational inertia" and "foster[ing] creative thinking." Michael E. Porter & Claas van der Linde, *Toward a New Conception of the Environment-Competitiveness Relationship*, 9 J. ECON. PERSPECTIVES 97, 99–100 (1995). He also argues that "stringent regulation can ... produce greater innovation and innovation offsets than lax regulation" because lax regulation "can be dealt with ... without innovation, and often with 'end-of-pipe' or secondary treatment solutions," while with more stringent regulation "compliance requires more fundamental solutions, like reconfiguring products and processes." *Id.* at 100. *See generally* Michael E. Porter & Claas van der Linde, *Green and Competitive: Ending the Stalemate, in* THE EARTHSCAN READER IN BUSINESS AND THE ENVIRONMENT (Richard Welford & Richard Starkey eds. 1996). There are anecdotal examples of compliance with environmental programs leading to cost

reductions—one cited by Porter involved an EPA program to work with businesses to reduce their energy consumption, which ultimately found that many steps which EPA recommended would save businesses money. *See id.*

406 Sumit K Majumdar & Alfred A. Marcus, *Rules versus Discretion: The Productivity Consequences of Flexible Regulation*, 44 ACADEMY OF MGMT. J. 170 (2001).

407 *See* Hodges, *supra* note 394.

408 William K. Reilly, *EPA's Cost Underruns*, WASH. POST, Oct. 14, 2003, at A23.

409 *See* ChemInfo Services, *A Retrospective Evaluation of Control Measures for Chlorinated Substances* (2000) (report to Environment Canada and Ontario Ministry of Energy, Science, and Technology).

410 Larry Dale et al., *Retrospective Evaluation of Declining Prices for Energy Efficient Appliances*, 9 ACEEE SUMMER STUDY ON ENERGY EFFICIENT BUILDING–PROC. 55 (2002).

411 U.S. CONGRESS, OFFICE OF TECHNOLOGY ASSESSMENT, GAUGING CONTROL TECHNOLOGY AND REGULATORY IMPACTS IN OCCUPATIONAL SAFETY AND HEALTH: AN APPRAISAL OF OSHA'S ANALYTIC APPROACH (1995).

412 Winston Harrington et al., *The Enhanced I/M Program in Arizona: Costs, Effectiveness, and a Comparison with Pre-regulatory Estimates*, (Resources for the Future Discussion Paper No. 99-37, 1999).

413 *See, e.g.*, T. Cackette, *The Cost of Emission Controls, Motor Vehicles and Fuels: Two Case Studies*, Presentation at the 1998 Summer Symposium of the EPA Center on Airborne Organics (July 9–10, 1998).

414 The OMB study also found that the benefits of regulation—like the number of lives saved—also tended to be overestimated, in part because analysts assumed full compliance with regulatory mandates. *See* OFFICE OF MANAGEMENT AND BUDGET, VALIDATING REGULATORY ANALYSIS: REPORT TO CONGRESS ON THE COSTS AND BENEFITS OF FEDERAL REGULATIONS AND UNFUNDED MANDATES ON STATE, LOCAL, AND TRIBAL ENTITIES 42 (2005).

415 *Id.* at 42.

416 *Id.* at 48.

417 *Id.* at 42.

418 Like the OMB study, the Harrington study also found that regulatory benefits were overestimated, although Harrington and his colleagues found that the ratio of benefit to costs was systematically underestimated, the opposite of the OMB finding. Winston Harrington et al., *On the Accuracy of Regulatory Cost Estimates*, 19 J. POL'Y ANAL. & MGMT. 297 (2000).

419 *Id.*

420 *Id.*

421 *Id.*

422 *Id.*

423 Robert W. Hahn & Paul C. Tetlock, *The Evolving Role of Economic Analysis in Regulatory Decision Making* (unpublished manuscript, on file with author).

424 *See supra* note 414, at 50.

425 *See* Michaele B. Abramowicz, *Information Markets, Administrative Decisionmaking, and Predictive Cost-Benefit Analysis* (George Mason Law & Econ. Research Paper No. 03-36, 2003) (discussing potential for "predictive cost-benefit analysis" using information markets) *available at* http://papers.ssrn.com/sol3/papers.cfm?abstract_id=430640.

426 David Leonhardt, *Odds Are, They'll Know '08 Winner*, N.Y. TIMES, Feb. 14, 2007, at C1.

427 Rana Foroohar, *A New 'Wind Tunnel' for Companies*. NEWSWEEK, Oct. 20, 2003 at 44.

Part III

428 These expanded transparency measures built on less formal revisions carried out in the administration of George H.W. Bush.

429 *See* Jo Becker & Barton Gellman, *Angler: The Cheney Vice Presidency*, WASH. POST, June 24–27, 2007 (four-part series examining Cheney's Vice-Presidency) *available at* http://blog.washingtonpost.com/cheney/.

430 Under certain administrations, OIRA has occasionally used cost-benefit analysis to increase regulatory stringency. Email from Sally Katzen, former Dep. Dr. for Mgmt. OMB (Jan. 7, 2008). However, even taking these instances into account, OIRA tends to review for undue stringency, rather than undue laxity.

431 It is possible that agencies will act strategically in the face of OIRA review by submitting overly strict regulations, in anticipation of having OIRA insist on reduced stringency. If this is the case, an economically efficient level of regulation may result, although the importance of OIRA's role is unclear. If anything, the interaction between OIRA and the agency would tend to introduce error into the decisionmaking process, as each agency attempts to out maneuver the other. There may be some benefit to this arrangement for administration officials that wish to obscure lines of responsibility, either as a way of short-circuiting special interest pressure, or to avoid public scrutiny. The general tendency, however, is to reduce the transparency of agency decisionmaking.

432 GENERAL ACCOUNTING OFFICE (GAO), OMB'S ROLE IN REVIEWS OF AGENCIES DRAFT RULES AND THE TRANSPARENCY OF THOSE REVIEWS 76–78 (2003).

433 *Id.* at 87.

434 David M. Driesen, *Is Cost-Benefit Analysis Neutral?*, 77 U. COLO. L. REV. 355, 369 (2006).

435 Oliver A. Houck, *President X and the New (Approved) Decisionmaking*, 36 AM. U. L. REV. 535, 542 (1987).

436 Deregulation can have an "annual effect on the economy of $100 million or more" Exec. Order No. 12,866 §3(f)(1). Therefore they fall under Clinton's Executive Order.

437 *OMB Circular A-4, supra* note 287, at 1.

438 Sally Katzen, former Dep. Dir. For Mgmt., OMB, Seminar and Subsequent Discussion at Georgetown University Law Center (Oct. 3, 2007).

439 OMB, *supra* note 358, at 21–22.

440 Letter from John D. Graham, Administrator, OIRA, to John Henshaw, Assistant Secretary of Labor, Occupational Health and Safety Administration (Sept. 18, 2001) *available at* http://www.reginfo.gov/public/prompt/osha_prompt_letter.html.

441 Letter from John D. Graham, Administrator, OIRA, to Benjamin Grumbles, Acting Assistant Administrator, Environmental Protection Agency (Apr. 16, 2004) *available at* http://www.reginfo.gov/public/prompt/epa_beach-act-2000.pdf.

442 John D. Graham, Presidential Management of the Regulatory State, Address Before Weidenbaum Center Forum (Dec. 17, 2001) *available at* http://www.whitehouse.gov/omb/inforeg/graham_speech121701.html.

443 GAO, *supra* note 432, at 109.

444 OMB Watch, *The Problems with Any OIRA Hit List*, Jan. 10, 2005 *available at* http://www.ombwatch.org/article/articleview/2596/1/309?TopicID=3.

445 GAO, *supra* note 432, at 103.

446 *Id.*

447 Public interest groups, naturally, put pressure on agencies to initiate new rules, but there is not a formalized and institutionalized mechanism akin to the "hit list" to deregulate.

448 *Id.* at 46.

449 Richard B. Stewart, *The Reformation of American Administrative Law*, 88 HARV. L. REV. 1669, 1675 (1975).

450 Administrative Procedure Act 5 U.S.C. §706(2)(A); *see also* Lisa Schultz Bressman, *Judicial Review of Agency Inaction: An Arbitrariness Approach*, 79 N.Y.U. L. REV. 1657 (2004).

451 *See, e.g.*, Corrosion Proof Fittings v. EPA, 947 F.2d 1201 (5th Cir. 1991) (holding that "[t]he substantial evidence standard mandated by TSCA [the Toxic Substances Control Act] is generally considered to be more rigorous than the arbitrary and capricious standard normally applied to informal rulemaking," under the APA).

452 Webster v. Doe, 486 U.S. 592 (1988).

453 *See, e.g.*, Thomas O. McGarity, *Some Thoughts on "Deossifying" The Rulemaking Process*, 441 Duke L.J. 1385 (1992); Richard J. Pierce, Jr., *Seven Ways to Deossify Agency Rulemaking*, 47 Admin. L. Rev. 59 (1995).

454 Cass R. Sunstein, *Cost-Benefit Default Principles*, 99 Mich. L. Rev. 1651 (2001).

455 Corrosion Proof Fittings v. EPA, 947 F.2d 1201 (5th Cir. 1991)

456 *Id.* at 1216.

457 *Id.* at 1216.

458 *Id.* at 1218.

459 *Id.* at 1218.

460 For a recent example where the D.C. Circuit agreed with plaintiff Public Citizen in finding that a cost-benefit analysis used by the Federal Motor Carrier Safety Administration was inadequate, leading to an unjustifiably lax rule regarding the hours of long-haul truck drivers, see Owner-Operator Indep. Drivers Ass'n Inc. v. Fed. Motor Carrier Safety Admin., No. 06-1035 (D.C. Cir. July 24, 2007).

461 This presumption would be rebuttable. *See* Sunstein, *supra* note 454, at 1694–98.

462 The first principle that stands in the way of judicial review is a doctrine of nonreviewability for agency non-enforcement decisions. In *Heckler v. Chaney*, 470 U.S. 821 (1985), the Supreme Court held that courts would not examine the non-enforcement decisions of administrative agencies. A second doctrine that limits judicial review of agency inaction is standing. The standing requirements are often harder to overcome for agency inaction than for agency action. The most important case limiting the ability of environmental groups to gain entrance to the courts in recent years, *Lujan v. Defenders of Wildlife*, 504 U.S. 555 (1992), was a case of agency inaction. In that case, the Court held that the plaintiffs lacked standing for a number of reasons, including because the groups had nothing more than a "generally available grievance about government." *Id.* at 573. The Court held that the Constitution sets limits on the kinds of cases that can be heard by the courts, and that even Congress could not create jurisdiction for private parties to bring suits to litigate generalized grievances.

463 While the *Chaney* doctrine of the non-reviewability of agency enforcement decisions does not apply to review of denial for petitions for rulemaking, the review of such denials is very deferential. Am. Horse Protection Ass'n, Inc. v. Lyng, 812 F.2d 1, 3–4 (D.C. Cir. 1987). Court's "will overturn an agency's decision not to initiate a rulemaking only for compelling cause, such as plain error of law or a fundamental change in the factual premises previously considered by the agency." Nat'l Customs Brokers & Forwarders Ass'n v. United States, 883 F.2d 93, 96–97 (D.C. Cir. 1989).

464 Matthew C. Stephenson, *The Strategic Substitution Effect: Textual Plausibility, Procedural Formality, and Judicial Review of Agency Statutory Interpretations*, 120 HARV. L. REV. 528, 537 fn. 23 (citing Cellnet Comm'n, Inc. v. FCC, 965 F.2d 1106, 1111–12 (D.C. Cir. 1992); *Nat'l Customs Brokers & Forwarders Ass'n of Am. v. United States*, 883 F.2d 93, 96–97 (D.C. Cir. 1989); James R. May, *Now More Than Ever: Trends in Environmental Citizen Suits*,10 WIDENER L. REV. 1, 28–33 (2003)).

465 *See* Kristina Daugirdas, Note, *Evaluating Remand Without Vacatur: A New Judicial Remedy for Defective Agency Rulemakings*, 80 NYU L. REV. 278 (2005).

466 Daryl Levinson, *Empire-Building Government in Constitutional Law*, 118 HARV. L. REV. 915 (2005).

467 *See, e.g.*, Katzen, *supra* note 133, at 1499.

468 *Id.*

469 *Id.*

470 *See* Michael A. Livermore, *Reviving Environmental Protection: Preference-Directed Regulation and Regulatory Ossification*, 25 VA. ENVTL. L.J. 311 (2007).

471 GAO, *supra* note 432, at 31.

472 *Id.* at 7.

473 *Id.* at 14.

474 Christopher C. DeMuth & Douglas H. Ginsburg, *White House Review of Agency Rulemaking*, 99 HARV. L. REV. 1075, 1082 (1986); Kagan, *supra* note 68, at 2361.

475 THE FEDERALIST NO. 10 (James Madison).

476 DeMuth & Ginsburg, *supra* note 474, at 1081.

477 Bob Woodward & David S. Broder, *Quayle's Quest: Curb Rules, Leave 'No Fingerprints'*, WASH. POST, Jan. 9, 1992, at A1.

478 OMB, *supra* note 287.

479 *See* Exec. Order No. 12,291, *supra* note 40; Exec. Order No. 12,498, 50 Fed. Reg. 1036 (Jan. 4, 1985).

480 *See, e.g.* Beryl A. Radin, Testimony to the Senate Homeland Security and Government Affairs Subcommittee on Federal Financial Management, Government Information, and International Security (June 14, 2005) *available at* http://hsgac.senate.gov/_files/Radin_testimony.pdf. Gary Bass & Adam Hughes, All PART of the Game (Mar. 25, 2005), http://www.tompaine.com/articles/2005/03/25/all_part_of_the_game.php.

481 Exec. Order No. 12,291, *supra* note 40.

482 Exec. Order No. 12,498, *supra* note 479.

483 Exec. Order No. 12,866, 58 Fed. Reg. 51,735 (Sept. 20, 1993).

484 Exec. Order No. 12,498, *supra* note 479.

485 Exec. Order No. 12,866, *supra* note 483.

486 Bragg v. Robertson, 83 F. Supp. 2d 713, 716 (D. Va. 2000).

487 *See*, Memoranda of Understanding Among the U.S. Office of Surface Mining, U.S. Environmental Protection Agency, U.S. Army Corps of Engineers, U.S. Fish and Wildlife Service, and West Virginia Division of Environmental Protection for the Purpose of Providing Effective Coordination in the Evaluation of Surface Coal Mining Operations Resulting in the Placement of Excess Spoil Fills in the Waters of the United States (1999) *available at* http://www.epa.gov/owow/wetlands/guidance/wv_mou.html.

488 *See* Guidelines for Ensuring and Maximizing the Quality, Objectivity, Utility, and Integrity of Information Disseminated by Federal Agencies, 67 Fed. Reg. 8452 (Feb. 22, 2002); Final Information Quality Bulletin for Peer Review, 70 Fed. Reg. 2664, 2667 (Jan. 14, 2005).

489 Comm. on the Institutional Means for Assessment of Risks to Pub. Health, Nat'l Res. Council, Risk Assessment in the Federal Government: Managing the Process 29–33 (1983).

490 *Id.*

491 *Id.* at 29.

492 *Id.*

493 *Id.* at 31.

494 *Id.* at 80.

495 *Id.* at 69–82.

496 *See* GAO, Chemical Risk Assessment: Selected Federal Agencies' Procedures, Assumptions, and Policies 158–59 (2001) [hereinafter GAO Report on Risk Assessment] (noting that FDA has not developed written internal guidelines on risk assessment and that external guidance documents that have been developed are suggestions with no legal force).

497 *Id.* at 40.

498 *Id.* at 46. The GAO report also examined the Research and Special Programs Administration (RSPA), a regulatory arm of DOT.

499 *See id.* at 190.

500 Draft Report: A Cross-Species Scaling Factor for Carcinogen Risk Assessment Based on Equivalence of mg/kg3/4/Day, 57 Fed. Reg. 24,152 (June 5, 1992).

501 Breyer, *supra* note 9.

502 In the case of Cancer Alley, there is significant debate about whether there are in fact elevated cancer levels caused by environmental pollution. *See* John McQuaid, *'Cancer Alley' Myth or Fact?*, http://www.nola.com/speced/unwelcome/index.ssf?/speced/unwelcome/stories/0524b.html.

503 Exec. Order No. 12,866, *supra* note 483, at §1(a).

504 Shavell, *supra* note 16.

505 Louis Kaplow and Steven Shavell believe that it is not necessary to analyze the impact of legal rules on distribution, preferring to look at overall indicators of economic inequality. *See* Louis Kaplow & Steven Shavell, *Fairness Versus Welfare*, 114 HARV. L. REV. 961, 994 n.64 (2001). Given the many ways that regulations affect welfare, however, we are doubtful that such an analysis will be sufficient.

506 Control of Emissions from New Highway Vehicles and Engines, 68 Fed. Reg. 52,922, 52,930–31.

507 Mass. v. EPA, 415 F.3d 50, 58 (D.C. Cir. 2005).

508 *Id.* (internal quotations omitted).

509 *Id.*

510 In his opinion concurring in the judgment with Judge Randolph, Judge Sentelle argued that the plaintiffs lacked standing to pursue their case. Focusing on the requirement that plaintiffs have a "particularized" injury—that "the injury must affect the plaintiff in a personal and individual way," *id.* at 59 (Sentelle, J., concurring)—Judge Sentelle found that, even "[a]fter plowing through their reams of affidavits and arguments, I am left with the unshaken conviction that they have alleged and shown no harm particularized to themselves." *Id.* at 59–60. For Judge Sentelle, because global warming is "harmful to humanity at large," plaintiffs presented "neither more nor less than the sort of general harm eschewed as insufficient" to support a case under constitutional standing requirements. *Id.* at 60.

511 First, Judge Tatel found that the standing requirements had been met because the Commonwealth of Massachusetts, one of the petitioners, was threatened by specific particular injuries—including the "permanent loss of coastal land," *id.* at 64 (Tatel, J., dissenting) (citing declaration of Paul Kirshen), while "other states may face their own particular problems stemming from the same global warming…these problems are different from the injuries Massachusetts faces," and therefore the harm faced by the state is "a far cry from the kind of generalized harm that the Supreme Court has found inadequate to support … standing." *Id.* at 65.

512 *Id.* at 73.

513 *Id.* at 75.

514 *Id.* at 74.

515 Mass v. EPA, 127 S. Ct. 1438 (2007).

516 The Court first found that the plaintiffs had standing, essentially agreeing with Judge Tatel's view. It also focused on the "special position and interest of Massachusetts," especially the fact that "the party seeking review here is a sovereign State." *Id.* at 1454. Tuning to the merits of the case, the Court found that Congress intended an expansive definition of pollution, such that greenhouse gases were included.

517 *Id.* at 1459.

518 *Id.*

519 *Id.*

520 *Id.* at 1459 (internal quotes omitted).

521 *Id.* at 1462.

522 *Id.*

523 *Id.*

524 *Id.*

525 *Id.* at 1472 (Scalia, J., dissenting).

526 *Id.* at 1467 (Roberts, J., dissenting).

INDEX

Americans with Disabilities Act
(ADA), 87, 88, 146
An Inconvenient Truth, 107
ancillary benefits
and air pollution, 63–64
and *American Trucking v. EPA*, 60,
71, 211–12n180, 212n181
and carbon pricing, 211n178
and citizens, 61
and countervailing risk, 58–65,
145, 212n184
and EPA, 60–62, 211–12n180,
212n181
ignored, 55, 58–61
OIRA guidelines, 212n184
overestimation of, 229n414, 418
parity with countervailing risks,
63–65
rarity of, 61–62
and risk-tradeoff analysis, 55,
58–62, 211–12n180, 212n181
and special interest groups,
61–62, 212n188
antiregulatory agenda
and the Clinton administration,
36–39
and Congress, 36, 42
and conservative groups, 21–22
antiregulatory bias
and the Bush administration
(1989–1993), 31
and the Clinton administration, 47
in court remedies, 159–61, 188–89
early research leading to, 38
historical basis for, 10–11, 151
institutional biases, 11, 151, 161
proregulatory groups and, 51, 145
and QALYs, 90
Reagan administration, 31

and regulations, 10–11, 43–45,
50, 63
results, 11
antiregulatory groups
and the Bush administration
(1989–1993), 168
and development of cost-benefit
analysis guidelines, 10
and health/wealth tradeoff, 71,
74–75
and homeland security
regulations, 43
impact on public policy, 24
and judicial review of agency
actions, 159–61
and QALYs, 88
and the Reagan administration,
168
and regulatory scorecards, 37–38
support of John Graham's OIRA
appointment, 40–41
use of political power, 38
See also conservative groups;
environmental groups;
progressive groups;
proregulatory groups; special
interest groups
Army Corps of Engineers, 165, 177
Arrow, Kenneth, 128
asbestos use and ban, 62, 96–98, 158
average values, 82–84

Bangladesh, 111–12, 222n335
Barnes, James A., 97–98
Breyer, Stephen, 57, 60, 71, 179,
212n181
Bulletin of the Atomic Scientists, 113
bureaucracy
bureaucratic language, 2

and economic growth, 21–22,
25, 30
presidential control over, 42
regulatory decisionmaking, 13
See also government agencies
*Bureaucracy and Representative
Government*, 21
Bush administration (1989–1993)
antiregulatory biases, 31, 189
and antiregulatory groups, 168
and asbestos ban, 98
Council on Competitiveness,
29–30, 167
and delayed rulemaking, 156–57
and OIRA, 168
proregulatory groups and, 11
See also Bush, George H. W.
Bush administration (2001–2008)
and agency appointments, 165
and climate change, 107–9, 185,
221n322
and conservative groups, 31
and delayed rulemaking, 157
and deregulation, 154
and discounting, 108–9
energy policy, 167
and environmental regulations,
39, 41
and Executive Order 12,866
(1993), 42, 152
foreign vs. domestic policy, 9
and OIRA, 40–42, 152, 171, 172
proregulatory groups and, 12,
34–35, 84
and QALYs, 88–89
and stated-preference surveys, 129
use of life-years analysis, 79–80,
84, 216n243
Bush, George H. W.
and Executive Order 12,291, 25

and Presidential Task Force on
Regulatory Relief, 26
See also Bush administration
(1989–1993)
business groups *see* industry and
business groups

campaign contributions and
deregulation, 30
cancer
from asbestos exposure, 97
clusters, 180, 234n502
guidelines, 179
rates, 27
carbon monoxide (CO) emissions,
59, 62–63, 213n194
Carter, Jimmy, 23, 24–25, 26
Cato Institute, 38
*CEI (Competitive Enterprise Institute)
v. National Highway Traffic Safety
Administration*, 57
Center for Risk Analysis, 40
Center for the Study of American
Business, 22
Center for the Study of Government
Regulations, 23
centralized review of regulations
and agency coordination and
harmonization, 175–79, 190
and the Clinton administration, 173
and cost-benefit analysis, 26
environmental groups impression
of, 26
and Executive Order 12,291
(1981), 151–52
and Executive Order 12,866
(1993), 42
as neutral tool, 32, 173
and the Reagan administration,
173, 175

reform measures needed for, 171

See also Office of Information and Regulatory Affairs (OIRA)

Chaney, Heckler v., 187

Cheney, Dick, 152, 167

chlorofluorocarbons (CFCs), 131–34, 140, 227*n*388

Chugachimuit, 120

Circular A-4 (OMB), 172, 181

citizens

and ancillary benefits, 61

participation in the cost-benefit analysis process, 51, 147, 151, 174, 190, 192, 194

civil rights, 18–19

Clean Air Act

and agency cost considerations, 69, 71

amendments of 1990, 56, 64, 136, 193

asbestos standards under the, 97

and the automobile industry, 135

and greenhouse gases, 185–87

New Source Review provision, 154

and ozone levels, 78

and power plants, 18

and QALYs, 88

Clean Air Interstate Rule, 41

Clean Water Act, 58, 125

Clear Skies Act, 79

climate change

and the Bush administration (2001–2008), 107–9, 185, 221*n*322

and discounting, generational, 108–9, 112–13

and the economic-incentive approach, 193

environmental implications of, 63

Climate Change: An Analysis of Some Key Questions, 185

Clinton administration

and agency coordination and harmonization, 176

and the antiregulatory agenda, 36–39

and antiregulatory bias, 47

and centralized review of regulations, 173

and cost-benefit analysis as neutral tool, 32, 205*n*77

and cost-benefit analysis guidelines for EPA, 10, 50

and delayed rulemaking, 157

and deregulation, 154

and EPA, 47

and Office of Information and Regulatory Affairs (OIRA), 171, 172

and proregulatory groups, 11, 34, 42

and regulatory inaction, 155

See also Executive Order 12,866 (1993)

coal consumption, 213*n*194

coal industry, 62, 63–64, 125, 137, 176–77

collateral consequences, 55

commodification of human life, 13–14

commodification of natural resources, 4

compassion, statistical, 3

Competitive Enterprise Institute (CEI), 57

Congress

antiregulatory agenda, 36, 39, 40, 42

and conservative groups, 21

Daniel, John, 28–29
D.C. Circuit Court, U.S. Court of
    Appeals, 128, 186
DeMuth, Christopher, 23–24
Department of Energy, 140, 165
Department of the Interior, 128
deregulation
    and the Bush administration
        (2001–2008), 156
    and campaign contributions, 30
    and conservative groups, 21–24
    and cost-benefit analysis, 9–10,
        15–16, 26–27, 29, 153–54,
        231n436
    and economic costs, 22–23
    and Executive Order 12,291
        (1981), 153
    and Executive Order 12,866
        (1993), 154, 231n436
    and health/wealth tradeoff, 70,
        73–75
    hit lists and prompt letters used
        for, 155–56
    and industry, 22–23, 27–30
    and proregulatory groups, 29
    and the Reagan administration,
        23, 25–29, 153, 156
    Reagan, Ronald on, 24–25
    and regulatory scorecards, 37–38
    and special interest groups, 231n447
Dingell, John, 27
disabled people, 87, 88, 89, 146
discounting
    and the Bush administration
        (2001–2008), 108–9
    defined, 95
    EPA guidelines on, 95–96
    inter-generational responsibility
        and, 218n284
    OMB guidelines on, 95, 218n287

OMB's preferred discount rate, 109
    using wage data, 101–2,
        219–20n305
discounting, generational
    and allocation of resources, 110–11
    and climate change, 108–9
    and consumption, 111–12, 115–16
    and corrective justice, 117
    and deferral of expenditures,
        114–15
    ethical considerations of, 110,
        221n330
    and future catastrophe, 112–13
    as moral issue, 107, 111, 146,
        221n321
    OMB guidance for, 110
    and opportunity costs, 113–14
    and pollution costs, 115, 222n339
    and sustainable development,
        116–17
    and utilitarianism, 117
    vs. discounting, individual,
        95–96, 100–101, 109–10
discounting, individual
    and dread, 103–4
    and future risk reductions, 101–2
    and involuntary risks, 104–5,
        146, 220n313, 316, 317
    and long-latency diseases, 96,
        99–100, 102–6, 146, 219n302
    and suffering, 105–6
    vs. discounting, generational,
        95–96, 100–101, 109–10
distributional analysis, 180–83,
    190, 235n505
Doomsday Clock, 113
drycleaner industry, 136
Dudley, Susan, 38, 41–42, 88–89,
    125, 126
Durban, Richard, 40

and ozone levels, 78–79, 215*n*238
proregulatory focus of, 164–65
and QALYs, 88
and regulatory biases, 11, 49,
    209*n*133
relationship with OIRA, 47,
    49–50, 174–75, 209*n*133
and results of cost-benefit analysis
    review process, 153
Science Advisory Board
    Committee, 34, 50
and stated-preference surveys, 129
and statistical life, 47–49, 70–71
use of life-years analyses, 79–80,
    216*n*243
use of science data, 178–79
*Environmental Protection Agency
    (EPA), American Trucking v.*
and agency cost considerations, 69
and ancillary benefits, 60,
    211–12*n*180, 212*n*181
and health/wealth tradeoffs, 69, 71
and QALYs, 88
and risk-tradeoff analysis, 57, 60
*Environmental Protection Agency
    (EPA), Corrosion Proof Fittings v.*,
    98, 158
*Environmental Protection Agency
    (EPA), Massachusetts v.*, 159,
    185–88, 235*n*510, 511, 516
environmental regulations
and the Bush administration
    (2001–2008), 39, 41
Clean Air Interstate Rule, 41
and Congress, 206*n*97
and cost considerations, 69
cost of, 9, 215*n*238
and discounting, 96
negative health consequences,
    68–69

off-road diesel rule, 41
and scientific research, 227*n*388
and statistical life, 33–34
See also regulations
Epstein, Samuel, 27
Evans, Mary, 81
Executive Order 12,291 (1981), 25
and centralized agency control,
    151–52, 173, 175
cost-benefit analysis required by,
    4, 152
and deregulation, 153, 180
fate of intellectual architects of,
    201–04*n*62
and industry influence, 28
requirements of, 25
See also Reagan administration
Executive Order 12,498 (1985),
    173, 175–76, 233*n*479, *See also*
    Reagan administration
Executive Order 12,866 (1993)
and centralized agency control, 42
and coordination and
    harmonization, 175–76
and delayed rulemaking, 156–57
and deregulation, 154, 231*n*436
and distributive impacts, 180–81
and OIRA, 31–32
revisions of cost-benefit analysis
    process, 152, 230*n*428
See also Clinton administration
existence value
defined, 119
and environmental groups, 119
and EPA, 125
excluding from cost-benefit
    analysis, 225*n*372
and the Exxon Valdez oil spill, 121
and industry groups, 125,
    225*n*373

and natural resources, 119, 121, 123, 146
nonexistence of, 126–27
for nonnatural resources, 125–26
and stated-preference surveys, 123–29, 146
and willingness to pay for benefit, 124–25, 127–29
Exxon Valdez oil spill, 120–21, 124, 128, 224n353, 357, 362

Fabian, Robert, 105
Federalist Papers, 167
Fish and Wildlife Service, 177
Food and Drug Administration (FDA), 132, 178, 234n496
Ford administration, 23, 24, 26
Ford Motor Company, 135
free market system and regulation, 23–24
fuel consumption rates, 57, 210n149
fuel efficiency standards for cars and light trucks, 57, 62, 64, 210n148

Gates, Bill, 74
General Accounting Office (GAO), 68, 153, 166, 178
generational discounting *see* discounting, generational
Gingrich, Newt, 56
Glenn, John, 68
global warming *see* climate change
Gore, Al, 27–29, 96, 107
government agencies
centralized control of, 16, 23–26, 29–30, 32, 42, 151–52, 163
considering ancillary benefits of regulations, 64–65
coordination and harmonization between, 175–79, 183

and delayed rulemaking, 156–57
evaluation of cost-benefit analysis, 141–43
inaction, 159, 188, 232n462, 463
and judicial review of agency actions, 157–61, 172
and the nondelegation doctrine, 88
and OIRA administration influence on regulatory review, 152
and overregulation, 151–53, 163–65, 168–69
regulatory agendas of, 173, 189–90
and regulatory inaction, 155–56, 231n447
and regulatory stringency, 153, 174–75, 189, 230n430, 431
submitting overly strict regulations, 230n432
use of science data, 177–79
See also bureaucracy; *specific agencies*
governmental decisions
consequences of, 2, 4
and natural resources, 2
personal decisions vs., 2–3, 197n3
and policy failure, 18
and statistical compassion, 2–3
Graham, John
and ancillary benefits, 61–62
commitment to cost-benefit analysis, 44
and delayed rulemaking, 157
and discounting, 95, 114–15
and government waste, 37–38
and life-years method, 79
nomination as OIRA chief, 40–41
and OIRA information, 172
and regulatory inaction, 155–56
and risk-tradeoff analysis, 55–56, 57–58, 60

and statistical life, 70, 71
and the war on terror, 43
Gramm, Phil, 40–41
greenhouse gases, 59, 62–64,
107–8, 185–88, 213n194
Greenwald, Peter, 16
Greer, Linda, 40
gross national product (GNP), 112,
222n335

Hahn, Robert, 38
Hammitt, James K., 44, 92
Haninger, Kevin, 92
Harvard Center for Risk Analysis,
44, 55, 92
Hassler, William, 62
Hauser, Philip, 69, 71–72
Haxthausen, Eric, 35
Hayek, Friedrich, 23
health and safety regulations *see*
environmental regulations
health care and the uninsured, 85
health care rationing, 86, 87
health/wealth tradeoff
and *American Trucking v. EPA*,
69, 71
antiregulatory result and claims
of, 70, 145–46
assumptions of, 67, 68, 71–73
and Congress, 68, 70–71
and deregulation, 70, 73–75
and education, 73, 214n225,
214n227
and income level, 74–75, 215n229
judicial support for, 70–71
and OSHA, 67–68
and productivity, 76
and regulations, 69–70, 73–76
See also statistical life
Heckler v. Chaney, 187

Heinzerling, Lisa, 41–42, 44, 96
Hewlett-Packard, 142
Hill, TVA v., 17–18
homeland security regulations, 43
Howard, Coby, 85
Hubbard, Allan, 30
human life
cost to save, 68–69
value of, 13–14, 26, 42–43, 192
See also statistical life

Iacocca, Lee, 135
income and health *see* health/wealth
tradeoff
individual discounting *see*
discounting, individual
industry and business groups
and development of cost-benefit
analysis guidelines, 10, 34–36,
205–206n84
and EPA, 134, 167
and existence value, 125, 225n373
and information markets, 142
and regulations, 22–23, 27–30,
61–62, 212n188
and regulatory costs, 134–35, 147
use of health/wealth tradeoff, 71
inflation and regulations, 24
information markets, 142
Information Quality Act (IQA),
177–78
institutional biases, 11, 151, 161
insurance and shifting of risk, 48
interest groups *see* special interest
groups
Iraq War, 44

judicial review of agency actions
and agency denial of petitions,
173–74

and cost-benefit analysis, 157–61, 188–89, 191–92, 232n460, 461
and court independence, 165–66
statutory requirements for, 157, 231n451
See also specific cases

Katzen, Sally, 134, 155, 164
Keeney, Ralph L., 69, 71–72, 74
Kenkel, Donald, 105
Kennedy, Edward M., 68
Kim, Hyun, 81
Kitagawa, Evelyn, 69, 71–72
Kniesner, Thomas, 81
Krupnick, Alan, 81
Kyoto Protocol, 59, 108

labor unions, 40, 61
League of Conservation Voters, 40
Levinson, Daryl, 164
liberal groups *see* progressive groups
life-years method
constant per life-year value, 77–78
and discounting, 219–20n305
and ozone regulation, 78–79, 215n238
and QALYs, 87–88
and value of older vs. younger people, 41, 77–78, 80–82, 84, 146, 216n245, 216n251
vs. QALYs, 92–93
and willingness to pay for benefit, 80–82, 146, 216n251
See also statistical life
lobbyists *see* special interest groups
Long Beach port, California, 16–17
low-income people and health/wealth tradeoff, 74–75, 215n229
Lutter, Randall, 69, 72

MacRae, James, 68, 71
Madison, James, 167
market-based regulatory systems, 138–39
Massachusetts v. EPA, 159, 185–88, 235n510, 511, 516
Medicaid, 85
Mercatus Institute, 38, 41, 88, 125, 126
Mica, John, 71
military spending, 44
Miller, James C., III, 23, 25, 26
Miller, Saul, 26
Molina, Mario, 132
Montreal Protocol on Substances the Deplete the Ozone Layer, 131–34
Moore, Michael J., 77
Morrall, John F., III, 37–38, 69
Morrison, Alan, 27
mortality risk, 92–93

Nader, Ralph, 26, 43, 44, 208n130
National Academy of Sciences, 132
National Acid Precipitation Assessment Program (NAPAP), 137
National Association of Administrators, 154
National Environmental Trust, 40
National Highway Traffic Safety Administration (NHTSA), 57, 64, 210n148
National Highway Traffic Safety Administration, CEI (Competitive Enterprise Institute) v., 57
National Oceanic and Atmospheric Administration (NOAA), 128
national parks, 62, 122
National Research Council, 178, 185

natural resources
  and commodification, 4
  and existence values, 119, 121, 123
  and future generations, 116–17
  and governmental decisions, 2
  nonrenewable, 60
  use and nonuse values of, 122–23
  and willingness to pay for,
    124–25, 127
Natural Resources Defense Council
  (NRDC), 16, 35, 40, 41
Nature, 132
Nature Conservancy, 124
Neurobiological Substrates of Dread, 103
New Source Review provision of the
  Clean Air Act, 154
New York Times, 79, 132
NHTSA *see* National Highway Traffic
  Safety Administration (NHTSA)
Ninth Circuit Court, U.S. Court of
  Appeals, 64, 121
Niskanen, William A., 21–22, 25,
  38, 164
Nixon Administration, 23, 24, 26
NOAA, *see* National Oceanic and
  Atmospheric Administration
  (NOAA)
nondelegation doctrine, 88
NRDC *see* Natural Resources
  Defense Council (NRDC)

Occupational Safety and Health
  Administration (OSHA)
  asbestos rule, 97
  and health/wealth tradeoff, 67–68,
    70–71
  and industry and business
    groups, 134
  and judicial review of agency
    actions, 157

and OIRA, 49
  and overestimation of economic
    costs, 140
  and regulatory biases, 11
  and special interest groups, 167–68
  use of science data, 178–79
Office of Information and
  Regulatory Affairs (OIRA)
  administration influence on
    regulatory review, 152
  and agency coordination and
    harmonization, 176–79, 183, 189
  agenda-setting and prioritization
    role for, 173–74, 189–90
  and the Bush administration
    (2001–2008), 40–42
  and Congress, 30
  cost-benefit analysis guidelines,
    212n184
  creation and role of, 25–26
  and delayed rulemaking, 156–57
  and deregulation, 153–54,
    231n436
  and distributional analysis,
    181–83, 190
  and environmental groups, 35, 41
  evaluation of cost-benefit analysis,
    141–43
  and Executive Order 12,291
    (1981), 151–52
  and Executive Order 12,866,
    31–32
  guidelines of, 172
  and health/wealth tradeoff, 68
  neutrality of, 165–68
  and OSHA, 49
  oversight, 171–72
  the president's relationship with,
    166–67
  and public meetings, 172

stated-preference surveys
  guidelines for, 128–29
  and OMB, 121
  reliability of, 128–29
  revealed preference technique,
    48–49
  stated preferences technique, 48
  use of, 123–25
  and willingness to pay for benefit,
    127–29
Statistical compassion, 3
statistical life
  and discounting, 103
  and health and productivity, 76
  and mortality risks, 92–93
  and regulatory spending, 37
  using average value, 82–84
  value of, 33–34, 47–50, 70
  willingness to pay for benefit,
    48–49, 77, 80–84, 146,
    216n251
  See also human life; life-years
    method; quality adjusted
    life-years (QALYs)
Stockholm Environmental
  Institute, 135
Stossel, John, 70
substitution risks
  see countervailing risk
sulfur-dioxide trading program,
  136–37
Sunstein, Cass
  and ancillary benefits, 60
  and the cost-benefit state, 36
  and discounting, 110
  and health/wealth tradeoff, 69
  and judicial review of agency
    actions, 158
  and QALYs, 87–89
  and risk tradeoff analysis, 55–56, 58

Superfund, 128
sustainable development, 116–17
Swedish Ministry of the
  Environment, 135

Tatel, David S., 186, 235n511
Taylor, Donald, Jr., 81
Tellico Dam, 17–18
Tengs, Tammy, 37–38, 79
terrorism, 43
Tolley, George, 105
Toxic Substances Control Act,
  97, 158
Tozzi, James, 26, 177
Trans-Alaskan Oil Pipeline, 120
TVA v. Hill, 17–18

United Auto Workers, 40
U.S. Army Corps of Engineers,
  165, 177
U.S. Constitution's nondelegation
  doctrine, 88
U.S. Court of Appeals, D.C. Circuit,
  128, 186
U.S. Court of Appeals, Ninth
  Circuit, 64, 121
U.S. Department of Energy, 140, 165
U.S. Department of the
  Interior, 128
U.S. Environmental Protection
  Agency (EPA) *see* Environmental
  Protection Agency (EPA)
U.S. Fish and Wildlife Service, 177
U.S. Food and Drug Administration
  (FDA), 132, 178, 234n496
U.S. General Accounting Office
  (GAO), 68, 153, 166, 178
U.S. gross national product, 112,
  222n335
U.S. Justice Department, 121